REBELHE

JOHN CAULFIELD

with Robert Redmond

www.**HERO**BOOKS.digital

HEROBOOKS

PUBLISHED BY HERO BOOKS
1 WOODVILLE GREEN
LUCAN
CO. DUBLIN
IRELAND

Hero Books is an imprint of Umbrella Publishing

First Published 2021

ISBN 9781910827130

Cover design and formatting: jessica@viitaladesign.com
Ebook formatting: www.ebooklaunch.com
Photographs: Inpho, Eddie O'Hare and Doug Minihane

DEDICATION

To my family, my ever supportive wife Gráinne and
our treasured daughters Aideen and Sinéad. Thank
you for putting up with me over the years and for your
commitment and love.

To my parents John and Nora who gave me the
drive, inspiration and opportunities to do anything I
wished and always had total belief in my ability.

To my brother Daniel who has given me many
words of wisdom over the years and has always been
there for me even though he lives far away in the USA.

CONTENTS

ACKNOWLEDGEMENTS

I HAVE BEEN privileged and honoured to have had so many great people who have helped me throughout my life and career. Sport has been a huge part of my life, especially football and GAA to a lesser extent.

I have had many dedicated coaches and mentors at various stages throughout my career. Bertie Fallon, in Lecarrow, who brought me to and from Athlone for many years. The late Jackie Quinn, in Athlone IT and manager of the Athlone B team, who instilled great confidence in me. The late Mick McGowan, in Summerhill College, who gave me guidance and confidence throughout my secondary school years in Sligo. And Albert Higgins, in Carrowroe FC and Sligo, who kindly took me out from boarding school on Saturdays to watch *Match of the Day*.

Thanks to you all.

I wish to acknowledge the support of friends in Wembley in Cork, especially Mick Punch. In Avondale United there was Tom Mullane, Noel Long, Brendan McCarthy, Paddy Scannell and the late Chris Herlihy. And in UCC there was Kieran Nestor, John McCarthy, Noel Healy and Conor Uhl. Again, thank you to you all.

There are so many others too, who have been there for me. Everyone in Riverside Athletic in West Cork, and in St Dominic's GAA club in Roscommon and, of course, my 'home town' GAA club, St Mary's Enniskeane and Ballineen, where I played for over 20 years and made so many great friends. St Mary's is a small club with a big heart.

There are too many great friends, who have sadly passed. Jim Hennebry, Avondale and Cork City, was a true gent and a constant source of invaluable advice. And Pat Lacey, who died tragically in 2019. 'Lacers' was an outstanding man to have by my side, and he is sadly missed by so many of us.

Seamus Kenny from Lecarrow and Dan Corcoran from Enniskeane... thank you for great friendships.

I must thank my late mother-in-law Nora O'Connell (mom Nora), who was an incredible support to me when I started living in West Cork. One of my best supporters, Nora attended all the Cork City games... before always rushing home to do a magnificent Sunday roast for us all.

Finally, the Cork City 'family'.

A special mention to Mr Cork City himself, Jerry Harris, and close friends in Cork City FC who are looking down from Heaven... Paul Bannon, Alex Ludzig, Noel O'Mahony, John Kennedy, Pat Shine, Noelle Feeney and Timmy Carey.

I remain sincerely grateful and appreciative to have had the greatest time of my sporting life... playing, captaining, managing and supporting a brilliant club. To my teammates, managers and staff... and the Rebel Army, a massive thank you to you all.

Lastly, thanks to Robert Redmond for all his hard work, countless chats, and numerous cups of tea and scones. And to Liam Hayes of Hero Books for his determination in convincing me to write *RebelHeart*, despite many refusals (from me). A sincere thanks to you both.

John Caulfield
September 2021

✦✦✦✦✦

I WANT TO thank John Caulfield and Liam Hayes for their patience, support and trust. I will always be grateful to Liam for commissioning me to tell John's story and helping me fulfil a lifelong ambition of writing a football book. He was extremely supportive, and I'll always be thankful that he put his confidence in me.

I jumped at the chance to work with a legend of Irish and Cork football. John is a detailed story-teller, an unfailingly honest person. I greatly enjoyed listening to and learning from him. It was a challenging but brilliant and rewarding experience. I'll always appreciate the trust and hospitality John showed me and retain fond memories of my trip down to West Cork and our meetings in the Lucan Spa Hotel. John represents the best of Irish football.

I want to thank my mother Betty for always reading to me as a child and buying a newspaper every day so I could read the sports section. She helped instil a love of books and reading that became embedded within me. She also showed me the value of hard work, getting up at half four every morning for 30 years to go to work in Guinness's.

I want to thank my father Tony for his feedback, advice and support, for reading my work and fostering my love of soccer and writing. A gifted writer, painter and artist, I'm aware that I inherited whatever talent for writing I have from him.

I want to thank my sisters Joanne and Lisa for their support, and Lisa for transcribing conversations John and I had. She was an invaluable help. This isn't my book to dedicate to anyone, but my late sister Anita and my late friend James are always in my thoughts. I'm sure they would be happy to see me fulfil this ambition.

I particularly want to thank Paula. She also transcribed hours of conversations between John and myself. But more importantly, she was there with me throughout – from when Liam offered me the chance to write John's book to the final stages of editing. Her support never waned.

I hope I have done John justice and repaid the faith he and Liam put in me. I agonised over word, comma and sentence and tried my best to capture John's story. If he is happy with the words on these pages, then so am I.

Robert Redmond
September 2021

PROLOGUE

I WENT BACK into the dressing-room a few minutes after we won. To sit down. Gather my thoughts. I was in there on my own, putting on my tie and I found myself shaking with nerves. Emotionally, I felt overwhelmed. It's hard to describe it, other than… I was suddenly a *free* man. I felt it the year before too. But I felt it more with the double. The spring and summer and autumn of 2017 were over. Our longest season had ended.

Freed.

CORK CITY LOST three of our starting team two-thirds of the way through the season. Seáni Maguire and Kevin O'Connor went to Preston North End in July. Johnny Dunleavy, our captain, got injured and was out for the season.

In the league, our form dipped after the lads left, which was understandable. We didn't hit the heights that we had, but that would have been impossible as we were 18 points clear at one stage. We were still in a commanding position for the second half of the season. There was no doubt that we were going to win the league, it was just when was it going to happen. But the cup was different.

All those players were missing for the cup.

We progressed well through the rounds without them and reached the final. For the third season in-a-row, it was Dundalk waiting for us.

We came from nowhere in 2014. And now for the first time in Cork City's history, we were on the verge of winning the double.

It was an extraordinary build-up to the cup final because we were still regarded as the underdogs, which was unusual for the league champions. It probably suited us in a way, but it smacked a bit that this bunch of players weren't getting the credit that they actually deserved. Twelve months earlier, we won the cup. The same group of lads then turned around and won the league.

Won 21 out of 22 games. Blew teams away. Yet, all some people seemed to want to say was… 'Oh, well, you had that player!' That player being Seáni.

That always made me smile. The same player was with Dundalk less than 18 months earlier and he wasn't even on their bench for the 2015 cup final.

CORK CITY WERE written off the previous year after we won the cup with Seáni scoring in the last minute.

Dundalk had been in the Europa League group stages. There was a lot of talk that their team had played so many games, that they were burnt out. We beat them in the cup final, but it felt like the reason given for that was that they had been tired – as though Dundalk *lost* rather than Cork *won*.

Yet, it was huge for us because it was the first major trophy we won as a team and the first major honour since the club was saved from extinction in 2010.

We then went to another level. For two-thirds of the 2017 season, we were unbeaten and our football was absolutely incredible. Our goalscoring was phenomenal. But, by the time Cork City won the league, it was like people had got bored of us because we had been so brilliant, and we had run away with the thing. We lost a few games, and it was like… 'Oh Cork City stumbled to win the league'. But we had created history with our record.

It was advantageous in some ways for me as a manager talking to the players.

'Look lads!' I would say repeatedly.

'You know people have never given you the credit.

'But if we can win this cup, it means then that they can say nothing about us. Whereas if we lose, they'll say, "Ah well, they weren't going to be good enough because they didn't have Seáni Maguire".'

THAT WEEK, GOING into the final, the team felt like they still had to prove themselves. We had lost a couple of brilliant footballers, particularly Seáni, but the other players in the squad were desperate to show what they could do on the biggest stage. They were a great group.

There was Mark McNulty, who was from Ballincollig. Nults was an excellent goalkeeper and so consistent – he never missed any games. In the 2016 FAI Cup final against Dundalk, he made a crucial save from David McMillan and he had been incredible again all season for us in 2017. Nults' attention to detail and his attitude in training was top class. He was incredibly fit too; we used to joke that he should have been in the Olympics.

McNulty was a serious player, but he was also the ultimate messer within the group, a real joker. Steven Beattie, a Dub, was another messer in the group, a joker. Beattie came to us from Sligo Rovers and he could play anywhere – right-back, right wing back, left-back and in midfield.

I liked him in that right-back position because he attacked so much. Beattie was very quick, and he was hard as nails. He was very much an unsung hero in lots of ways, but extremely popular within the group and vocal. The lads would laugh because some days he and I would knock the heads off each other. He took a bit of managing, but I valued him highly as he would run through a wall for us; a really influential player.

He was one of the few players who said no to signing for me at first, but I then went back for him. He would often say that the biggest mistake he made was that he didn't join City sooner.

IN MIDFIELD WE had Gearóid Morrissey, a very popular player in the group. He was a great guy with a really nice manner and a fantastic attitude.

Gearóid was from Mahon in Cork. It is a real strong soccer area; they have a great football club down there and some brilliant players. But a lot of them don't progress for whatever reason and fall out of the game by the time they are 16 or 17 years-old. Gearóid was one who fought through a lot and I think people appreciated that. He went to Blackburn Rovers at 16 but came back because of homesickness. He was a *real* home bird. He then spent a year with Cambridge United between 2014 and '15 and did okay – he made his debut at Old Trafford against Manchester United in a cup game.

I think he realised though that English football at that level – League Two – was hyped up to be something it wasn't. He got it out of his system and became a big player for us. Gearóid was probably the most talented and skilful player within the group. Stephen Dooley though was a genius.

Dooley was special; a highly intelligent guy, but a total introvert. A very quiet fella with absolute magic in his boots. I drove from West Cork to Portstewart at the top of the country to convince him to come to us after Derry City decided not to sign him. I couldn't believe they passed on him.

He was an incredibly talented player. Seáni got all the glory, but Dooley was often the one setting him up. If he had more self-belief, I've no doubt that he certainly would have played in the Championship in England. He was that talented.

DOOLEY WAS PROBABLY the most underrated player in a team of underrated players, a team that was on the verge of creating history by being the first Cork side to win the double.

In 2005, City had the chance to win the double and they lost against Drogheda. They didn't take the opportunity because they celebrated too much after winning the league. Some of the players from that era – Bennett, McNulty – were able to tell us those stories. They were two local players, born and reared in Cork; they knew what it was about. They realised that they had blown it in 2005.

I was a supporter at the time looking on. They played Drogheda in the final having been celebrating for some time. They lost 2-0. Whether they would have won it if they hadn't been celebrating, well that is another story, but they weren't prepared for it.

This was something we talked about within our group. The boys had spoken about it and swore... *We must give ourselves every opportunity.*

The night we got the league trophy after the last game of the season we didn't celebrate because we had the cup final 10 days later. We took the trophy and went around the ground, and went to a small reception in town.

But that was it. We trained the following morning.

There were no celebrations but there was a real togetherness. The motivation was twofold. There was the chance to make history and win the double for the first time. And there was the Maguire and O'Connor scenario; after they left the rest of the team never got the credit they deserved.

Then we had the Karl Sheppard situation.

I SIGNED KARL in 2015. He was out of contract with Shamrock Rovers and there hadn't been a massive demand for him.

He had a big reputation, but he had a season where he didn't play much or start many games. Yet he still took a massive gamble coming to us.

In my first season we didn't know what we were going to do and the next thing we ended up in the last game of the season against Dundalk going for the league title. *Were we one season wonders?*

There was a lot of talk that it was just one of these freak seasons and the bubble would burst… that we hadn't really established ourselves, even though we had come second.

Sheppard had been over with Reading. He then went to Shamrock Rovers and was part of their double win. He had a bad season, but he still had a bit of clout. Shep also told me that people had told him that we wouldn't be a good fit. And the amount of people who told me that he wouldn't suit me… that he was a flash boy… he was lazy, and he was this or that.

I met him and I sold him the Cork dream. For me, as someone who came from outside the county, I wanted players living in Cork.

I played with Cork City teams when we were very good, and we had a good core of players from, and living, in Cork. When we had players travelling from Waterford and Limerick, or over from the UK, it just didn't work.

We needed players to come to Cork, to buy into it and to walk around the streets. People knew who they were, there was pressure on them.

But, at the same time, if you won, Cork was a great place to be. Whether it was something I said to him or not, I don't know, but the following day he rang me.

'I'm going to sign,' he told me. It happened very quickly, and it was significant for me to get him. Shep bought into what we were straight away. He was very intelligent, trained hard and scored goals. He was great. I put him in a different position, one that was unusual for him, but it turned out to be perfect for him and us.

Shep had been viewed as a centre-forward. He ended up playing wide, coming in off the line.

We had a front three of Seáni central, and Dooley and Sheppard either side. They all had pace, they could all score and they were all intelligent players.

They were lethal.

SHEP JOINED and did very well for Cork City.

He was part of the cup final team in 2015 and won the cup with us in '16. Shep was also a real pain in the backside to Dundalk. There were matches in those couple of seasons where he had really caused Dundalk a lot of problems and scored quite a few goals. He got taken down for a couple of penalties and had been a thorn in their side.

Shep's contract with us was up at the end of the 2017 season so I had talked with him in September, before we won the league, about a new deal. We never got into discussions about money for next season because Shep indicated to me that he would probably go back home to Dublin.

He was from Portmarnock and his girlfriend was from Dublin too. It felt like his time with us had come to a natural end. He had been down in Cork for three years and now he was moving back home.

That was fine. While I wanted players to stay, if someone wasn't happy or was moving on and had legitimate reasons, I had no problem with that.

Ultimately, when you're managing a group of people, you need everyone happy. They may not be pleased about being taken off or dropped or whatever, but they have to be overall happy coming in every day to train.

Shep told me that a couple of clubs had been on to him, which was fair enough. The problems began the week of the cup final.

I DID MY press conference on the Monday, which meant that some stories about us appeared on the Tuesday and some were kept for later in the week. But press day was over for us… everyone was finished their interviews until after the cup final. That suited us perfectly because I wanted to lock down and get everyone's head focused. Dundalk's press conference was on the Tuesday.

At it, Stephen Kenny just casually said to the press that Dundalk had agreed to sign Karl Sheppard.

There was no doubt in my mind that he said this to throw us and create problems, absolutely. We had won the league title and he had to do whatever he felt necessary as manager of Dundalk. It was his job to make sure that they won the cup. But, professionally, if you look at it from manager-to-manager, should you do something like that? Of course not, no.

It crossed a line. When you lose in sport you have to shake hands; when you win you have to shake hands. In 2015, they won the double against us in the Aviva... Richie Towell scored. Afterwards, I congratulated Dundalk as a group of people in the dressing-room because it was the right thing to do, they were the best team.

While you might lose and be unhappy, you have to take it on the chin, and say, 'Lads, you were the best team and you deserved to win the double'.

A year later and the following year we were neck-and-neck in the league, and we were getting the better of them in our games. We had a very good record against Dundalk in the league and we won the President's Cup against them as well. Relations between the two sides started to sour around that time.

The relationship between myself and Stephen was much better when they were beating us regularly. When I saw the clips of his press conference, I thought... *That was below the belt.* I knew straight away that it could cause us major issues.

IT WASN'T THAT I didn't know that Shep was going to Dundalk. Everyone in the dressing-room was aware that he was moving on; players talk to each other, we all knew he was off.

The feeling was that he was going to go to Dundalk or Rovers.

The problem for us was that it had gone public.

That was *different*. It meant our supporters knew and it was a different challenge. I had headaches all that day thinking about how I would deal with it.

As a pure coincidence, I came up to Dublin the same week to meet Philly McMahon. I saw his interview on *The Late Late Show*; I was really impressed as he chatted with Ryan Tubridy about his new book, which was much more than just the life of a Dublin footballer. I admired him and the story of where he had come from.

We used to have what we would call 'The Last Supper' on the Thursday before the cup final. It was a light-hearted get together for the squad and coaching staff.

I was conscious that a team changes every year. The same group of people will never be together again; there will always be someone missing the next year, that's just the way it is in football, especially Irish football.

I wanted to buy the lads something as a token.

'Basically... this *is* The Last Supper, I'm giving this as a gift to thank you.'

That's what I always told them.

After that, at least they will remember that book or whatever was offered

REBELHEART • JOHN CAULFIELD

to them to mark the occasion. I thought Philly's book was a great read. There were parts of it that were really challenging and parts that were really positive. If some of the lads after The Last Supper could read it before the final, or read some of it, I thought it might help them. Or at the very least, take their minds off cup final nerves.

I MET PHILLY in Dublin on the Wednesday morning. We had a cup of tea and, of course, we spoke a bit about gaelic football. He was a lovely fella, very genuine.

We were just having some general chit-chat when the cup final came up. Philly was close with Trevor Croly; he had done strength and conditioning training with Shamrock Rovers when Trevor was the manager.

Philly said he had worked there for a little while when Sheppard was at the club. Philly then passed a comment about Shep. He noted how well he had done for me and mentioned he hadn't done as well for Trevor.

Then he said it.

'How are you going to deal with the elephant in the room?' He was referring to Kenny's comments about Shep signing for Dundalk.

I was taken aback. In my head I was thinking about it non-stop.

Yeah... I know I have to sort this out. I need to work out how?

And here was a guy who had absolutely nothing to do with me and nothing to do with Cork City, yet out of the blue, he just went, 'You have a problem there!'

Philly was presenting me with the Dublin mentality. They had won several All-Irelands with Jim Gavin as their manager, but they were a seriously strong-willed group. There was a lot of talk that Dublin were a very player-led group and that they sorted lots of things themselves.

'You have to sort that out before Sunday... or you have no chance!' Philly said to me. I didn't disagree. I wasn't expecting it, but what he said underlined that the issue had to be tackled head-on. I got the books and drove down the road back to Cork. But what Philly said was still in my head. *What way will I deal with this?*

Between Tuesday, meeting Philly on Wednesday and driving home, I decided that I was going to deal with it at The Last Supper.

I had different ideas about what was the right way to sort it. On the Thursday morning I came in and asked the management staff for their thoughts. They were helpful but some said... 'Just let it go.'

I couldn't. I said, 'No… we have deal with it'.

The lads had left on Tuesday and they were off on Wednesday, so this was the first time they were back in. On the Thursday afternoon following training, I called Shep into my office. He was extremely annoyed.

WE HAD A discussion for three or four minutes. He was really wound up.

'Look John… this will not affect me on Sunday,' he assured me.

'Fine,' I replied. 'I'm not doubting you.' And I wasn't, but it wasn't that simple.

'The problem for you is… it's your reputation.

'If the game goes against you, your career, your reputation… who you are, all of it could be damaged because of this.

'Since I met you, and brought you into the club,' I continued, 'You've been impeccable, professional… brilliant.' A part of me felt sorry for him. But, on the other hand, from my perspective as manager, we had a cup final to win.

We had a chance of winning the double!

I needed to make sure he played well. He was a key player.

'Look… I'll be fine,' he told me. 'I'll be one hundred percent.'

'I'm not doubting you,' I repeated.

'I'm only telling you that you need to be mentally strong because you have been thrown into the fire here.' He told me again he would be ready for Sunday.

He had his say… I had my say.

I looked him in the eye. I could see he was really hurting, but I was confident that he would turn that into a proper performance. When I left him that day, I was feeling more content. I still had to bring it up at The Last Supper, however.

WE WENT TO Fota Island resort just outside the city, and after we had our meal I stood up. 'I've a little presentation for you,' I began.

'But just before… I just want to say one or two things.'

The lads might have thought I was going to go through Dundalk and the tactics for Sunday or whatever. There was none of that.

'Lads, is there an elephant in the room?' There was silence.

'Look lads… there are 20 of you, is there an elephant in the room?'

Again, silence. 'Is there a problem?'

They were all looking at each other.

I pointed at Shep. 'What about him?'

Eventually, Alan Bennett said, 'We've no problem with Shep.' That comment would have meant a lot within the team. You need fellas to pass on good information and Benno was a phenomenal leader on the pitch and within the group. He had a great presence.

It wasn't about roaring and shouting, he was not that type of guy. Benno had played over 200 games in England and earned Ireland caps before coming home. He was always in the right position, a brilliant defender and excellent at organising the defence.

Benno didn't need to do loads and loads of training, we just had to manage him. Off the field, he minded himself. I think that a lot of the younger lads could see how he progressed his career. Benno made other players better, he helped change their mindset about how to look after themselves.

He was also born and bred in Cork, all his family were from Cork.

Benno knew more than most what it meant to play for the club and his support of Shep would have helped the others. I didn't really doubt it before, but I knew now that there would be no issues within the group.

'That's great,' I told them. 'Absolutely, because he's going to be brilliant on Sunday… don't worry about him, because he's one of us.'

Conor McCormack then piped up. 'We'll be right for Sunday!'

McCormack was another one I could rely on completely. I like to sign what I call… *Good honest players.*

Lads who can play and have the skill, have a good mentality – you don't have to be minding them and you're not worried that they're out on the town. They just have the right attitude. They're here to play football. Conor was all of that.

Before I had him, Michael O'Neill told me that he was a brilliant player, that he could play anywhere. *Was he a footballer to pass 40-yard balls?* No, but he was hard as nails, tenacious and had true grit.

We played Derry one day when he was playing with them, and I said something. I was actually roaring on the sideline and Conor was standing about 20 yards away. He turned around and shouted at me.

'F**K OFF!' he roared.

Sometimes in management, when you look back, you take your hat off and just think… *Fair play to him.* He was a tough man, you knew by him it meant something. There are a lot of players just going through the motions; some in it for money. You see it all over England at every level. Whereas, over here in Ireland, for most of them, the money isn't great so they're busting themselves for the love of the game, their own personal pride and for their teammates.

Conor was like that, the whole squad was. *They were honest players.*

I knew from the reaction of Benno and McCormack that Shep's situation wouldn't be an issue within the group. The players were fully behind him. I didn't need to hear any more from them. As far as I was concerned, the issue had been dealt with, so I picked up the Philly McMahon books and handed them around to the players.

'By the way lads, here's a book… a great book. You can read it before Sunday… if you can't, read one or two chapters.'

Walking out the door, you could sense a real togetherness. Sunday was a massive day for us, but we were ready for it. I was one hundred percent happy. We couldn't control anything else. There had been a lot of social media talk about Shep and Kenny's comments. Some people were saying, 'Oh, Sheppard shouldn't play… he should be left out of the cup final team'.

Our chairman Pat Lyons had even phoned me saying, 'There's been a lot of speculation about him'.

I had a great relationship with Pat, but I shut it down immediately.

'Absolutely not… the team is my baby,' I assured Pat.

'There's no problem with Shep.'

ON FRIDAY MORNING we had training, and then we left on the Saturday for Dublin.

Like the previous year, we stayed in the Clayton Hotel in Leopardstown. It was on the other side of the city away from anyone travelling up from Cork for the night. We knew it would be quiet on that side, there would be no one over there and there would be no Dundalk crowd either. These are the sort of considerations you have to make when preparing for a final.

When I got up on the morning of the game, I was surrounded by the management staff and the players. It can become a bit stuffy, people living in each other's pockets – especially when there is a lot of nervous energy hanging around ahead of such a big match.

I needed time to myself. After breakfast, I left the hotel, and I was away for maybe an hour and a half.

We had travelled up by coach… we had no cars with us. So, I hopped on the Luas into Dundrum and I went to Mass. I did it the previous year too on the day of the cup final. I always go to Mass.

It just gives me space to myself. There was no one with me, there was no one who knew me and there was no one asking me any questions.

It was an hour and a half all to myself. I needed it.

I was able to think about the game, how it was going to go. My mind raced, thinking back to where the club was when we came in, the progress we had made. But it was still a bit of tranquillity before the day started.

When I came back, I had a pre-match meeting with the management team at noon, and we then had a brief team meeting for about 10 minutes.

At that point, I never want to bog the lads down with too much information. We had gone through everything we needed to during the week – video analysis, set-pieces… the whole lot was done.

Lisa Fallon was our video analyst and opposition scout. She was really top class. The year before, Lisa came up with an idea of having a motivational video for the final. So, once we got to the semi-final, she got clips of the year together from training and games.

She made a three and a half minute motivational video and we played it in the hotel before we left for the stadium.

Did it make any difference? It's impossible to know, but it couldn't harm our chances of winning. Like with a lot of things in football, the outcome determined everything you tried beforehand.

I went in and named the team.

Mark McNulty… Steven Beattie, Alan Bennett, Ryan Delaney, Shane Griffin… Conor McCormack, Gearóid Morrissey, Jimmy Keohane, Garry Buckley, Stephen Dooley… Karl Sheppard. Subs… Greg Bolger, Achille Campion, Conor Ellis, Conor McCarthy, Kieran Sadlier, Robbie Williams… Alan Smith.

I wished them well and we left for the stadium.

THIS WAS THE biggest day of the year in Irish football. The two best teams in the country playing in a magnificent stadium, in a game live on national television on a Sunday afternoon.

It was a showcase for everything good about Irish football.

Two brilliant teams, two historic clubs and two passionate sets of supporters. If we were playing most teams other than Dundalk, and the game was televised, we always reckoned that our attendance would be down round 700 or 800 from our usual crowd at Turner's Cross.

On cup final day though, we didn't have to worry about the attendance. There were almost 25,000 in the Aviva Stadium. The noise and colour from both sets of supporters was special. It added so much to the event and showed the potential of the league and the teams.

As a manager, I didn't really get the chance to soak it all in beforehand, even if, before kick-off, I was at a bit of a loose end.

The players and coaches went out and did their stuff with the warm-ups. I stayed around the dressing-room and went out halfway through the warm-up. I watched on and said a word to one or two players.

That was generally my routine.

I'm not really superstitious.

Not anymore, anyway.

For years and years, I was unreal, especially as a player but also as a manager. Maybe one or two years into the City job, I just went away from the superstition because it gets into your head and, in the end, sure it's all rubbish anyway.

Will I wear the same suit? Oh, I wore it last week... And we won!

Eventually, you just break from it because otherwise it almost becomes *too* important.

For the cup final, I had to be focused on the sideline and composed. But the adrenaline was absolutely running one hundred percent through me.

I thought about winning and losing beforehand, visualising how the game would play out... *What it would mean to win the double.*

Cork City had never done it before. Something like this seemed so far away when I came in as manager at the end of 2013, when we had five players signed with the club.

I was shaking inside with nerves, but I couldn't show it. I had to be strong and try to be controlled, give the impression I was relaxed.

It's a lonely place to be.

IT WAS AN even game.

There weren't a lot of chances. It was a bit like a chess match.

For both clubs, both sets of supporters, it was intriguing and probably great for a soccer guy watching at home. *Was it great for a neutral sitting back to watch the game?* Probably not. The match finished 0-0 and went to extra-time.

And then, Niclas Vemmelund scored for Dundalk after four minutes of extra-time, a header after Ryan Delaney lost him.

At this point, the easy thing might have been to think… *It's the cup final, it's only been a one-goal game for the previous couple of years.*
We're done.

But straightaway I looked to the big screen at the Havelock Square end and saw that there were 20 minutes to go.

We brought on Greg Bolger and Kieran Sadlier, and changed the system.

When we won the cup the previous year, Greg wasn't at his best and he had an injury for most of the second part of the season. As the 2017 season had progressed, he wasn't involved in lots of games because McCormack was flying.

But you need that competition, you need players to respond. Greg did. He went to the middle of the park and made a huge difference.

Sadlier went to the number 10 position. Sads was English-born but from Irish stock. He came in when Seáni left in the second half of the season – one of the few times we actually paid a transfer fee for a player.

We couldn't get a direct replacement for Seáni, because he was unique, and he was an out and out centre-forward.

Sads was more of a wide player who could play the 10 role and give us more options and score goals. He had incredible technique, and on both left and right striking the ball he was absolutely brilliant. He was deceptively good in the air as well. He was one of those players who had loads and loads of natural talent.

It was my job to try to make him consistent, because he had that X-factor where he could drop the shoulder and go past a fella and could score from 30 yards.

ACHILLE CAMPION also came on for us up front. Some of the lads that came off had tired a lot, which was inevitable at the end of a long season.

Up to the half-time break in the first period of extra-time, we had come back into the match and the fresh lads who came on looked lively. We had a chance from a corner, but it was still 1-0.

Dundalk probably thought they were over the line because one goal had decided it in our other finals. When we changed for the second-half, I sensed that they backed off.

'They've dropped off, let's get at them!' I said to the players at the break.

Nine minutes from the end of extra-time, Sheppard chipped a ball over the top... Campion was in.

H, as we called him, was French. A big, fit guy, he was 6'2", he was strong, and he could run. He wasn't bad in the air either and could hold the ball up. But he wasn't a prolific goalscorer at all – he had only scored once that season. The lads used to give him unbelievable stick in training.

When I saw him, I was wondering if he was offside because he was so far ahead. I was looking, but the flag stayed down. He was in. H controlled the ball, turned and hit it low. Gary Rogers got a hand on it but eventually the ball went in.

It's in the net!

H was a smashing guy. I will always remember one story about him, and had never seen it happen before, but at training one morning someone said an ice-cream van was outside. We were confused. *Why the hell would there be an ice-cream van outside the training ground?* We could hear the music playing.

H walked in.

'Oh yeah, it's my birthday,' he announced.

'I brought the ice cream van.'

So, the players all went out and got their ice-cream and stood outside eating their cones. He brought an ice-cream van to training to celebrate his own birthday!

Until extra-time in the cup final, he had scored as many goals in the season as he had brought ice-cream vans to training.

After his goal, I'd always say to the players when they were slagging him, 'Remember, he got us that goal'.

We were back in it.

There were eight minutes to go, it was 1-1 and I felt then we could win it.

I thought we could get the second because Dundalk had backed off. They got hit with the goal and now we were in the ascendency.

After that, we had one more chance with three or four minutes to go.

But we had to go to penalties.

SOME PEOPLE SAY that penalties are a lottery. But we had consistently worked on them for a long time.

We had a formula that Lisa brought in two years previously.

We practiced them every week in training… and every player got one penalty each. A guy couldn't practice five. They would take one and go off.

It seemed to be working because we had never missed a penalty in a match until that point. Cork City's record was incredible.

We knew who their takers would be, and ours were… McCormack, Beattie, Sheppard, Bolger, Sadlier.

And it wasn't like as if… *It's cup final day, I'm not sure.* All our players were thinking… *I'm in for it!*

We also did a lot of work with Nults on where they put their penalties. But at the same time, it's going through your head… *If we lose, we'd be desperately unlucky, we've given it everything.*

But it's a penalty shootout… We could win the double.

The margins are almost unfair, everything coming down to 10 kicks of the ball after such a long season, when we'd been incredible.

Years of work… defined by this.

It's almost wrong… but… it's how it is!

All of this was running through my head as the teams prepared to take the kicks. At this point, a manager is ultimately powerless.

Shep stepped up first and scored his penalty. It was brilliant to see the ball hit the net. He had done his part, proved the doubters wrong and could be happy with his contribution. He had played really well and, no matter what, no one could say anything to him now.

McMillan scored his penalty for Dundalk.

Bolger scored for us.

O'Donnell scored for them.

McCormack scored.

Benson scored.

Beattie scored.

The standard was brilliant.

And then Duffy stepped up.

McNulty steadied himself on the line. He dived the right way. Saved it. Our fans went nuts, we celebrated on the line.

But I had to bring myself back down to earth almost instantly because it wasn't won yet.

SADLIER WAS NEXT.

The last kick of the shootout.

He was unbelievable at taking penalties and free-kicks. Absolutely brilliant at dead ball situations. But still my heart was pounding. You know anything can happen, momentum can turn *like that*.

As he picked up the ball and walked to the penalty spot, my mind was racing.

He never misses… it's the last kick of the game.

We're a kick away from winning this thing… everything!

When he scored, I just… my whole body just went!

The relief was incredible, the adrenaline rushed through me… I could physically feel it. Relief, not joy, was the main feeling.

In that instant, that split second, it was the *only* feeling.

I put pressure on players, I know the knocks that are there for a player. I had been there as a player myself, but I felt it 10 times over now as a manager.

The pressure, the intensity… it all evaporates with one accurate kick of the ball. We had won the double, something no one expected at the start of the season.

I was so thrilled for the lads and what they had achieved, they deserved it. I was so happy for the supporters, they had travelled up the country; everyone's family came up. It felt like a collective effort; the fans, the players and the management staff all in sync, all united in this one goal.

The relief and the mix of emotions, it probably took about five or 10 minutes for it to sink in.

The year before when we won it with Seáni scoring in the last minute, I went back into the dressing-room two or three minutes after the final whistle, just to sit down… to get my thoughts again.

The year before I also put on a tie for the presentation and the interviews.

My superstitions had gone, but to gather my thoughts I went back in again after we won the double. It gave me precious minutes to myself.

I was in the dressing-room, on my own, putting on the tie and was just shaking with the nerves, with the emotions.

I was just tying my tie up, well… trying to, and getting myself ready. I could still hear the noise and celebrations from outside; the noise echoed down the tunnel and hung outside the dressing-room.

But I was detached for a moment or two.

Minutes to just compose myself. Because in the same dressing-room afterwards with the cup, they would all be celebrating, all the players, the staff. Bedlam.

I was just thinking… *There's no one here.* Like at Mass earlier that morning, in Dundrum, it was a bit of space. My space.

I WENT BACK out to the pitch and looked for my family who were in a corporate box. Our crowd were electric. *Euphoric.*

The excitement was palpable. They were emotional, I could feel it. The club was on the brink seven years earlier and had been saved by the supporters.

When I was appointed manager in 2013, we had no idea that we would be here a few years later. We had won the double, beaten the team so many had said was the best to ever play in the League of Ireland, the team that had received all the plaudits. And we had done it without some of our best players, when outside influences had tried to bring us down.

Fittingly, Seáni and Kevin were there in the stadium. Seáni was one of the greatest goalscorers in League of Ireland history even though he was only with the club for 18 months. His record was incredible.

Yet, we won it without him. The lads had done it, they had proven beyond any doubt that they were anything but a one-man team.

At the same time, he was still a crucial player for us. So, I called him and Kevin down from the stands. In fairness to the two lads, they didn't really want to join us.

But I was going, 'Look lads… you won the league! You need to be with us'.

I walked with them over to the City supporters and they got a great cheer. I'm sure Kevin felt a bit awkward because they were all chanting Seáni's name, but Kevin had still been the left-back and played his part.

It was fitting that everyone who helped us complete the double was there, and Johnny was up getting the cup as well with Benno.

ROY KEANE AND Martin O'Neill came into the dressing-room to congratulate the lads. I wasn't there… I was on the *Six One* news doing an interview.

Roy had said a few words to the team. I met Roy on loads of occasions. *Had he any passion for Cork City?*

I'm not sure. Roy never played for City, but he seemed to enjoy going to our games. I think he enjoyed watching us competing, when clubs with bigger budgets than ours, like Shamrock Rovers, were *not* competing.

We were the only team that were, and we had come from *nowhere.*

Dundalk and Stephen had a year's start on us, because he was in his job a year ahead of me. They had won three leagues and a double. We had started off and won a cup and now we were after winning the double too.

After the cup was presented, and everyone did their lap of honour, I went into the dressing-room to try say a few words to the players.

I congratulated them, but I didn't say much because there was mayhem.

It was a hyper time, the fellas were all over the place, looking for their families to celebrate with them. They were roaring and shouting, they were wired. The drug testers were in the room, all the management staff were there… the chairman was in.

It's not the time for a manager to speak.

The year before, we stayed in Dublin after the cup final. We decided this time we would come home late on Sunday night ahead of the parade on the Monday.

We stayed in the Poitín Stil in Rathcoole until 10pm. Everyone was still as high as a kite and the boys were in good form. There was no drinking culture within the group, but because the season was over, and due to the emotion of winning the cup, they were in great form.

We all assumed Shep was gone, there was no reason to think he wasn't.

But before we left to get on the bus to Cork, he called me out and asked, 'Can I have a word?'

'Can I meet you tomorrow morning?' I asked.

'I don't want to go to Dundalk!' he told me.

I was conscious that he was after having a couple of drinks, so I wasn't getting into it there.

'Okay, Shep. I'll meet you in the office at two o clock,' I said.

On the way back to Cork, the management staff and I chatted about it.

Has he signed for Dundalk or not?

As far as we knew, he was gone, and I was expecting him to join them. But all the boys had it on the bus coming back that Shep wasn't going to Dundalk.

We got home to Cork at about half one in the morning and went upstairs to Soho; there were maybe 80 or 90 friends and family there.

We had a low-key, relaxing night.

SHEP AND I met at 2pm the next day. The first thing he said to me was, 'I don't want to go to them'. He was adamant.

'I want to stay here!'

There were two things in my head.

One... *If he hasn't signed officially for them, do I want to keep him?* Absolutely. And two... *What am I going to offer him?*

There were rumours of what he was getting from Dundalk and there was no way we could offer him that. Rumours of €1,200 a week? I didn't know that for sure, but we wouldn't have been able to come up with anything like that in Cork. If he wanted a couple of hundred more, I'd be stretching it.

'The problem here is Shep, you're not going to get the deal that they gave you... just to be clear.'

'I know, but this is not about that,' he replied.

What we could afford would still be a long way from what he could get at Dundalk. I then said to him, 'I thought you were going to move back up to Dublin with your girlfriend?'

'No,' he said. 'Look it, I had a good chat with her last night and this morning... she's going to move to Cork.'

'Okay, but what have you signed? Have you got it?' I asked.

He had left the form at home, so we said we'd meet the next day at noon.

The following day, Seán Ó Conaill, the club solicitor came in. He just looked at the paper Shep had on the table. 'That means nothing,' he told us.

There was no legal obligation hanging over him after signing the pre-contract agreement. All it meant was both parties agreed that these were the conditions of the contract, but it wasn't a contract in itself.

At the end of the day, Seán said, it probably favoured the player. If a club pulled out, a player, if he pushed it, might get something. But, ultimately, he said it wasn't worth anything and didn't mean anything.

Shep and I spoke. He was going away the next day for three and a half weeks and seemed anxious to do a deal. We verbally agreed on one.

'What about Kenny?' I then asked.

'You have to ring him.'

He asked me if I would.

'I won't, you have to do it.

'Sometimes you just have say it as it is. Ring him from here, I'll go outside the door and all you say is… "Stephen, thanks very much, I've had a rethink and I've decided not to take up the offer, I'm going to stay with Cork. Thank you very much, good luck".

'Don't say anymore.

'Twenty seconds!'

I left the room and stood outside the door. I heard a conversation and there was a lull. I heard Shep say, 'Well I've made up my mind, that's it. I'm after telling you… good luck!' And he hung up.

WORKING IN IRISH football isn't a stable job. The money isn't great for the majority of players, and most contracts are for 42 weeks. A career could be over with one injury, form can dip, and some players don't have anything else to fall back on.

It said a lot about Shep that he rejected Dundalk, that he turned down the money and the chance to live back in Dublin.

In football, you get guys who only want money. There are other lads who might think… *The set-up is good, the club is good, and I like the manager.* They see the value in that.

If they act the maggot, overstep the mark and take advantage of the decency, well then, that's a different story. But people would have seen within the club and the management team that we were all decent, good people.

The players were all young lads, half my age, their lives only starting off; they were thinking about money, mortgages, bills, cars, partners, kids… which is all stressful.

I was at an older stage where I had done all that. We always tried to do our best for every fella and that stood to us.

Within a few days, the whole situation had turned. We thought we had lost a player to our main rivals, but we got him back. It worked out for us.

CORK CITY OFFERED me a new two-year contract about 10 days before the cup final. I didn't sign it until after the final though because I was wondering… *Am I doing a good job?'*

Does the board have full confidence in me?

The board had to be totally supportive.

If they weren't, I wouldn't stick around.

I had only ever done two-year spells, because in football you can only do so much, and you only get so much time. I always felt that I should do two years and then assess the situation.

We were now into a new cycle.

The only problem this time was that Seáni was gone and we were looking for a centre-forward. Campion was a good guy, but he wasn't going to fill *those* shoes, even though he got us one of the most important goals in the club's history.

The two weeks after the season finishes are the worst two weeks of the year – no matter how the season ends. Everyone goes on holidays, they're all away from the club for six or seven weeks and the manager is left trying to put his panel together.

I had a plan for them all to come back in January, and we would do a few days training at the start of the month. I had re-signed most of the players that I wanted to keep but I was still five or six players short of where I wanted us to be. I had a couple of players lined up to sign, but the other three top clubs had those same players lined up as well. I knew that! It's just how it always is. I was trying to bed things down, so I could go off on holidays myself!

Up until then in Irish football, only Dundalk paid 52-week contracts. It was something we had never done, though we had begun to try to match that full year's commitment as well. That gave us a bit more clout, even if it was still difficult to get players who were, of course, looking for the best deal.

Generally, the Cork guys would stay, but the guys from outside the county, if they could go back up to Dublin and earn two or three hundred quid more, it was a no-brainer.

We had the 'sell' of Champions League and European football and challenging at the top, playing in front of over 5,000 people at Turner's Cross every second week. It was huge exposure for a player. If he was good enough, everyone would know him and it would be a great place to play; he would be a big fish in our city.

We did well with that pitch to players.

But those two weeks after a season finishes were always a nightmare, even after we won the double.

THE EMOTION FROM winning, the relief and the joy, it all goes so quickly. It's hard to explain, even to the management team.

I had responsibility for the whole footballing structure in Cork City… all that responsibility was mine, so everything fell to me.

My coaching staff were absolutely brilliant. They mightn't always have agreed with me, but they were very loyal.

While they would be disappointed when they went home if we lost, I was the guy who was taking all the flak. I was the guy getting abuse.

Ultimately, the management staff would never understand that because they would never have had that pressure.

I was responsible for working within the budget signed off by the board, signing and letting players go, dealing with the board and the media.

And the job was in my head 24/7. I was probably fully stressed every day. I was just flat out. I knew it was a strain on my family; my wife Gráinne, my daughters Aideen and Sinéad.

I would lose a game and for two days I'd be absolutely wrecked. I would take results personally, I could never relax in the job.

People would say to me, 'You've gone grey, you've lost your hair… is that from the stress… the hours that go into it?

'Would you do it all again?'

Of course, I would.

There's nothing else that can give you that adrenaline rush. The intensity of matches leaves you shaking.

As managers, we just live for that adrenaline, that's just the way it is. There is very little time to take stock, to pause and reflect.

The pressure is always building because it's always about the next match, the new season. *Jesus, I must make sure next year we can go again.*

THE DAY AFTER the cup final, the Cork City squad and coaching staff met in Bishopstown, our training ground.

We needed a team photograph of everyone in their suits with the two cups. But Ryan Delaney left his jacket somewhere in town. He knew where he had left it, but the jacket was gone, and no one ever copped it.

When we saw the photograph afterwards, it was immaculate – but then there was Ryan in the middle of it in his waistcoat and no jacket! No one noticed that until after we saw the photograph.

From there, we went to the grand parade in the city centre. They had the stage set up and there were somewhere between 9,000 and 10,000 fans out on the street for us. It was a beautiful night, lovely and mild for November in Cork, really nice.

The crowd was massive, there were loads of kids there and it was an absolutely fantastic atmosphere. It was a great night for the supporters because they were in amongst the players. There was a real feel-good factor and it carried on for weeks.

The team had delivered and everywhere we went, we could feel it. We went around with the cups to the schools, to the schoolboy clubs and the kids were getting into photographs with the players and the cups.

It was absolutely brilliant. This was what I always wanted.

When I did my first interview as Cork City manager, I said I wanted to bring the crowds back, bring the passion back and get the team competing again.

Four years later, we had achieved all of that and more. The passion was back, we were winning trophies, and kids were wearing jerseys around the city and county.

The club was in the right place.

That gave me a great sense of pride.

AFTER THE TROPHY presentation and celebrations at the Aviva, I had gone back out to the pitch. The last two or three hundred City fans were leaving the stadium behind the bottom goal, the City end. They were all singing… 'CHAMPIONS OF IRELAND… CHAMPIONS OF IRELAND.'

I could hear them as they moved away in the distance… their songs and chants echoing through the tunnel as they left the ground.

The double… I thought to myself. *What a magic day.*

And it was.

PART ONE

Choices

CHAPTER 1

I WAS BORN in The Bronx in New York City on October 11, 1964, a long way away from where my parents were from.

My father John was born and reared in a place called Kilmovee, which is in Mayo, near the Roscommon border.

At the time, the eldest son stayed with the house and the parents and everyone else had no choice but to get out of town. Other than working on the land, there were no jobs or prospects in the village, especially not in the 50s.

So, my father left home when he was 16 and went to England. He ended up in Middlesbrough in the north-east. He worked down the coal mines for a time and always told me it was incredibly difficult and dirty work.

After about two years in Middlesbrough, he left with a friend for New York City. He was only 18 years old.

In New York, he got a job working on the buses in the city, and soon settled in The Bronx. To go from Kilmovee to The Bronx must have been such a culture shock. Kilmovee was a small border village, with no more than a few hundred people living there. In The Bronx alone, there must have been well over a million people at the time.

My father spent a huge part of his life in the city and loved it there. It was where he lived through his formative years between his late teens and mid-30s. If you mention it to him now, he will say that he loved that part of his life.

My mother Nora O'Keeffe is from a place called Cullen, just outside of Millstreet, near the Kerry border in north Cork. Like so many Irish people in the 50s, she emigrated too. She and two of her friends also went to New York.

At the time, New York City and The Bronx were full of Irish emigrants, especially people from the west of Ireland, as well as second generation Irish.

The Bronx, with its strong Irish community, made settling there easier for my parents. My mother met my father within a few years of arriving in the city. They got married and then I came along. I only spent four years in New York before we returned to Ireland, though.

Through the years, many journalists have made a lot out of the fact that I was born in New York City. I saw it mentioned before, that I was the first American-born coach to win a top-flight league title in Europe. But I don't really have any connection to the city or America as a country other than being born there.

My brother Daniel came along eight years after me and he would take the opposite journey to me. He was born in Ireland but has spent most of his life in America. Daniel was a natural athlete and got into running. He was a national champion at 1,500 metres and, when he was 16, got a scholarship for a school in America. He went to The Bronx. My parents moved back to New York with him and they stayed there for a long time, over 15 years.

Daniel never made it to the Olympics and missed out on qualification by a fraction of a second during his prime. He was a brilliant athlete, and raced in the World Championships, but would often say to me, 'In athletics, no one in Ireland would know you unless you win an Olympic medal. That's just the way it is'.

There was no funding in Ireland for athletics at that time. You wouldn't get a penny unless you went and won something in the Olympics, and there were very few Irish runners going to do that.

But Daniel has been involved in athletics ever since he left for America and has made a life for himself in the United States. He married Jackie, an American girl, and is the head athletics cross-country coach at a university in Pennsylvania.

My life has always been in Ireland.

FOUR YEARS AFTER I was born, we moved to Roscommon where my father bought a pub and a farm in a place called Curraghboy, a small village about 35 miles or so from where my father was born and reared in Kilmovee. While our house in Lecarrow was being built, we lived in Roscommon town for a couple of years.

Lecarrow, Knockcroghery is on the south side of the county, around 13 miles from Athlone and close to Lough Ree. It's a small village.

Knockcroghery once had a massive clay pipe industry. A factory in the village operated for 250 years, and exported pipes all over the world… until 1921, when the village and the factory were burned to the ground by the Black and Tans.

The village's other claim to fame was the presence of Jimmy Murray, who captained Roscommon in gaelic football when the county won All-Ireland titles in 1943 and '44. People travelled from all over the country to visit Jimmy's pub.

Jimmy coached me at underage level for the local team, St Dominic's. Later, when I was playing with Cork City, he used to say to me, 'How did you end up playing soccer for Cork?'

It was a fair question. And, from his perspective, it was easy to see why he was confused by my sporting career path. Roscommon was a big gaelic football county and soccer was almost non-existent there at the time.

I LOVED ALL sports and played everything I could, looking for any way I could to get off the farm. It was fair to say that I was never planning on being a farmer.

I played gaelic football at minor level for Roscommon and loved it. It was very much GAA country. The Roscommon District League, which organised junior level soccer in the county, wasn't formed until 1971, when the ban on 'foreign games' was lifted by the GAA.

At schoolboy level though, there was no organised soccer in the county. Athlone had a big soccer heritage – Athlone Town is the oldest League of Ireland club in the country, founded in 1887 – and there would be summer leagues in the town. I would go in to the town each summer and play in those leagues. But I didn't take part in any regular organised soccer until later, when I played in the Community Games.

I suppose my love of soccer stemmed from when I was seven or eight, maybe earlier. I distinctly remember watching the FA Cup final on television each year. If there was a stand-out game for me, it was the 1971 FA Cup final between Arsenal and Liverpool.

It is the first soccer match I remember watching on television. There were

100,000 at Wembley and the television coverage lasted the whole day. Arsenal had won the league and were going for the double – which was a rare achievement in those days. The Gunners won it in extra time – Charlie George and Eddie Kelly scored – and I was hooked on Arsenal, but particularly soccer, from that day onwards.

Soccer just had a certain glamour that gaelic football didn't have at that time.

This may seem strange to a younger person now, but what I particularly loved about soccer was that the players all had their own kits – their own jerseys, their own togs and their own socks.

Arsenal just looked brilliant in their red jerseys with white sleeves and white shorts, or in their yellow and blue 'away' kit on the day they beat Liverpool. It caught the eye.

While, in gaelic football, there was no such thing as each team having its own kit. We wore the jerseys that were used in our club. The under-12s, under-14s and under-16s all shared kits, and jerseys were thrown on the ground for the next team to pick them up the following day, unwashed and oversized.

I always loved the organised element of soccer – the kit, the gear, the boots, everything seemed to be the best in class. Just to have a nice pair of boots as a young lad made us all feel 10-feet tall walking onto the pitch.

I had caught the soccer bug.

MY PARENTS WEREN'T particularly sporty, so we are not quite sure where my brother or I got the sporting genes from.

My father went to a couple of soccer matches when he was living in Middlesbrough, to Ayresome Park. He followed sport when we were back in Roscommon also, and he was involved in the local GAA club. He was a GAA man. But he never played any sport, which isn't a surprise given he left home so young.

He very much helped foster my love of sport though, as he brought me to games, both gaelic and soccer, from an early age.

As I've explained, I was a soccer fanatic from around 1972 onwards. I reckon from between 1972 to maybe around '87, when I entered my twenties, I could tell you about any player from any team. I was obsessed.

My father knew that and therefore made an extra effort to bring me to matches. In 1975, we went to the famous UEFA Cup match between Athlone Town and

AC Milan in St Mel's Park. It was the first match I attended. I had just turned 11.

Athlone was a big soccer town, a garrison town, with a great passion for the sport. The team had finished second in the league the previous season under Amby Fogarty, a Dubliner who had spent a large part of his career in England.

After beating a Norwegian side in the opening round of the competition, Athlone drew AC Milan, and the interest was massive. The entrance to the ground was narrow and tight. It was absolutely packed on the day. They say there were 10,000 people at the game, which must have been almost the entire population of Athlone.

But it was hard to tell exactly how many spectators were there. From my vantage point, it was just a sea of people, the place was heaving.

I remember my father protecting me, shielding me from the crowd and keeping a tight grip on my arm. There was no health and safety regulations then, no ticket scanner, no security to try to keep order.

St Mel's had a fence running around the pitch – it was only a few yards from the pitch, you could almost reach out and touch the players – with a wall further back that people were sitting and standing on. There were no stands or cover over the ground. We were open to all the elements and it was a sharp, windy day in October.

The breeze whipped across the ground, fluttering the flags on the side of pitch – well, 'pitch' might be a stretch. It was essentially just muck with some lines painted on it. I don't remember seeing much grass.

But the atmosphere was absolutely electric.

There is a famous photo of the AC Milan players getting off the team bus outside the ground and stepping into mucky potholes wearing their immaculate Italian leather shoes. It must have been an alien experience for them. I didn't realise it at the time, but they had some brilliant players, like Gianni Rivera. Giovanni Trapattoni was on their coaching staff.

We knew that it was a big deal to be playing AC Milan and they were this massive club from this glamorous, prestigious league, but I suppose we didn't really know who they were.

They were famous Italian footballers and that was enough for us. Milan came onto the pitch with their pristine gear – their famous red jerseys with black stripes, white shorts and black socks with a red trim. They looked like Gods.

The two teams were led onto the pitch by a pipe band and Athlone's mascot – which was a goat.

It was surreal.

ATHLONE PLAYED GREAT on the day and should have won. They got a penalty and the crowd started celebrating and cheering. We thought Athlone were going to win it. John Minnock missed with his kick, however.

The Italian goalkeeper dived to his right and stopped it.

You could hear a pin drop in St Mel's after the penalty was missed. The air was sucked from the crowd. People weren't even cursing or giving out. It was stunned silence. All we could hear were the Italian players shouting at each other, and the flags blowing in the wind.

The game ended 0-0, which was still an incredible result for Athlone Town and Irish football, one of the best ever achieved by a League of Ireland team.

Everyone left the ground happy.

I was hooked on the game, even more so.

A few weeks later, I listened to the second leg on the radio. Athlone lost 3-0 in the San Siro after holding out for most of the game. The experience left a big impression on me. My love for, and affinity towards, the League of Ireland started that day, and it sparked my interest in domestic soccer.

There was man who lived up the road from us in Knockcroghery named Bertie Fallon. He used to go to all the Athlone home games every second week – League of Ireland matches were played on a Sunday afternoon back then – and I would head along with him if my father couldn't bring me.

I played more gaelic football than I did soccer at that point, a lot more, but I remained fascinated with soccer.

Other than the summer leagues in Athlone though, and the Community Games, I didn't have the chance to play the sport as soccer remained almost non-existent in Roscommon. In some counties at that time there was a serious resentment towards the sport from hardened GAA people.

But I never encountered that attitude in Roscommon. Soccer just wasn't a threat to gaelic football… it was a non-entity. There were no teams to join, so there no chance of the GAA losing players to the sport.

BACK THEN IN the country, the Community Games was like the Olympics. If you won your event, for instance, in athletics – the 100 metres, 200 metres or whatever – you got to go to the Community Games in Mosney.

It hosted events for almost every sport, including gaelic football, hurling, rugby and soccer. There was one team per sport, per age group. But you could only play for one team in one sport.

There was a strict Community Games rule that you couldn't go forward for two teams. So, we had to make a choice between gaelic football and soccer.

In Roscommon town, gaelic football was very strong, and soccer was also popular amongst the lads, especially the townies. Out in the county though, it was *all* gaelic football.

This was the first time I experienced a conflict between the sports.

Everyone else on the team that played the two sports opted for gaelic football. I wanted to play soccer.

I was the youngest on the team, but I was saying, 'No, I don't want to play gaelic'.

I was adamant. However, it was the one and only time in my life that my father blocked me when it came to sport.

It was under-14, and we were up against the very best teams representing every county in Ireland.

We won that Community Games title in Mosney, which was a big deal for the team and for the town in 1975.

It's funny, even now, all these years later, if I meet any of the lads that were on that team, they will always laugh and remind me I wanted to play soccer ahead of gaelic.

In the team photo, you can see me with my white boots! Playing gaelic football with white boots was unheard of, but there I was!

Still a boy, but already a soccer man at heart.

CHAPTER 2

WHEN THE TIME came to go to secondary school, I could have gone to the Christian Brothers in Roscommon.

But the school had no soccer team and I had made up my mind; I wanted to play soccer. The only way to do that was to go to Summerhill College in Sligo.

Sligo was a massive soccer town, another garrison town like Athlone, and Summerhill had a very good soccer team. They were a *big* soccer school. But, the school was 60 miles away from home! Summerhill was also a boarding school.

I'm not sure if all of this registered with me. I was young and fearless, perhaps? I begged and pleaded with my parents to send me to the school.

They were baffled and just couldn't understand it, understandably so. They said that there was a bus passing our door every day to bring me to a school 10 minutes away, and a bus to bring me home every evening.

Why did I want to go to Summerhill... *A school that was so far away?*

Why did I want to move an hour and a half away to a boarding school?

The world was a much bigger place back then. To go to school in another county, it was almost like there was no coming back.

You couldn't come home every weekend. And as I was the eldest in the family, it was tough for my parents to see me so keen to leave home at such a young age. I was incredibly determined and enthusiastic, however.

This was the only way I could get to play organised soccer and play it every day. This was the type of school I was looking for. In my head, I was going to Summerhill to play soccer and that was that.

My parents gave in eventually and off I went to boarding school in Sligo.

THE FACE OF Summerhill College is a grey stone, and very austere looking, imposing. It was built in the 1850s and, by the time I got there in the mid-70s, it was starting to show its age. But I loved the school.

Summerhill was just an absolutely fantastic place to go to school.

It might sound strange to people, for someone to love going to boarding school. If you mentioned that you went to boarding school, some people might think you were being sent there by your parents.

But it wasn't like that at all for me.

There were so many lads in the boarding school who were there because they *had* to be there. Their parents might have sent them against their will, or because they couldn't look after them at home for whatever reason. Those lads were generally unhappy in the school.

For me, though, boarding in Summerhill was great. I loved it. It was perfect for me and what I wanted to do. I played soccer all the time – at break-time in school, after school, and for the school team and for the local team. There were organised soccer competitions within the school.

Summerhill boarders were allowed to go home at weekends. But I would usually stay in Sligo and play for a local team, Carraroe. I played for them at under-14, under-15 and under-16 levels. I went home maybe once a month.

The boarders were lads from counties in the midlands and the north-west – Roscommon, Leitrim, Mayo and Donegal. They were mostly from rural backgrounds and into gaelic football.

The local lads from Sligo were known as the 'day boys', as they never had to board in the school and got to go back home to their own beds every night.

As a massive soccer town, the locals were undoubtedly more into soccer than GAA. The townies were soccer heads. There was an obvious divide between the students, between sports, and between urban and rural. A lot of the townies wouldn't even play GAA for the school, even though they were good at the sport.

It was strange to me, as I loved all sports, but they wouldn't entertain the thought of playing gaelic football for the school.

The only lads from Sligo who played GAA were from rural areas. I felt conflicted between the two games. I was one of the few boarders who played both. It was unusual in the school for someone to play both, but I thought nothing of it. I was the only boarder on the school soccer team, everyone else were townies… the 'day boys'.

In my Leaving Certificate year, I was captain of the team when we made it to the All-Ireland Schools final. We played Drimnagh College from Dublin. Niall Quinn would have played for them, but he was suspended after getting sent-off in the semi-final. We still lost; Conor Flynn, who went on to play for Bohemians, scored the winning goals.

I WENT TO school in Sligo for six years and my experience was very positive. It had everything I was looking for. I was never a home bird, so being away never bothered me. I was always on the move.

When I was a young fella, I was either playing in a game or going to matches. I would even go over to England to matches every chance I could. My uncle lived in London and I would go over to him for my holidays, when I was 14 or so, in the late-70s. It just so happened that he lived in Highbury, in north London, right next door to Arsenal almost.

Every time I went over, I went to an Arsenal game. It was incredible. They were brilliant at that time and had such a strong Irish connection, so there was a great excitement around the team amongst soccer fans in Ireland. Four of their best players were 'ours' – Liam Brady, Pat Jennings, Frank Stapleton and David O'Leary. There were seven Irish players with Arsenal at one point.

I loved going to the Showgrounds to watch Sligo and I loved going to St Mel's to see Athlone Town. But going to Highbury was something completely different. There, I entered a place I viewed as Heaven.

There were around 35,000 or so at Arsenal home games, all the supporters on top of each other on the terraces, penned in and chanting. The experience was unlike anything you would experience at a game in Ireland.

At holiday times, it was easier to get to a few games as the fixtures list was stacked during those periods. I had become a keen Arsenal fan at this point, but I would go to watch Tottenham Hotspur if The Gunners were playing away. I would even go over to Fulham in west London. They were in the Second Division at the time, but it didn't matter to me. Or, I would then take the tube to Stamford Bridge to watch Chelsea.

Tourists in London spent their time going to see the famous sights, to Buckingham Palace or the West End or whatever, but all I wanted to do was go to a football stadium.

BACK IN IRELAND, there were only three television channels when I was a boy. RTE, BBC and ITV. To see a match – any match live – was such a treat because we only ever got the FA Cup final shown live on television every year.

Match of the Day was on the BBC on Saturday nights, with highlights of one or two games – we might get to watch it the odd time if the signal held up in Roscommon and Sligo. ITV had *The Big Match* every Sunday afternoon, with more highlights of two or three more games, which many felt hurt the League of Ireland attendances. Live soccer matches on television were a rarity, however, so you would have to find other ways to follow the English game.

Every Saturday, after my own match for the soccer team in Sligo, I listened in to BBC Radio 5. The signal would often be crackling and fickle, but I would be glued to the radio, listening to the scores from England as they came in.

Looking back, I think that's why I remember so much about soccer during that period; it's why I still remember the names of players from that era.

The rarity of football on television made attending live games all the more special and exciting. I loved the buzz of going to games, gaelic Football or soccer, it didn't matter.

I just loved going to matches… in England, or to Irish international matches in Dublin. I even went to a few international rugby matches on a bus rented out for the day by Sligo Rugby Club.

THE FIRST IRELAND game I remember attending was against England in 1978, a few weeks after my 14th birthday.

The matches were always held on Wednesday afternoons, because there were no floodlights, which meant I had to try to get a half-day from school to go up to Dublin.

I asked my father to write a letter to the school to ask for special permission to take me out of school early so we could go to the Ireland game. Summerhill didn't like that. It set a precedence for other students, who might have wanted to do the same. But they still let me go.

Ireland had yet to qualify for a major tournament, and England had not reached the World Cup finals since 1970 – but it was still a big game, a Euros qualifier, and there were some brilliant players on the pitch.

Ireland had Liam Brady, David O'Leary, Mark Lawrenson, Tony Grealish, Don Givens and Frank Stapleton. John Giles was the manager.

The Ireland team had not captured the attention of the wider Irish public at this point, which was a shame because they were a very talented team, who played great football. It was a massive treat to watch these players, and such a novelty.

The match finished 1-1.

Gerry Daly scored for Ireland, and the place erupted. There must have been 50,000 at Lansdowne Road that day. The terraces, with high fences in front of us, were full of Irish flags; it was such a thrill.

I went to a lot of those Wednesday afternoon Ireland games. I was there at Lansdowne Road a few years later in 1981 when Ireland beat a great French team 3-2 in a famous match. Michael Robinson and Frank Stapleton scored for Ireland, Michel Platini got a goal for the French.

I would get the train from Sligo up to Dublin and meet my father up there. He would collect me at Houston Station, and we would make our way to Lansdowne Road – always Lansdowne Road, as the Irish matches had switched from Dalymount Park at that point.

I remember going back to school, to Summerhill, and telling the lads in my class, 'I was there yesterday'. It was unusual for fellas from the country to go to these games. They were long days, but they were always worth it and special; it was fascinating to be there. As a GAA man, my father mostly followed soccer because I did. But he made the effort for me.

Looking back, he did whatever he could to help foster my love of sport.

I WAS IN Croke Park an awful lot as a young fella too.

One of the first gaelic football games I remember going to was Roscommon against Kerry in a National League final in 1974; it went to a replay and Kerry won it well. I was nine.

Going to these games are some of my earliest sporting memories.

Obviously, the biggest GAA matches in the championships were played during the summer when I was off school, so my father would always bring me to the inter-county games. It helped that the Roscommon team, led by the legendary Dermot Earley, was very strong during the late-70s and early-80s.

From 1976 to '80, Roscommon were one of the top teams in the country and played in Croke Park every year.

They won the Connacht Championship four times in-a-row, they won the National League in 1979 and regularly made it to All-Ireland semi-finals. Then, in 1980, they reached the All-Ireland final, where they played Mick O'Dwyer's amazing Kerry team.

The excitement of going to Croke Park late that summer for the semi-final and final was incredible – heading up in the car early on the morning of the match with my family and neighbours, being out for the whole day, with over 65,000 people in the stadium.

What I distinctly remember from those games, and the 1980 final in particular, were the nerves. I was so nervous at the match. I was almost shaking, just absolutely desperate for Roscommon to win. That whole team were heroes to us.

That Roscommon team was my team, too, like Arsenal. And I knew every player and every statistic, and supported them at every game I could.

Roscommon were such a tough side and had excellent players like Harry Keegan, Gerry Connellan, Danny Murray and, of course, Dermot Earley. They started the 1980 final brilliantly and went ahead very early in the game.

John O'Connor, who was known as 'Jigger' because of his brilliant control of the ball under pressure, scored a goal after about 30 seconds. Kerry worked their way back into the match though. They were a formidable team, going for their third All-Ireland in-a-row, and they had the brilliant Jack O'Shea and Pat Spillane leading them. In truth, every man on their team was a household name in every county in the land.

In the end, despite an heroic performance, particularly in defence, Roscommon lost by three points, 1-9 to 1-6. Roscommon had got so close but couldn't get over the finish line, though there was no real expectation within the county that Roscommon would win.

The county had not won the All-Ireland since 1944. But, for me, it was gut-wrenching to lose. The disappointment within me festered for months.

I PLAYED FOR Roscommon at minor level.

My father always maintained that I was a better gaelic footballer than I was a soccer player. I was half-decent, but I was never one of the top players on the Roscommon team.

I played with Paul Earley, a younger brother of Dermot's. Paul was one of our top players and was recruited to play Australian Rules for the Melbourne Demons club, before coming home and starring for Roscommon at senior level for a decade.

I suppose, what held me back was my height. I was quite small as a teenager. In my Leaving Certificate year, I was only about five and a half feet tall, and I was on the county minor team with big country fellas, many of them farmers' sons.

I was a farmer's son too, but I was anything but a farmer. I was never on the land or doing the tough manual labour that is necessary on any small holding. Even in the summer, when I was home from Summerhill, I would work in the town in the local shop.

I just never enjoyed working on the land. I was more of a townie and was probably perceived that way. I suppose that extended to my sporting preference in the end.

Soccer, one hundred percent, had become my No.1 sport.

CHAPTER 3

IN MY LEAVING Certificate year, I had to start thinking about what I would do after I left school.

Working on the farm wasn't going to happen!

I was strong at accountancy and business in school, but I hadn't a defined idea of what I wanted to do at that point – I had no career plan of any kind – other than playing soccer.

I wanted to be a professional soccer player.

That was the goal.

Like all young Irish soccer fans, I dreamed about playing in England, of course. That was just a dream, though. To get a move over to an English club, you generally needed to go on trials as a teenager, and there weren't any players from Roscommon going across the Irish Sea.

In those days, there were a handful of teams in Dublin and Cork that acted as feeder clubs for English teams. If you didn't play for one of these teams, you didn't have much chance of getting a trial with an English club.

THERE WERE A couple of exceptions to the rule at that time.

Kevin Moran went from playing gaelic football for Dublin, and winning two All-Irelands, to playing for Manchester United in 1978. Most others followed a more traditional route, like in 1982, when Paul McGrath also joined United from

St Patrick's Athletic, and Jim Beglin signed for Liverpool from Shamrock Rovers around that time too.

They were all exceptional players and I was never in that league; I was never capped at underage level by Ireland or in contention to go on trials.

At that point, I realised that the chance of getting over to England had passed – or was probably never there.

Playing football was still all I wanted to do, however.

A month before I sat my Leaving Cert exams, when I was 18, I went to the FAI Cup semi-final between Sligo Rovers and Cobh Ramblers. Cobh were non-league at the time, and the semi-final really caught the attention. The tie went to four games. They played twice in Cork and twice in Sligo, and three of the games went to extra time. It was incredible.

Eventually, in the fourth and final match, Sligo won 3-2 in extra time.

I was in the Showgrounds for the match. The place was absolutely packed – there were about 7,000 or 8,000 in the ground and the whole town was transfixed by the match. It was like it hit me then, all of sudden. Looking around the ground, at the players on the pitch, I thought to myself… *I would love this.*

I would love to be playing in the League of Ireland.

I had always followed the league, from the days of going to St Mel's Park with my father to watch Athlone Town.

I loved going to Sligo matches at the Showgrounds. I loved how the whole town got behind the team and how it was part of the town's culture. I loved the way people invested in the team, how the mood of the town could be lifted by a good result.

It wasn't that I had never thought of playing in the league before, or that it was a consolation prize for me, but the goal very much became crystallised for me that day.

Don't get me wrong, it wasn't as if I was going to walk into any League of Ireland team. I was still thinking to myself… *How am I going to get started?*

The standard was so high. But that day in Sligo convinced me of my future.

AFTER MY LEAVING Certificate, I went to Athlone Regional Technical College, which is now Athlone Institute of Technology. It was the next place to go, I suppose.

Some college students know from an early age what they want to do, or have a general idea; they are focused. I wasn't.

At that point, it felt like every one of my year was going to college, whereas 10 or 15 years previously, most wouldn't have. It was almost essential that you should go to college and get a qualification. It was perceived that you should go. The regional colleges were another avenue you could take if you didn't get into university.

I did Business Studies, but still had no real career path in mind.

If I am to be blunt, looking back, I was probably just doing it for the sake of it, not knowing where I was going.

I was playing soccer for my local team in Roscommon, a junior team called Knockcroghery Rovers, and I was playing for the college. We would play against the other regional colleges that would become Institutes of Technology – DIT, Blanchardstown, Tallaght, Bolton Street, Rathmines.

I felt like I was probably going nowhere. Like a lot of young men at that stage in their life, I was drifting. That began to change when I joined Athlone Town reserves, or the B team as they used to call it.

At that time, Athlone Town were doing very well, experiencing the best period in their history. Turlough O'Connor was the senior team manager.

Turlough was strongly associated with Dundalk and Bohemians. He scored a lot of goals for both teams during his career. He also played for Fulham in England, and won a couple of Ireland caps in the 1960s and 70s.

At the end of his career, he became player-manager for Athlone Town, his hometown team. O'Connor used his connections from his time with Dundalk and Bohemians and brought in a lot of Dublin-based players.

He helped turn Athlone into a serious team.

They won the League of Ireland twice while he was manager – in 1981 and '83. It was amazing for the town, the only times in the club's history that they won the league.

I joined the reserve team in 1983; playing as a sweeper, where I had always played growing up.

I greatly enjoyed my time with Athlone Town reserves. The B team was made up mostly of young lads trying to make their way in the game. But there were also a few first-team players coming back from injury, dropping down to play a couple of matches to get their fitness levels back up.

Turlough, the first-team manager, played for us, as did Fran Hitchcock, a Dublin player who would go on to play for several League of Ireland clubs. Fran also scored for Athlone Town in the European Cup.

We played in the B division against the other reserve teams of League of Ireland clubs.

Matches were played every Saturday and our away games were at League of Ireland grounds. We got to play against Bohemians reserves at Dalymount and Shamrock Rovers reserves at Milltown, the famous Glenmalure Park which would be knocked down a few years later.

There was nobody at the matches, no supporters, but it was nice to play at these famous grounds.

We managed to win the reserve league twice in two seasons. It was a good time.

I also played for the college's gaelic football team and we reached the final of the regional colleges' final, which was played at Croke Park. It was always a dream to play at the stadium where I had spent so much time watching Roscommon.

It was surreal playing in a stadium that vast, but so empty. I just remember the echo of players shouting with no fans to drown out the voices.

We were beaten by a handful of points on the day. But it was still good to say I had played at Croke Park.

AFTER TWO YEARS of the Business Studies course in Athlone, I spotted that AnCO – which was the forerunner to FÁS – were running two sales courses and were paying people to do them. One was in Dublin, the other was in Cork.

I decided to go to Cork and give it a try.

I chose Cork because I knew it well from visiting the county as a child with my family. As my mother was from Millstreet, I had loads of relations and connections in the county. So, in 1985, I moved to Cork. I lived in the city at first.

I was still playing for Athlone Town's reserves and continued to travel up for games at the start of the season, when I would stay for the weekend.

Early in the season, Athlone's first-team had a game against Home Farm at Tolka Park. I was told that I would travel with the team for the match and be part of the squad. It was a nice surprise.

The game was open, with lots of chances. Home Farm were amateurs but looked like beating us when they scored with about 15 minutes to go. We equalised with about five minutes left to make it 2-2.

And then, with about three minutes to play, I was substituted on to play at right-back. It was a week or two after I had turned 21 and I had managed to achieve my goal of playing in the League of Ireland, even if I was only on the pitch for a few minutes.

It happened so fast I didn't really get the chance to let it sink in.

I had made a breakthrough and got into the first-team squad, and made my first appearance for the club. But, it would prove to be my one and only appearance for Athlone Town.

AT THE END of the previous season, Turlough O'Connor left the club and took the Dundalk job. Turlough had brought tremendous success to Athlone Town but left after the club started to tighten their budget.

Athlone had built a new clubhouse and attendances were down from the previous season. They were in debt. Turlough's departure was a shock to most people associated with the club, if not entirely unsurprising. He had spent six years as Athlone manager, and it was going to be a tough job to rebuild the team.

At Dundalk, he would win another two League of Ireland titles.

Athlone's new manager, Con Flanagan had to work with a smaller squad, and work with some of the younger players, because Athlone were in such a tight spot financially. But he didn't seem to rate me, or any of the local players.

He was preoccupied with the Dublin players, who were coming down on the bus to play. He brought in a new batch of players to replace many of Turlough's gang, who had already won leagues and would go on to win league titles elsewhere. Con brought in a bunch of lads from the Leinster Senior League.

The decline was sharp.

Athlone Town went from being very competitive, to dropping down a division. I think they finished eighth that season, having been third the previous year.

Yet, he still wouldn't play the young lads. It felt to us as though he didn't want any of the local players. The commute up and down from Cork to Athlone each week also wasn't working out for me. So, after my one and only appearance for the first-team, I went to Con and told him there was no point in me travelling up from Cork. And that was it, I left Athlone Town.

I joined a team in Cork called Wembley, who played in the Munster Senior League. I played with them until the end of that season, while I did my sales course.

During the course, I did work experience in a business called Soundstore and after the course was finished I got a full-time job with the company. They were an electronic company, selling televisions and electronic items and technology which, at that time, was new age. Fax machines and video recorders would become all the rage in businesses and homes.

After a few months, the owner of the company asked me would I move to their store in West Cork. He offered me a company car as part of the deal. I had no idea where the store was; I knew nothing about West Cork either, but I agreed and moved to the store.

I have been in West Cork ever since.

I joined St Mary's GAA club in Enniskeane and played gaelic football during the summer. The two sports perfectly complimented each other at the time.

The soccer season ran from mid-September to the end of April. The GAA season was from the middle of May to August. It meant I was keeping fit and playing away for a full 12 months.

Around the same time, I experienced some luck with soccer too.

Wembley's assistant manager Mick Punch also happened to be Cork City's assistant manager under Noel O'Mahony. Ahead of pre-season training for the 1986/87 season, Mick brought me up to Cork City. And, for the next 33 years of my life, 22 of them would be spent with Cork City.

PART TWO

Learning My Trade

AFTER MOVING TO West Cork, Cork City became central to who I am for almost all of my adult life. Here I am **(top left)** in action in 1991. The man who moulded City into a winning team in the 90s with his fierce passion was Noel O'Mahony **(top right)**.

IT WAS NOEL who wanted a Cork City team filled with as many proud Cork lads as possible, which led the way to our European adventures, including facing the brilliant Bayern Munich in 1991 **(centre)** and winning the league title two years later. The team that played Bayern in the home leg was... **Back row (from left):** Mick Conroy, Dave Barry, Phil Harrington, Gerry McCabe, Paul Bannon and Stephen Napier. **Front row (from left):** Pat Morley, Declan Daly, me, Liam Murphy and Anthony Kennelly.

I CELEBRATE WITH the lads after winning the league title two years later.

CHAPTER 4

WHEN I JOINED Cork City in 1986, it was still a new club, just starting over.

The club had very little money, and attendances were low; we had a squad mostly full of young players, nowhere to train and a dilapidated stadium.

I got in on the ground floor.

Cork City had been formed two years earlier, in 1984. For two years before that, there had been no team from Cork in the league.

Cork United were expelled from the League of Ireland in 1982. They ran into financial trouble and lost money after they brought Manchester City over for a friendly in 1981. City said they were owed around £8,000. Cork United appealed to delay the payment, but they were still expelled. It became bitter and acrimonious.

CORK CITY ENTERED the league in 1984.

The club was formed by some of the people who had been involved with Cork United and Munster Senior League side, Avondale United.

The squad had a lot of young players like me, lads just making their way in the game. Most of us had been playing in the local leagues or the Munster Senior League. There were also a few experienced League of Ireland players in the squad who had been playing in Cork, players from the old Cork United group.

Looking back, it was perfect timing for me to arrive in Cork in 1986. I went to Cork purely for work reasons, to do the sales course, and playing in the League of Ireland wasn't part of the plan. But it led to me signing for City.

I'm not sure how my football career would have played out if I decided to do the sales course in Dublin instead of Cork, or if I had stayed in Athlone.

This was my first proper chance to make a career for myself in the league, though quite frankly Cork City, in 1986, were a very weak team.

The season before I arrived, City didn't win a single game at home in Flower Lodge. They only won three games in total, and stayed up ahead of Shelbourne and UCD on goal difference.

Those first few years were a steep learning curve for all of us.

We had a very solid Cork core to our team. It wasn't like we had lads who had played for four or five different clubs.

Cork City was our team and the bulk of our squad, around nine, 10, 11 of us, were all local lads – me, Dave Barry, Patsy Freyne, Philip Long, Deccie Daly, Liam Murphy and, when he joined us in 1989, Pat Morley.

I count myself as a local, despite being born in New York, growing up in Roscommon and going to school in Sligo.

When I moved to Cork City in 1986, most people thought I was from West Cork. And when I moved to West Cork for work, they thought I was from Cork city. It was only later that most Cork people realised I was from Roscommon, and most were surprised!

The world was a lot bigger back then, there were no mobile phones or social media, so I suppose it was easier for me to integrate, and I had a load of relations and connections in the county.

The answer to where I'm from is never going to be a one word answer, but I suppose if I was to go into a pub in Roscommon now, and was asked, I would say, 'West Cork'.

All these years later, I'm still in West Cork. My own family was born there, so I think I've earned my status as a local.

MOST OF OUR team, as I've said, had been playing in the local leagues. As a group, the City team developed and matured as one.

Patsy Freyne was probably our most naturally talented player. He was only a young lad, just learning the game like the rest of us at this point. He was physically slight, and not the tallest either, and neither was he the strongest or the fastest player in our group, but the man was magic with the ball at his feet. Patsy had a wonderful touch. He was a brilliant passer and his vision was simply exceptional.

He was a step ahead of so many players in the league.

Over time, we would bring in some outside players who integrated and added to our core group. Phil Harrington joined us when Eamonn O'Keefe was manager in 1988 and stayed long after Eamonn left. Phil was a goalkeeper from Wales. Mick Conroy joined us at the same time. Mick was a Scot, who had played for Celtic and Hibernians earlier in his career.

It was a tough learning curve for us in those early years. So, the most important thing for any player coming into our squad was to buy into it and what we were about, which all of these lads did.

They settled in Cork and we became a very tight group.

NOEL O'MAHONY was the Cork City manager when I joined. Noel was a tough man, steeped in Cork football.

He had been a legendary Cork Hibernians player in the 60s and 70s. Noel was part of the Cork Hibs team that won the league and two FAI Cups in the early 70s. I never saw him play live, but he was said to have been one of the most feared defenders in the league. He played in an era when tackling was vicious, and you had to mind yourself.

By all accounts, he was a very tough player, and he carried that attitude into his managerial career.

For young players like me coming through, Noel put fear into us. If you didn't play well, he'd come for you. He wouldn't hesitate to turn on you in the dressing-room at half-time or after a game.

He would pin you to the wall, shout and scream. That's how it was with managers then and it could be very intimidating.

We used to joke that, if you were having a nightmare of a match, you should sit beside Patsy Freyne at half-time. Patsy was a chain-smoker and would light up at half-time in the dressing-room. There would be so much smoke, Noel wouldn't see you if you sat beside Patsy! That was the line we trotted out to one another.

But Noel was incredibly passionate about Cork football, and his disposition and displeasure was due to that passion turning brutal sometimes. He drummed it into us about being a Cork team, about the pride in that and representing the county and the city. He was always particularly wound up when we played Dublin teams.

I wouldn't say it bordered on hatred or anything like that, but he definitely fostered a 'Them vs Us' attitude.

IT WOULD TAKE time for Noel to see some type of pay-off for this approach. At City in 1986, he was tasked with turning the team around. It wasn't easy for him.

And to be fair to him, his frustration in that first season stemmed from how poor we were at that time. He was tasked with managing young players who just weren't good enough yet, lads who were out of their depth.

We were at the bottom of the table, whereas he had been such a good player with Cork Hibs, a successful team that won leagues and cups and played in Europe. We weren't up to the task at that point.

Cork City only won seven games that first season.

For those first three years, in fact, between 1986 and '89, we were mostly struggling, finishing near the bottom of the table.

It was a great achievement for us to stay in the league and we always celebrated when we weren't relegated. These were probably bigger celebrations than when we started winning trophies.

Noel helped mould us into the team we would become. And he was very much about Cork teams being aggressive. Ahead of games, he would tell us to make sure we sorted the other side out, to never let them intimidate. Or bully us. Never.

Over time, we became a very talented team but we were also a very hard, aggressive team that other sides hated playing against. They ended up hating coming to Cork and to Turner's Cross.

We revelled in being this remote team, down in the south of the country, away from all the other sides. It did become very much about representing the county and the city.

Noel played his part in helping us develop good traits that would stand to us as the team improved. He left us ahead of the 1987/88 season and was replaced by Eamonn O'Keefe, but he returned to City midway through the following season.

WHEN I JOINED Cork City, it was probably one of the lowest points in the League of Ireland's history in terms of attendances and finances. The crowds from the 50s, 60s and 70s had declined and weren't coming back.

Shamrock Rovers lost Milltown around this time, when the stadium was sold to property developers and was knocked down.

Clubs couldn't even get away with short-term efforts in an attempt to gain attention and boost gates, such as signing up big-name players – the likes of George Best, Bobby Charlton and Geoff Hurst – at the end of their careers on short-term deals. That had been a common tactic.

In the season before I joined, Cork City signed Terry McDermott, formerly of Newcastle United and Liverpool, and West Ham legend Trevor Brooking. Both had been brilliant players in England but were at the end of their respective careers and only lasted a few games in the League of Ireland.

The problem was that the Irish public knew that these guys couldn't really play to their previous levels anymore.

The novelty never lasted. Television and newspaper coverage of the English game was growing, rapidly. As the League of Ireland was at a low point in the mid-80s, clubs were left to their own devices, operating from week to week, and just doing their best to get by, fending for themselves.

No one was ever going to get rich playing in the League of Ireland. The City lads certainly weren't in it for the money. There were one or two professionals on the books at the club, and a few semi-pros, but we were all working day jobs and most of us were amateurs.

I was paid expenses of £10 a week, which is probably the equivalent of around €40 now. It was effectively just petrol money.

I lived in West Cork, in Enniskeane, and there was no dual carriageway, so I had to drive around 60 miles three or four times a week for training and matches.

ALMOST ALL OF the League of Ireland clubs were struggling financially at the time... Cork certainly were. But there were still some top quality teams and players.

For my first couple of years in the league, I was struggling, no question about it. I would say that it took me maybe two seasons to adapt – it was the same for most of the local lads.

I was eager, the whole Cork team were, but we would often get hammered by teams like Shamrock Rovers, St Patrick's Athletic, Bohemians and Dundalk.

These were such strong teams. This was the Shamrock Rovers side that won four in-a-row. Derry City came into the Premier Division in 1987 and were a top team with a massive following. They managed to become very good, very quickly.

Derry hired Jim McLaughlin as manager, after he left Shamrock Rovers. McLaughlin, who was from Derry, brought a lot of the Rovers team that had been so successful with him to the club.

Derry paid wages in sterling, so they were able to pay more than anyone else and they got a lot of top players from Dublin. They won the treble within two years of entering the Premier Division, an achievement no League of Ireland team has matched since.

We could only dream of success like that in Cork at that time.

It was a tough league to play in. What really struck me about these teams was how strong they were. Even I was taken aback by the physicality – and I had grown up playing gaelic football against rough and tough country lads.

Some of the League of Ireland players were vicious, incredibly physical and tough. Imposing. It was men against boys.

The gap between us and those teams was so big at one point and it wasn't just a physical gap. They were far superior footballers. But, in hindsight, those couple of years turned out to be exactly what the City squad needed.

We gained the experience of playing against these tough teams, which helped us understand the league. Over time, we learned how to look after ourselves. We became physically and mentally stronger and fitter.

Within a couple of years, we lost our rawness.

IN OUR FIRST match at Turner's Cross in my first season we played Shamrock Rovers, who had just won three league titles in-a-row and the double on two consecutive seasons.

I started the match on the bench but came on at right-back.

Mick Byrne scored twice for them, one in each half, and they were undoubtedly the better team. But we managed to score a goal of our own. I was involved in it. I played a one-two with Patsy Freyne and he scored from about six yards out.

This felt like my proper League of Ireland debut, even if the record books will show I made that one appearance for Athlone.

I would say there were no more than 600 people or so at the game; that was the average crowd that season. When it came to the Cork sporting public and crowds, you had to earn their attention.

Noel O'Mahony told us about the Cork Hibernians team he played for in the 70s. Cork Hibs won the League of Ireland in 1971 and the following year they had a title decider on the last day of the season against Waterford, which they lost.

There was always talk of there being a crowd of 26,000 at the match.

Noel said there probably was, but for their first league game the following September, there were only around 5,000 watching. When they were going for the title towards the end of the season, the crowds increased to around 10,000 plus.

These were crowds we could only fantasise about.

CHAPTER 5

GAA IN CORK in the late-80s was on top of the world. The Cork hurlers and Cork footballers were absolutely flying.

The footballers were in four All-Ireland finals in-a-row, lifting the Sam Maguire Cup in 1989 and '90.

The hurlers won the All-Ireland in 1984, '86 and '90.

Meanwhile, Cork City were lucky to get any air-time or coverage in the newspapers. With small crowds, and a struggling team, we were quite far down the pecking order.

City had a small, devoted base of supporters, who would attend every game. But we weren't good enough yet to capture the wider support. We hadn't got the old Cork soccer supporters on board yet... the fans who had followed the old Cork Hibs and Cork United teams.

There was also that Cork mentality, with people from the county expecting all of their teams to be winners. This belief didn't naturally bring patience, and we were probably expected to win from the get-go.

It was something of a culture shock for me living in Cork in this regard. In Roscommon and Sligo, there was never an expectancy to win in gaelic football or soccer. Roscommon did very well in gaelic football in the 70s and were competitive, but nobody in the place expected an All-Ireland title. It was just great to get to Croke Park every year.

It was similar with Sligo Rovers. It was brilliant to watch them win the League of Ireland in 1977, but there was never an expectancy to win every game and every trophy; the supporters knew ultimate success would be infrequent, despite the town being soccer mad.

It was a different story in Cork, though.

Very different!

THERE WAS A confidence about Cork people, beginning with the fact that they were incredibly proud to be from the county.

It was the same in West Cork – it was almost as though West Cork was a separate county.

People from areas like Bantry or Clonakilty or Skibbereen would say they were from West Cork, rather than Cork itself.

National newspapers, such as *The Irish Times* and the *Irish Independent*, weren't widely read in Cork. It was always the *Examiner*, the *Echo* and local newspapers. Local pirate radio stations were more popular than national radio.

Cork and West Cork were very much their own entities, almost living in their own bubbles. It was Cork first, and everything else second.

They were very proud, confident people and their sports teams were an extension of that. There was that unbelievable confidence within the county when it came to sport. No matter what the sport was or who the team were or the wider context, Cork teams were expected to win.

It may not have made sense to expect success – it especially didn't when it came to City in the early years – but that didn't matter. That was just the way it was.

Cork people *expected* you to win.

There was a confidence that some might have perceived as arrogance. Cork people had a swagger, and even among the young Cork lads coming up, you could see that confidence. And Cork people followed everything, all sports. It struck me instantly how invested they were in sport.

Everyone in the county seemed to know and take an interest in how the teams were performing – how the gaelic football team, the hurlers, and Cork City were doing. Most of them might not have been at all of the matches, but they knew how the teams were getting on and had strong opinions about it.

Cork was also unique in the sense that there was no single dominant sport.

The county had pockets where soccer was very strong, and other pockets where hurling was the main sport. It was the same with gaelic football and, to a lesser extent, rugby. Even basketball was hugely popular in some parts of the county.

From the outside, people might think it is a particularly strong GAA county, and that GAA is the top sport, but from my experience that view is wide of the mark.

The Cork crowd go where the success is – and there wasn't a lot of that for us in the early years with Cork City.

IN OUR FIRST season at Turner's Cross, the ground had no stands. The Cross was just clay banks all around the pitch, with no terraces.

Our 2-1 loss to Shamrock Rovers probably flattered us because they would give us some tough beatings over the next few seasons. They had some tremendous players. It was a tough upbringing, but I loved every minute of it. This was where I wanted to be.

I was young and I just wanted to try and play in every game. For that first season, however, I was in and out of the team.

I played as a sweeper growing up when I was in Summerhill, and for Athlone Town's B team. For Wembley in the Munster Senior League, in the season before I joined City, I played either as a sweeper or part of the back four.

In my first year with Cork, I mostly played at right-back. I was happy to play anywhere all the same. I was a team player and would try my best, work as hard as I possibly could. I also had a bit of pace and kept myself fit.

I was a grafter.

I think Noel realised that and in one match that November he switched me to the right wing for a game against Sligo Rovers at Turner's Cross. It was our fifth game of that season and we had yet to win a match. Sligo, like us, were struggling near the bottom of the table. I had played with a few of their players at Summerhill.

They went ahead early in the game with a shot that hit off the crossbar and bounced down – the referee gave it as a goal, saying the ball crossed the line. A few minutes later, Sligo scored their second.

It looked like we were going to be beaten again.

At this point, we were bottom of the league.

Our confidence was rock bottom.

But we dug very deep and started to turn the game around. I was moved from right-back to the right wing. We had a goal disallowed and then, just after half-time, I took a shot and their goalkeeper spilled it into the net. A few minutes later, the ball landed to me after their defender mishit it and I struck a low shot into the bottom corner.

I then scored a header near the end to get my hat-trick.

We won the game 3-2.

It was brilliant.

Our first win of the season, the first hat-trick I had ever scored and, as I found out after the game, the first hat-trick in the club's history.

I was absolutely buzzing. And it was nice that the goals came against Sligo, where I went to school and a place that played such a big part in my soccer development.

The win over Sligo got us off the bottom of the table and kicked us on.

A week later, we beat Home Farm 4-1 in Dublin. I started on the right wing again and scored twice.

For the rest of the season, we were always hovering above the bottom two or three, but we managed to stay above the relegation zone. I was in and out of the team for the year, mostly still featuring at right-back. I was still learning my trade.

We ended up finishing seventh that season in a 12-team league, which wasn't bad considering how inexperienced most of us were. Noel stepped down at the end of the season and Eamonn O'Keefe came in.

Eamonn was from Manchester and of Irish descent. He had played for Everton, Wigan Athletic and Blackpool, and had a spell playing in Saudi Arabia. He also won a few caps for Ireland. He played for Ireland against England at Wembley. He had been a decent player by all accounts, but was winding down his career after suffering a knee injury.

Eamonn became the player-manager. He wanted to introduce more professionalism to the club. He brought in more training and better coaching, which wasn't an easy thing to do considering we weren't a full-time team and had no training base or facilities of our own. Cork City trained in a public park the previous season.

The only light we would have during the winter months was from the street lights. We then went to a place near the airport; they called it Farmers Cross. It was beside a hockey club.

So, we would go out there to the field and train beside the hockey pitch, using the light from their floodlights on the other side of the fence.

THE PLAYERS NEVER complained, it was just accepted that this was how it was. We had no choice. This was the reality for many clubs in the country.

When Eamonn came in though, he wanted to try and make things more professional. We started to train in a college in Blackrock.

This time we were actually *on* a hockey pitch and we had more light than when we were in the park. But the pitch was full of sand and gravel, and it was far from ideal for football training.

Again, we didn't complain because it was the only place we could rent. We didn't have showers or our own clubhouse, so we just got on with it.

I'm not sure what Eamon thought of it, though it must have greatly frustrated him. He had played in the English First Division with Everton! Whereas, on the hockey pitch, if the ball hit a floodlight, the light might go off and we would have to find the switch to put it back on.

I BENEFITED FROM Eamonn's arrival and his emphasis on coaching. Bill Haydock was his assistant manager, an older guy also from Manchester, who had played in the English leagues.

Bill noticed I had a bit of pace and started coaching me to play as a striker. Every night in training for 10 or 15 minutes with the other forwards, we would work on movement, criss-crossing, timing runs and finishing.

This was all new to me.

I had some coaching in secondary school – a few ex-Sligo Rovers players did a bit of work on shape with us and work on defending. But I had never been coached at this level. And I had always been a defender.

If Eamonn and Bill had never come over and taken the Cork job, I probably would have played out my career in the League of Ireland as a defender, with the occasional game in midfield.

They started to play me up front and I started to get a few goals.

I never went back to playing in defence.

We lost our opening game of the league at home to Dundalk before winning away to Bray Wanderers. We then beat St Patrick's Athletic, who were managed by Brian Kerr, in the League Cup semi-final, a win which got us into the cup final. We won the match 2-1 at Turner's Cross.

Eamonn scored a penalty after I was taken down in the box by Curtis Fleming. I then scored myself a few minutes later. Pat's got one back, but we saw it out. It was the first final Cork City had reached since being formed in 1984 and it was the first final for a Cork team for well over a decade.

It was great and a sign of progress for the team and the club.

We were brought back down to earth a few days later, however. In our third game of the season, we went to the Brandywell to play Derry City. They absolutely hammered us.

It finished 7-2.

They were a super team, with brilliant players such as Felix Healy, who had played for Northern Ireland in the 1982 World Cup finals. They also had a massive, passionate support – there were about 7,000 people at the game.

We had been on a good run ahead of the game, and went on a good run after it, but Derry showed how far we had to go.

A FEW WEEKS later, we played Shamrock Rovers in the League Cup final at Turner's Cross.

There were 5,000 at the match, which was by far the biggest crowd we had ever had at home up to that point. It was easily 10 times more than our average attendance that season.

This was the great Rovers team. They were heavy favourites to beat us.

Yet, we won 1-0.

Kieran Myers, a local lad, scored the only goal of the game.

It was a big shock, no one was expecting it, but, in truth, we could have won by more and probably should have. We had plenty of chances and deserved to win.

The League Cup wasn't as prestigious as the FAI Cup or winning the league, but it was massive for us.

It looked like this would be a big turning point for us to kick on and compete regularly for trophies and move up the league. But it didn't quite work out that way.

We were still finding our feet in the league and ended up finishing seventh again. This time we won more games than we lost, and were closer to the top of the league than the bottom.

The City squad, nevertheless, went into the following season feeling that, maybe, *just maybe*, we'd be a tougher nut to crack for other teams.

Ahead of the new season, the club signed Phil Harrington, a goalkeeper from Wales who had played for Preston North End, and Mick Conroy. Mick was a Scot and he had played for Celtic earlier in his career.

There was a sense that, with the mix of the younger local lads, some experienced outsiders and the increased coaching, that we could kick on, challenge the better sides in the league and potentially qualify for Europe.

BY CHRISTMAS, WE had only won three games and were at the bottom of the table.

At one stage, we lost eight games in-a-row.

Our crowds were down, and the club was strapped for cash. It was awful. Eamon got the sack after a 0-0 draw with Bohs at Turner's Cross. There was an issue between Eamonn and the chairman Chris Herlihy, who also owned the club. There was talk for a while that he would be moving on, so it wasn't a surprise.

It was a typical League of Ireland scenario, really.

Eamonn was a full-time manager, he had a full-time assistant manager and he brought in full-time players from England. He had guys in the squad who had been getting decent pay, even though we were a part-time club.

The club over-reached and couldn't sustain the high costs after our form collapsed and the crowds declined.

Eamonn lost his job as a result and also suffered because of our run of poor results. It was a reminder of how uncertain life could be in Irish football.

There was talk of the club losing £1,000 a week, and that we would have to switch to amateur status for the next season. There was even talk of us potentially not fulfilling our fixtures for the rest of that year. There was a lot of uncertainty.

I was personally very disappointed to see Eamonn leave. He was a big backer of mine and changed my career by moving me up front. When a manager likes you, it's tough to see him leave. Players are selfish in that way, always thinking about how something directly affects them on a personal level and their chances of playing.

Noel O'Mahony came back, initially as caretaker manager.

For Noel's first game back, we were to travel up to play Derry City at the Brandywell. I had to miss the match due to work commitments, which was a regular enough occurrence for players.

Derry were top of the league, with their massive support and big money behind them. One of their players, John Coady, cost them £15,000 from Chelsea, a transfer fee that was far beyond anything Cork City could offer for a player.

We ended up losing 4-2, which probably wasn't bad considering how good they were and how poor our form had been.

THE LEAGUE OF Ireland was a winter league at the time, and there was always a busy schedule over Christmas.

Cork City played Limerick at Turner's Cross on St Stephen's Day. We lost 1-0. Two days later, we played Dundalk at home. We lost 2-1. And then, on New Year's Day, we travelled up to St Mel's Park to play Athlone Town. We lost 1-0.

It was terrible, we were desperate... shockingly bad.

We were level on points with Waterford at the bottom of the table. After 20 games, City had only won three times. It was another grim few months for the club, probably the lowest point in City's history.

Relegation would have been a disaster.

A week later we had an absolutely crucial game against Cobh Ramblers at St Colman's Park. Cobh were struggling like ourselves at the bottom of the table, two points ahead of us – no Cork City team should ever find themselves below Cobh on the table.

We didn't have Dave Barry for the match; he was suspended, and there were a few lads just coming back from injury, such as Mick Conroy, Philip Long and Donal Madden, who had been out injured for well over a year.

Donal was a veteran of Cork football. He first played for Cork United in the late-70s, and he started up front for us against Cobh. St Colman's was absolutely packed, there was about 3,000 at the game, which was a huge crowd in Cobh.

We started the game well and were probably the better side in the first-half. In the second-half, they were probably the better team and had a few chances. We were short on quality but determined and aggressive, and we managed to fight it out.

With about four or five minutes left in the game, Philip took a throw down the line to Donal, who cut the ball back across the box for me.

I hit it on the volley, as hard as I could.

Thankfully, the ball went past their 'keeper and into the net. One-nil to us and we held on to win the game.

The relief was immense.

It was our first win in two months, and we moved off the bottom of the table. It was my first goal in two months too.

A week later, we played Waterford, our other relegation rival. We won the match 3-0 at Turner's Cross. I scored twice.

We then played St Patrick's Athletic at Richmond Park. St Pat's were challenging for the league title, but we were the better team on the day and held them to a 0-0 draw.

Eamon O'Keefe played for Pat's in that game. Although Eamonn was good for my career, it was fair to say that Noel's return had a galvanising effect on us.

Momentum is massive in sport and it started to go in our favour.

CORK CITY WENT on a run of positive results and didn't lose again in the league until March, when Derry beat us.

O'Keefe's coaching had made a massive difference to me in particular, but there is no denying that Noel's return was exactly what we needed at that time.

This was an era when the football in the League of Ireland was extremely physical and tough. You needed to have lads alongside you who had your back, who were prepared to give as much as you, fight for every ball and back each other up.

Noel was still his old self, very much about *that*, about us showing who we were. He wanted us to show our passion and to take no hassle from anyone. No team coming to Cork was to be given an easy day; we were told to sort them out, to be very physical and leave a mark.

Overnight, we became a much more physical team and known for our aggressive approach.

Our decent run of form in the league helped us pull away from relegation trouble and we also managed to put a run together in the FAI Cup.

City beat Sligo Rovers at the Showgrounds in the third round, and got past Cobh in the next round at St Colman's. In the next round we drew Dundalk, who were double-winners, the reigning league and cup holders. They had a great team and were managed by Turlough O'Connor. Dundalk were big favourites for the match.

We started very well, were the better team in the first-half and were leading at half-time. But it looked like we were heading out, as we were losing 2-1 with a few minutes to go. Dave Barry then popped up with a header to take the game to a replay back at Turner's Cross.

Ahead of the replay, the draw was made for the semi-finals.

If we got past Dundalk, we would avoid Derry City in the semi-finals. Derry were to play Shamrock Rovers, and the winners of our replay would play Drogheda United or Bray Wanderers.

But most people expected it to be Derry against Dundalk in the final, a repeat of the previous year's FAI Cup final and the top two teams in the country at the time.

Yet, we were the better side again in the replay. Patsy Freyne scored, and we went ahead.

Dundalk had a few chances after the break – most of them landed to Terry Eviston, but we held on and deserved to win.

It was brilliant for us to beat such a strong team and get the better of them over two games.

In the semis, which were played over two-legs, we came up against Bray, who were a First Division side. We lost the first leg 2-1 at Turner's Cross.

Bray got a lucky goal near the end, and long before then their goalkeeper had earned himself the Man of the Match award.

It was disappointing to lose, but we had another game to try to reach the cup final.

There was a lot on the line for us.

CHAPTER 6

IT HAD BEEN 16 years since a team from Cork had made it to the FAI Cup final.

Something to bring to an end!

Plus, the winning team would qualify for Europe!

Derry were lying in wait. They had cruised past Shamrock Rovers. They had already won the League Cup and were going for the league title, which meant that the other side in the final would automatically qualify for the UEFA Cup Winners' Cup.

In the second leg against Bray, we won 1-0, levelling it on aggregate 2-2. It went to a third game, and we won the toss.

It was a lovely sunny day at Turner's Cross. The place was packed, with about 6,000 in attendance, even though the match was played on a Wednesday afternoon. And we played very well.

Dave Barry was back in the team and he scored twice in a 4-0 win.

All the City fans were chanting...

'WE'RE ON OUR WAY TO EUROPE'

It was brilliant, an absolutely fantastic achievement for us to reach the FAI Cup final.

We spent most of the season in the bottom two or three in the league and were only averaging about 1,000 people per game.

At one point that year, the future of the club was in doubt once again.

So, to knock out the teams we did and get ourselves into a final was a massive effort. In the final, however, we were up against Derry City; a good and a bad thing from our point of view.

Derry were going for the treble and had a super team with players like Felix Healy, Paul Carlisle and Paul Doolin. They had crowds of up to 10,000 at the Brandywell and had a massive following for away games.

To qualify for Europe was huge to us… to go from fighting for our lives in the League of Ireland to playing in Europe, whatever the result in the final!

DALYMOUNT PARK HOSTED the final.

As we hadn't been challenging at the top of the league, we had less than 5,000 supporters at the match. Our following hadn't really grown yet, and we were still working to capture the old Cork football support.

But it was an incredible day, with over 21,000 at the match.

Derry's following was absolutely massive, their supporters covered two thirds of the ground, making it a sea of red and white.

As usual, we weren't given much of a chance. But we were the better side and took it to them. We were aggressive, and refused to let Derry settle and play their normal game.

We were so determined to make sure it wasn't an easy day for them, and to try and silence their crowd. It worked because we remained the better side for long spells.

Derry were rattled at first. It felt like they were expecting us to roll over for them because they were the champions and the superior team.

But they gave as good as they got too. I needed stitches after the match, after getting a smack to the face from Stewart Gauld, their captain, when we were jumping for a ball.

It was a tough game, but we had the better chances. Dave Barry came within inches of winning it for us. He had a shot in the second-half that beat the Derry goalkeeper Timmy Dalton and hit off the inside of the post.

The ball then rolled across the line.

If it went in, we would have probably pulled off one of the biggest shocks in Irish cup history.

The game finished 0-0 and went to a replay the following Sunday.

I think Derry were relieved; they had another chance to beat us and knew they hadn't been at their best.

Apparently, Alex Ferguson's assistant manager at Manchester United, Archie Knox was at the game to scout Liam Coyle, who played for Derry.

Coyle was a young lad coming through, and he was fabulous player. He had already played for Northern Ireland at senior level; he was gifted and was rated extremely highly.

However, Liam had a quiet game against us that day.

Meanwhile, we had a tall centre-back playing for us, a young lad named Brian Carey. Brian was named Man of the Match, and Manchester United signed him.

He was with United for a few years but never played for the first-team. Yet, he managed to carve out a career for himself in England with Wrexham and Leicester City.

Coyle, meanwhile, suffered a terrible knee injury a few months later and was forced to retire temporarily. He was only 21. He managed to make a comeback a few years after and had a successful career with Derry.

The final was replayed a week later, back at Dalymount Park. Derry had the bulk of the crowd again. This time though, they had most of the chances too.

It was a warm May day.

And it was harder than it had been a week before to disrupt them. They also started much better than they did in the first game; they were all over us in the first 20 minutes or so.

Phil Harrington made three or four great saves and really kept us in the game. Finally, Felix Healy scored. It ended 1-0, but they beat us well.

Derry had already beaten us three times that season. But, we could take some pride from our performance. It showed that we had grown and developed as a side.

Looking back, playing Derry in a final was almost the ideal preparation for European football – playing against a superior team who were expected to beat us, in front a big crowd and having to fight and scrap for everything.

THE CITY PLAYERS were hoping for a tie against a Mediterranean team. We wanted to go somewhere warm, to get some sun on our backs for a few days.

Instead, we were drawn against Torpedo Moscow. Needless to say, none of us had ever been to Russia. We were trying our best to get some roubles for the journey!

No one knew what to expect in Moscow. Our only impression of the place came from what we had read or seen on television about life in the Soviet Union.

This was a few months before the Iron Curtain fell and we had read that life was gloomy in communist countries – people were in bed by 10pm, we even heard.

We found the Russian people we met friendly, but downtrodden. We stayed very close to Red Square, about 500 or 600 yards away from it. We went down to see the Changing of the Guard, and had a look around.

The Russian capital was a cold, bleak place.

Our hotel, the Rossiya, was the largest hotel in the world at the time. It was a huge, grey structure, old and very basic and there was no western European food.

It wasn't like any of the Cork players were complaining though. We were in our own bubble and made the most of the experience.

Torpedo Moscow were an army team and there were plenty of Soviet soldiers at the game, sitting in the front row in full uniform. It was surreal.

There were about 6,000 people at the game in what was a modest stadium.

There were two huge clocks at either end of the ground. After 22 minutes I looked up at one of the clocks.

The score was 0-0.

When I looked back up to the clock, 32-minutes were gone, and we were 4-0 down.

TORPEDO WERE A serious team.

We wanted to do our best, but we were never going to progress. It was the first time that I was exposed to what you might call 'real football'. All their play was on the ground. They didn't play a long kick out from the goalkeeper to the far end.

Everything was passing through midfield.

If they played a pass of 20 or 30 yards, it was straight through you.

They pinged the ball around… fizzed it along the surface to each other. Everything was one and two-touch football.

It was the first time that I was ever involved in a match where I saw in front of my eyes what the opposition were doing, but also found myself and my teammates powerless to stop it.

City were used to the physicality and the rough and tumble of our own league, getting stuck in and clattering each other. But this was total football. I think Torpedo actually felt sorry for us; it seemed to me like they took their foot off the gas.

We lost 5-0 in the end.

After the game, we wanted to have a few drinks, but there were no open bars at the time in communist countries; all the bars were underground, protected by the police and there was a mob and KGB presence everywhere in the city.

But, we were a determined bunch off the field too. Eventually, we got into an underground bar.

Looking back, we were oblivious to any danger; we didn't see it, we were in our own bubble enjoying the trip.

IN THE SECOND leg in Cork, I had a header that hit the post and I possibly could have scored. It would have been City's first goal in Europe. But it wasn't to be.

They beat us 1-0.

The experience was massive for us, however, just being to Russia, feasting on the excitement of the unique experience, playing such a top team.

To the City players, this was it.

Over the next few years, we would come up some against serious teams and go to places we never would have seen otherwise. Qualifying for Europe, every time, was like a mini-holiday for the players, as we were away from work for a few days.

It was also a novelty. On the trips, we actually trained in the mornings, as if we were full-time professional players, something we never got the opportunity to do before. Being away for those three or four days as a footballer was special.

A few months later, the Iron Curtain fell, and the Soviet Union started to collapse. And a part of the old Eastern bloc had followed us back to Cork.

When we were out in Russia, our chairman at the time, Pat O'Donovan had met an agent, who told him that he could get four Bulgarian internationals to sign for City. Around October, the players arrived.

Sasho Borisov, Ilya Velichkov, Mario Vulikov and Stefan Vasiliev. Their agent, who also acted as their translator, arrived too.

I understood why they wanted to get out of Bulgaria. Other countries behind the Iron Curtain, such as Hungary and Poland had broken with communism and overthrown regimes earlier in the year. Bulgaria was on the brink and in a bad spot, and these lads evidently wanted out.

But my first impression was... *What are they doing over here?*

I couldn't see why they wanted to join Cork City.

WE WERE TRAINING out by the airport, up at Farmers Cross, still using the lights of the hockey pitch next to us. You could hardly see the ball it was so dark. We were semi-professional, training three times a week.

Whereas the Bulgarians would have been used to being based in the army with training facilities, playing as professionals.

There was a lot of hype around the foreign lads joining us too.

The City players were told that this was a real coup for the club.

The four lads played in a trial game against UCC, and they did okay. After that, there was talk of scouts from England attending our league game, where they would make their debuts, against Shelbourne.

There was even a press conference at Jury's Hotel announcing their arrival.

I remember a report in the *Examiner* said that they had over 100 caps between them. But it became a disaster, a farce.

Only two of them had international experience, and only one had played regularly for Bulgaria. That was Borisov. He was the only decent player, and he was probably in his late-thirties. Most of them appeared to be mid- to late-thirties.

Borisov actually scored an own goal on his debut against Shelbourne, a match we lost 1-0. Noel O'Mahony had to play the four of them again a few days later against UCD, and we lost 2-1.

It was a different type of football to what they were accustomed to. They were used to playing it on the ground, but the League of Ireland pitches were mud baths.

They couldn't speak English, so it was impossible to communicate with them. We ended up feeling sorry for them. The experiment only lasted about four weeks.

Noel got fed up. He just wanted them out of the way.

WE USED TO meet for away matches at the Imperial Hotel in Cork, which is in the South Mall. If we were playing in Dublin, we always met at eight o'clock on the Sunday morning because generally the games were at two in the afternoon.

We would have to drive up through all the villages, because there were no bypasses or dual-carriageways. Motorways were decades off!

It took about four hours to get to Dublin at that time.

The morning we were playing Dundalk, we were all in the hotel about to leave when Noel spoke to us.

'I want you all to get onto the bus straight away!

'We're going to leave the Bulgarians behind… so everyone get on before them.'

Noel was standing at the door of the bus and as the Bulgarians went to get on, he let on two of them, and then he stopped the other two. The interpreter was with them and he was protesting, arguing with Noel to bring the other two.

But Noel wouldn't budge.

'NO… NO… NO!' he insisted.

Noel then turned around to the bus driver and told him to close the door and get going. And off we went.

It was a strange situation. In those days, teams were only allowed to have two substitutes, and our two subs were the Bulgarians. But, in the dressing-room before the game against Dundalk, Noel surprised us all again.

'We are 11 fellas here from Cork, now,' he began. 'And we'll have none of this. You go out there and do your best.

'I don't want to hear any more about this… we're going to win the match and we're not bringing these fellas on.

'They're no use!' We beat Dundalk 2-1.

It was a huge result for us because they were a big team at the time. We went back to Cork high as kites, buzzing after the win.

Not long after that, the Bulgarians were gone.

Noel said that they weren't able to cope with the physicality of the league. They were also either past it, or not good enough to begin with. It was a farce from the start, really.

The club probably thought it would boost attendances, but we lost every game they were involved in. It didn't help that we were a struggling team at the time, down at the bottom of the table.

Before the Dundalk match, we hadn't won a league game in two months.

THE PRE-SEASON OPTIMISM that we could push on after our positive end to the previous season – our run to the FAI Cup final, and the European adventure – had evaporated quickly.

We were back in a relegation fight, scratching around at the bottom of the table. But the win against Dundalk helped us and, in hindsight, the creation of a new, better team over the next few years had begun.

The Bulgarian signings had been a mistake, but we had more luck with two other players we brought in at that time – both of whom scored against Dundalk.

Paul Bannon, who joined City a month or two previously, scored our first goal that day. Paul was a Tipperary man, his father won an All-Ireland in hurling with the county. He was an excellent footballer and played most of his career as a centre-forward in England with Carlisle United and Bristol Rovers. He also played in The Netherlands and in Greece.

Paul was 32 when he joined us, but he was still a quality player... he ended up switching to centre-half.

He was comfortable in himself; he knew he was a good footballer and wasn't short of confidence. Paul had a sharp tongue too and could cut guys down to size quickly. But he was great fun on a night out, a real joker and storyteller.

He would be an important player for City over the next few years. Our other goalscorer that day would also make a big impact.

Pat Morley joined us after he couldn't get clearance to sign for a team in Australia. He had previously played for Limerick and Waterford in the League of Ireland. A Cork native, his father had won the league with Waterford in the 70s.

Pat was a prolific goalscorer.

He and I would form a great partnership up front across 10 years with the club. On the pitch, we just clicked.

We had different qualities. He was a brilliant striker, a natural goalscorer who came alive when the ball was in the box.

Was I one of the best players on the team? Certainly not, but I was a team player. I worked my backside off, I had a bit of pace and I started to score goals. In that first season I scored nine goals in the league, and he got 10. Our styles complemented one other. And, although we didn't realise it at the time, the City team of the next few years was starting to fall into place.

The gimmicks like bringing in a raft of outsiders and short-term fixes didn't work. It was a slow, tough process, with a lot of defeats along the way, for us to form a team that could compete.

CHAPTER 7

OUR FORM IMPROVED after the win against Dundalk at Oriel Park. We went on a great run and were unbeaten for three months. They were all close games, but we had momentum, and we were improving as a team.

St Pat's beat us 1-0 in March, and went on to win the league under Brian Kerr. We hadn't lost since New Year's Eve before that.

The following season, we went on a phenomenal run, we went to another level again. City went 20 games unbeaten between the start of the 1990/91 season in September and the following January. We beat everyone we came up against in the league, home and away, and were full of confidence.

In one game after Christmas we beat Limerick 6-1 away. I scored twice, Pat scored… the whole team was playing great stuff.

When we eventually lost, Shamrock Rovers beat us 4-0 at the RDS. We didn't even play badly in the game, everything just seemed to go Rovers' way. Pat's won on the same day to go top of the league. After the match, we were devastated, almost inconsolable after losing.

Looking back though, that defeat really showed how far we had come.

It was our first loss in the league since the previous March. A season or two before, we would have been used to getting beatings like that in away games. Rovers, Dundalk, Bohs, Derry – all these teams would regularly hammer us. But on that day, we were disgusted, and the result was a shock.

THE TEAM WAS maturing and coming to its peak years.

After a few seasons of getting hammered, of being pushed around physically and generally just being out of our depth, things started to click for us.

We dusted ourselves down and went on another run.

After the Rovers loss, we beat Sligo Rovers, Athlone Town and Shelbourne ahead of a game against St Pat's, who were looking to retain the title. Dave Barry, Phil Harrington, Patsy Freyne and Paul Bannon – four of our best players – were missing for the match. Yet, we won 3-0 in Harold's Cross. It was brilliant.

The win put us top of the table, four points clear of Pat's. After the game, Brian Kerr said that they wouldn't be able to catch us.

It was between City and Dundalk for the title, with seven games to go.

Dundalk were a point behind us, and we were due to play each other on the last day of the season at Turner's Cross.

During the run-in, we dropped a few points we shouldn't have. Phil's absence in goal cost us. He got injured and we had to bring in a reserve goalkeeper, Craig Nelson. He was only a young lad and a bit out of his depth.

We dropped points in matches we definitely shouldn't have, drawing with Bohs, Shamrock Rovers and, worst of all, Limerick, who were down at the bottom of the table. But we went into the last game of the season level on points with Dundalk. The team that won on the day would win the league. If it was a draw, there would be a play-off.

Dundalk were a top team. Turlough O'Connor was still their manager and they had a lot of players from the team that won the league in 1988... lads like Terry Eviston, Gino Lawless and Martin Lawlor.

But there was nothing between us.

In the two games between Dundalk and City already that season, both were draws. And we had home advantage this time.

WE WERE GETTING a lot of coverage in the media. We were front page news on the day of the game. It had been a long time since a Cork team won the League of Ireland.

There was a lot of talk about Cork dominating sport in Ireland.

The county did the double in the GAA in 1990, winning the All-Ireland hurling and football championships. Cork's Neptune had also won the national basketball title, a sport that was strong in the county even if it wasn't popular nationwide. As I've said, if any Cork team was doing well in any sport, it tended to be popular in the county.

There was a lot of talk that, if City won the league, Cork would become the sports capital of Ireland.

The Dundalk match really captured the attention of the Cork public. For us, this all made the enormity of the game sink in.

We had a chance to be the first Cork team in 17 years to win the League of Ireland... the first since Cork Celtic in 1974.

TURNER'S CROSS WAS packed on the day.

It was a sell-out with anything between 12,000 and 15,000 at the match, depending on who you speak to. And about ninety-five percent of those in attendance were supporting City.

It was late April, and the weather had changed.

It was a lot milder, and the ground had gone from soft and damp to hard and dry... the ball was bobbling all over the place.

It made for an absolutely horrible match.

Dundalk were a very experienced team, who had won the league a couple of times already with a very experienced manager, Turlough. He had brought a lot of the Athlone players to Dundalk, lads who had won a league with Athlone before City were even founded.

They were used to winning trophies and we weren't.

Maybe it stood to them on the day.

The crowd was probably expecting us to get them on the edge of their seats, to take the game to Dundalk and to break them down. But it turned into a real scrap.

It was a battle between two aggressive teams who didn't want to lose, but it was a poor match, with very few chances.

It looked like the game was going to end 0-0 and go to a play-off. And then, about 20 minutes from the end, Tom McNulty broke through from midfield for Dundalk.

He went one-on-one with Phil Harrington.

He scored.

I could feel the air suck out of the crowd.

The City team was floored too.

We pushed hard to get a goal back, but Dundalk hung on to win and clinched the title. We had been at the top of the league for almost all of the season but lost it with 17 minutes to go.

It was desperately disappointing.

At Turner's Cross, the dressing-rooms were together with a thin wall separating the two squads. The showers were open plan.

So, as Dundalk were celebrating winning the league, we were in the same room! They were chanting and singing in the showers. And we could see them.

On one side of the dressing-room, it was a party. On the other, it was like a wake.

It was a bad, bad day for us.

WE DIDN'T PLAY well enough.

We left points behinds us in the run-in. We should have won the league. To miss out on the title was deeply disappointing.

Of course, you're thinking… *Maybe we have blown our only chance at this!*

League of Ireland football is precarious.

Teams can rise and fall, very quickly.

Things change quite quickly, too – one or two players could leave, the club may not be able to afford to replace them, and before you know it, the team drops down the table, back to square one.

But luckily, we were able to hold onto our core group.

Other than Patsy Freyne, who fell out with Noel O'Mahony and left us for a few years. Patsy was a brilliant footballer, an incredible talent and a fan favourite. It was very disappointing to see him leave, especially as he left for Cobh Ramblers. Yet, we had developed a hardness as a team, a maturity and kept pushing on.

When you're 20 or 21 going into the League of Ireland, your eyes are wide open, and you're not used to that environment. The only way to get used to it is to take the kicks and hammerings from other teams. It was so physical, and fellas weren't shy about sorting us out, about leaving their foot or their elbow in.

But within a couple of years, we'd learned how to look after ourselves.

City also had incredible team spirit. We spent most of our lives travelling together up and down the country on the bus. It was difficult being a Cork team in the league. Every second week, we were on the road.

Even if were playing teams in Munster, such as Waterford or Limerick, it was still a two-and-a-half-hour or three-hour trip each way, never 'missing' even one town or village. If we were playing in Dublin, which we were regularly, as there were so many teams from the city in the league, it was a four-hour trip up and four hours back.

We had no choice, and no one ever complained.

This worked to our advantage, though.

There was no one driving up on their own or meeting us at the ground. Everyone had to be on the bus, which helped develop a team spirit and camaraderie. Due to the time we spent on the road, in training and socialising after matches, the City squad became very close.

We would all have a drink on the bus on the way back… maybe stop into a pub.

We were all good buddies.

Most of the team, bar one or two guys who came from England, were all Cork fellas. At this stage, I suppose I qualified as a Cork man too.

And we had a manager who was very much into us showing who we were, about representing the City and the county, showing passion and taking no crap from anyone who came down to play us.

We were a local team. It was something the Dublin teams at this time probably couldn't understand.

If you played for Shamrock Rovers or St Pats' or Shelbourne, you were playing in Dublin every second week, or going up to Dundalk or maybe down to Athlone.

All of these experiences, being on the road every second week, driving on all those backroads, playing in all weathers, coming up against these top teams and getting battered, all of this was the making of Cork City in the early years.

By this point, midway through 1991, we were a proper team.

PART THREE

RebelHeart

CHAPTER 8

IN THE EARLY-90s, before the Premier League exploded in popularity, and English clubs went around the world for pre-seasons, they would come to Ireland because it was handy to get a game here.

We were both on the same season, and going to Asia or the U.S. on lucrative tours just didn't happen back then.

You didn't have to pay the English clubs anything either, they just came in for a game, or for a week away.

Cork City played Manchester United at Musgrave Park the summer after they won the Cup Winners Cup in 1991. We used to play a lot of pre-season friendlies in Musgrave Park because it had a seated stand and could hold more spectators than Turner's Cross. We also played Liverpool, Chelsea and Tottenham Hotspur.

The one that really sticks out was a friendly against Celtic in July 1991, a few months after we lost the league to Dundalk on the final day. It was one of Liam Brady's first matches as manager of Celtic and he brought over his strongest team for the game. There were 6,000 at the match, a tremendous crowd, and Celtic obviously had a big following.

This was the Celtic of Charlie Nicholas. Tony Cascarino had just joined them for a million pounds, and they had Paul McStay in midfield. Packie Bonner was in goal. These were players who had been at the World Cup the previous year.

But at that stage, we were hardy bucks. We were all in our mid-twenties, we were all fit and confident and we fancied giving Celtic, or any team that came to Cork, a rattle. I suppose they probably wanted a nice, easy game and didn't want us to be getting stuck in or kicking them because they were *Celtic*. But we were having none of that.

I scored the opening goal. Dave Barry hit a great strike from about 25 yards out. Bonner saved it and pushed the ball back into play, I dived and headed in the rebound. We brought on a young fella called Fergal Giltinan, an absolutely fantastic player, who didn't have the ambition to go on to be a top League of Ireland player and packed up within a couple of years. But Fergal got us the second goal, a brilliant header.

We beat them 2-0.

The Celtic players were really unhappy about it. In hindsight, it probably showed where they were at the time, or where Liam Brady was at the time.

I used to watch him when I went over to see Arsenal play at Highbury in the 70s; he was a phenomenal player, so it was nice to score against one of his teams.

But when he took over that Celtic team, it never worked. He had a horrendous run for a year or two before it ended badly for him.

It was only a friendly, but we completely outplayed them. It was a fantastic moment for City. And a sign of what was to come. Celtic weren't the only team we caused an upset against that season.

When we lost out on the league on the final day of the season to Dundalk, it was a double disappointment for the club. We also missed out on qualification for the European Cup, which would have netted the club a fortune.

There was a chance to be drawn against massive clubs, like Barcelona or Arsenal or Marseille. We could have even drawn Rangers, which would have been a money-spinning tie for the club. Instead, we had to settle for the UEFA Cup – though that turned out to be a massive blessing for us.

Dundalk were drawn against Hungarian side, Honvéd in the European Cup. With the greatest of respect to Honvéd, it wasn't exactly a glamour tie.

Meanwhile, we were drawn against Bayern Munich.

BAYERN MUNICH, THE German giants, were coming to Ireland, with the first leg in Cork.

This was like winning the lotto for the club.

We had played big teams in friendlies, but to be drawn in a competitive European game against Bayern Munich, one of the biggest clubs in Europe, was the greatest draw that Cork City ever got and ever could have got.

We celebrated drawing them like we had won a trophy. This was a once-in-a-lifetime draw and a massive opportunity for us, a part-time team. The excitement of the draw actually affected our league form; the hype took our focus away.

The first leg was moved to Musgrave Park. Munster Rugby ran the stadium and they were good to us, they made sure there were no rugby matches played on the pitch before our game against Bayern.

Although, that probably would have helped us to have the surface scuffed up!

Ahead of the game, there was a huge uproar about the admission fee for the match. Pat O'Donovan, our chairman, was a bit greedy.

The average price of a ticket for a league game was a fiver. For the Bayern game, it was raised to £20 for a stand seat, and £8 for the terraces.

It caused incredibly negative publicity against him and the club for charging our own people that amount. The supporters were saying they wouldn't pay it.

In the years since, I've had countless people come up to me and tell me they were there that day. But the attendance at the ground was way below capacity. Many people decided not to go.

It was partly out of principle, but also, they just couldn't afford it.

Cork suffered badly in the mid-80s from the closure of Ford and Dunlop, big employers in the city; unemployment was huge in the city, and still was in 1991. People didn't have a lot of money, especially not £20 pounds for a Wednesday afternoon game, even if it was Bayern Munich.

Through a combination of people refusing to pay the ticket price, supporters being unable to pay it and others just boycotting the game, there was only about 4,500 at the match.

It was outrageous because Musgrave Park could have held 15,000 or more, but O'Donovan thought he would sell it anyway because we were playing a giant of a team.

THE CITY PLAYERS were living in our bubble though, preparing for such a big match. No matter what, we were still playing Bayern Munich.

They had reached the semi-finals of the European Cup the previous season.

We were determined to give our best, even if we were missing a few players through injury. Before the game, Noel O'Mahony told the press that a 2-0 defeat would represent a great result for us. And he wasn't wrong.

Bayern had some brilliant players – Stefan Effenberg, Manni Schwabl, Christian Ziege, Brian Laudrup, Markus Babbel. All these fellas were internationals. Three members of their squad had won the World Cup with West Germany the previous year.

There was only going to be one winner and we were expected to have no chance.

But we absolutely tore into them, put everyone behind the ball and chased them down every chance we could.

Mick Conroy was 34 at this time, our player-coach and only playing because we had so many injuries. He was brilliant that day. Midway through the first-half, Mick won the ball in the centre of the park. He passed it on to Pat Morley, who knocked it onto Dave Barry breaking from midfield.

Dave carried the ball towards the edge of the box, sold their defender a dummy and cut inside on his right foot. Dave had a very forceful shot.

He connected with the ball brilliantly and smashed it past Gerald Hillringhaus, who dived early and got a hand to the ball, but was never going to stop it.

1-0.

The place erupted.

I jumped on Dave's back as he ran away celebrating! It was surreal.

We were part-timers up against World Cup winners, guys who won league titles and European trophies.

I won't say we had them on the ropes or anything like it, but Bayern were rattled. We were stunned to score so I can only imagine how they felt!

It was a lovely, clear sunny day for late-September in Cork and Musgrave Park was bouncing after the goal.

We were closing them down, whacking into them and were defensively strong. I was playing on the right wing; we had one up front, Pat, and we packed midfield and tried to put pressure on them, stop them where we could.

I was up against a guy called Manfred Bender.

It was exhausting but utterly exhilarating… we were wired with adrenaline.

I remember looking up at the scoreboard.

Cork City 1, Bayern Munich 0.

BAYERN GOT BACK to basics quickly.

They were totally in control, far superior and they completely dominated the game. Right on the stroke of half-time a shot deflected, and the ball broke to their captain Stefan Effenberg on the edge of our box.

He controlled it with his knee, held off a tackle and buried it past Phil Harrington into the bottom corner.

A goal from nothing.

That was the difference playing against top players.

In the second-half, it was an avalanche. We were defending on the edge of our own box, putting our heads on the line and Harrington made a couple of brilliant saves.

Mazinho was through on goal and his point-blank shot was stopped by Phil. Another Bayern player followed up and hit the crossbar with his shot.

For us, Dave had a powerful shot from a free-kick that was saved, and Anthony Kenneally had a half-chance where the keeper made a second fantastic save.

They were probably the only times in the second-half that we got near their area.

We hung on though.

The final whistle went.

Cork City 1, Bayern Munich 1.

It was incredible… the relief, the emotion, and we were absolutely shattered. The hype, the adrenaline, we were buzzing and were almost unsure what to do.

We were in disbelief.

We went straight to the bar and celebrated!

What else were we to do? That was part of our DNA and culture. Bayern wanted to batter us, they expected to and we expected them to. But we got a 1-1 draw against Bayern Munich.

We were the lead story on BBC *Sportsnight* that night… 'Fantastic Cork City got a result against the mighty Bayern Munich.'

Brilliant. But we were all back in work the next morning.

That was just the way life was then. You trained hard, you worked, and you might have had sore legs and a sore head, but you wouldn't miss work. Even if you got a draw against Bayern, the greatest result of any Irish side in Europe up to that point.

BAYERN RESTED A few players for their league match ahead of the return leg. Meanwhile, we had a 400-mile round trip to Sligo Rovers on a bus a few days before the game. We lost 2-1.

Bayern, of course, were embarrassed to draw with a part-time team. The press back in Germany was heavily critical of them.

Juup Heynckes, the Bayern manager, questioned the players' commitment and said they didn't put in even thirty percent of the effort that they should have. The Bayern players probably knew we fought hard and did our best, and that they had been complacent.

Effenberg, though, was a different story. He was completely dismissive of City, especially after the first leg. He promised the Bayern supporters that they would hammer us in the return leg. He said that we were a 'team of 40 year-olds' – which made me laugh because I was 26 at the time!

Effenberg also said something about Dave Barry being old enough to be his father. When he was asked about this by the German press after the second game, Dave said, 'If he thinks I was like his father, he played like my mother tonight'.

The German reporters loved that because Effenberg wasn't a popular figure and he was a problem within the club at the time. He was incredibly arrogant. Which was fair enough, he was a brilliant player and we were part-timers. It was strange though.

It's not like we thought we had a chance of winning the tie. Noel told the press ahead of the second game that a 4-0 or 5-0 loss would be a good result for us.

For the players, it was another 'holiday'.

We wanted to do ourselves justice, of course, but this was such a novelty. A trip to Germany mid-week, a few days away from work and the chance to train every morning as professionals.

THE SECOND LEG was on a Tuesday night at the Olympic Stadium in Munich.

We arrived on Sunday morning and Bayern representatives showed us around their training ground.

Bayern Munich claimed that they were the biggest and wealthiest club in Europe and they probably were, judging by their facilities. The car park was full of Mercedes cars, all the first-team was sponsored by them.

Bayern had 4G pitches. No one in England had this. They showed us their hydro-pool. None of us knew what a hydro-pool was. The Bayern representative explained that it was for when players get injured, it speeded up recovery. They had an oxygen chamber too to aid recovery.

We were gobsmacked.

We had never seen anything like this. No one in British football, and especially not in Ireland, was doing this or even knew about it.

The Germans were the best at everything.

The dressing-rooms were incredible, everything was absolutely massive. Every player had their own number over the seat... they were all allocated their own space. It was phenomenal to be there.

When teams visited us, someone from the club would show them Blarney Castle or some other landmark. You couldn't show them our training ground anyway, because we didn't have one – and there was certainly no hydro-pool!

The Oktoberfest beer festival was on that night and the Bayern representatives asked us would we like to go?

One hundred percent of hands shot straight up.

Absolutely.

TWO OR THREE of the Bayern staff brought us.

Noel O'Mahony, knowing that there was a drink culture within the league, told us we could only have two drinks each. But they didn't serve pints there.

The drink came in these huge pitchers.

We got there at 7pm and there were already about 5,000 people in this massive marquee. The music was blaring. Everyone was clapping and singing, standing on tables.

After a few pitchers, one of our centre-backs, Paul Bannon decided that he'd go up to the orchestra in the middle of this and he'd conduct a song or two. The crowd was loving it!

That was it for Noel though.

He called the representative from Bayern and said we were out of there.

We protested, everyone was singing, having a good time, but Noel was like, 'No... no, the bus is coming... we're going now!'

It was only about 10pm.

Everyone was steamed. I don't know how many of the pitchers we had, but they were simply massive. And on the bus back to the hotel, there was a sing-song. The following morning we trained beside the Olympic Stadium.

Noel ran us for an hour and a half.

We did 12 minute-runs.

He ran us and ran us… *And ran us.*

After about an hour, we were over at the corner of the pitch lying down, absolutely gasping for air when an aul German fella on a bike cycled by, stopped and looked at us.

'You will not be able to run tomorrow,' he said.

We were all thinking… *You're f**king right there!*

WE WENT BACK to the hotel and were meant to get ready and then do a tour of the city. We cancelled it. Everyone stayed in bed; we could barely move or talk after the morning of training.

That night, we went to Olympic Stadium to do a warm-up – well, a kickabout – and take a look around it.

The stadium was built for the 1972 Olympic Games and had also hosted the 1974 World Cup final. It was spectacular. We had never seen anything like it. The dressing-rooms were designed for the Olympics and we were told could hold up to 100 athletes. We were used to League of Ireland dressing-rooms or portacabins, everyone cramped in a tiny room no bigger than two wardrobes.

At the Olympic Stadium, they had a plunging pool, a hydro-pool and oxygen tents in the dressing-room. It was phenomenal. At that time, English football was oblivious to the benefits of these things and remained so until Arsene Wenger came along. The Germans were miles ahead.

We were staying in this incredible hotel, it was top notch.

When we came down to breakfast on the morning of the match, there we were on the cover of the two Munich newspapers. They had photographed us at the beer festival on the Sunday night.

Cork City enjoying themselves at Oktoberfest, the headline read.

We were all laughing about it, joking with the waiters and waitresses who recognised us from the photos.

It was all good craic, although Effenberg probably didn't find the photos funny.

THERE WERE AROUND 15,000 at the match, including tennis legend Boris Becker, who was a Bayern supporter. City fans were over for the game too. But, in a stadium that could hold 80,000, it felt empty.

It was an enormous pitch, far from the stands, with an athletic track running around it. We were buzzing for the game – it was live on TV in Germany.

Another part of us was probably thinking... *Let's get the game over... and we'll get back out to the beer festival!*

Munich were expected to walk all over us.

Our approach was the same as the first game. Everyone behind the ball, keep it compact, leave one up front and make it as hard for them as we could.

As expected, they controlled the ball. They had all of the possession and we were defending on the edge of our box, but it wasn't as if they were battering us... they didn't create a lot.

We defended brilliantly. They were finding it hard to break us down.

0-0.

Bayern were booed off by their supporters. They were going through because of the away goal they got at Musgrave Park, but it was another embarrassing night for them, and the supporters weren't happy.

In the second-half, we got one or two breaks and all of a sudden, the thought crossed our mind that maybe these guys were there for the taking.

WE GOT A free-kick on the edge of their box.

Gerry McCabe laid it out to Dave Barry, who hit it well.

Hillringhaus saved it.

The ball broke to Paul Bannon about six or seven yards from goal, dead centre of the box. He was a fraction away from putting it in the net; it spun through his legs, and Bayern cleared it.

Paul just didn't expect the chance.

We couldn't believe it. *We nearly scored.*

If Paul had put it in the net, Bayern would have needed two goals to go through. For the next couple of minutes, maybe we had the wind in our sails, but we started gambling and going for it.

We got caught on the break 15 minutes from the end.

It's still incredible to think Bayern scored against us from a counter-attack, and that it took so long for them to get past us.

Effenberg played a pass into midfield and they got it forward to Wolfharth, sprinting forward on the right wing. We couldn't stop him. He got to the edge of the box and squared it across for Labbadia to score. Phil Harrington couldn't do anything about it.

And then, with the last kick of the game, they scored a penalty after the referee said Liam Murphy handled the ball in the box from their corner.

Christian Ziege scored it, but Phil got a hand on it and almost saved the penalty.

That was the story of the tie for us and for them; we were so close to stopping them and they were quite lucky.

The Bayern supporters gave us a standing ovation at full-time and Heynckes, the Bayern manager, was complimentary of us after the game. He said we, 'sold ourselves very well' and that we were, 'a good advert for Irish football'.

He also said that we had been, 'more committed' then the Bayern players.

They were probably expecting to beat us 5-0 or 6-0, so 2-0 was like a win for us after the draw in Cork.

There was a lot of disharmony within Munich at the time, they were struggling and Heynckes was under immense pressure.

He was sacked two days later.

THERE WAS A UEFA rule at the time which stated that a player couldn't take off his jersey in front of the cameras. So, we couldn't swap shirts with the Bayern players on the pitch.

When we came back into the dressing-rooms, they were all throwing their gear into this big laundry basket.

We asked the Bayern kit guy could we take some jerseys from the basket?

'Go ahead!' he told us.

All the Cork players went into Bayern's massive dressing-room and we started pulling jerseys and togs and socks out of the basket, to take home as souvenirs. I got Manny Bender's shirt.

When we turned around, all the Bayern players were sitting across from us in silence. Staring at us.

They must have been thinking, *This shower of...*

Playing in Europe then wasn't like it is nowadays for Irish sides, where you might play a team from Iceland or Norway or Estonia and you might stand a chance.

This was Bayern Munich, one of the biggest clubs in Europe. It was very much, from our perspective, about not getting battered.

Don't lose 10-0.

That's why the 1-1 draw at Musgrave Park is probably one of the greatest European results, if not the greatest, an Irish side has ever had.

Unless an Irish team draws Barcelona or Real Madrid or Juventus, and gets a draw or a win against them, it's hard to see how it could be topped.

Cork City had come a long way in the six years since I joined the club.

CHAPTER 9

OUR LEAGUE FORM suffered from the hype of the Bayern Munich experience. It took our focus away.

We went six weeks without a win in the period before and after the two matches.

I suppose it was almost inevitable that we would take our eye off the ball in the league, although it was disappointing given we had lost out on the title on the final day of the previous season.

Three days after drawing with Bayern, we lost 3-0 away to Dundalk. There had been nothing between ourselves and Dundalk the previous season, but our attention wasn't on the task at hand.

The day before we left for Munich for the second leg, we lost 2-1 away to Sligo Rovers, which was a bad defeat for us.

We eventually kicked back into gear and started to be in contention again near the top of the table.

City ended up finishing third, a point behind Derry in second and six points behind Shelbourne. And I finished the season as the league's top scorer. I got 16 goals. It didn't compensate for missing out on the league title, but it was a nice personal accolade.

Finishing as the league's top scorer was certainly something I never could have imagined when I came into the league as a defender from Athlone Town.

At this point, I was probably at my peak. A lot of the City team were. Pat

Morley and I had developed a great relationship on the pitch. We had been playing up front together for a few years and we had a near-perfect understanding.

Neither of us were the tallest but we both could move around, we were quick and could cause defences trouble.

CORK CITY WERE one of the strongest teams in the country and we reached the FAI Cup final again, where we played Bohemians.

Bohs were a good team with some excellent players like Pat Fenlon, Robbie Best and Paul Whelan, brother of Ronnie, the Ireland and Liverpool midfielder. They had finished fifth in the league.

It was going to be a big day no matter who won. It had been 19 years since a Cork team won the FAI Cup – Cork Hibernians won it in 1973. Bohemians, meanwhile, hadn't won the cup since '76.

We were heavy favourites. We had a very strong, experienced team and weren't going to be bullied or pushed around.

We were a physically imposing side too. I would say maybe half of our team was six foot or more – Dave Barry, Paul Bannon Liam Murphy, Declan Hyde, Johnny Glynn. We had Pat and myself getting goals up front, and there was quality throughout the team. Gerry McCabe, a Scottish winger, was a very good player who spent a few seasons with us. He was probably the best of the outside players we brought in.

So, we had a strong team, and we also had the support of the Cork crowd. There were only about 17,000 at the FAI Cup final at Lansdowne Road – we had about 10,000, maybe 12,000, at the game.

The City fans took up the entire West Stand in the stadium and most of the South Stand. There was talk of five trains coming up from Cork with supporters. We had earned the support of the old Cork football fans.

The support had come back. Over the previous couple of years we were attracting decent crowds, averaging 4,000 or 5,000 for big games and we could get anything up to 8,000 or 9,000. At this stage, we were challenging and that's what Cork supporters want. They'll follow you once you're competing for trophies and doing well.

And to be honest, it felt like we were going up to Dublin just to pick up the cup.

We had a better team than Bohs, our league position was better, we had more experience, and we had a massive following.

We all fully believed we were going to win the cup.

Yet, it turned into the worst day of my League of Ireland career.

It was an absolute nightmare of a match.

We were awful.

THE FINAL WAS played in May, but it was like a winter's day – grey, rainy, windy. It was difficult to play any football in the conditions and it was a very stop-start game. The referee was fussy and pulled both teams up on *nothing fouls*.

It was just a horrible match, made even worse by a gale sweeping across the pitch. The fans on the terraces were drenched.

We had more of the ball, but huffed and puffed without creating much. Phil Harrington made a few saves to keep us in it. After about five minutes, I had a chance and went through on goal one-on-one with John Connolly, the Bohs' goalkeeper. He saved my shot from point blank range. I was disgusted.

Connolly was only a young lad and he was shaky in goal. We thought he was there for the taking and he should have been, given the form Pat and myself were in. But it just wasn't our day at all, and the team didn't create much after that early chance.

Bohs had the wind in the first-half. But then the wind changed after half-time and it was into our faces again in the second-half! *Incredible.*

Even the elements were against us.

With about 10 minutes to go, Connolly kicked the ball from his hands up the pitch. Alan Byrne won a header and knocked it on to Pat Fenlon, who headed it on again. The ball, massively assisted by the wind, bounced between our centre-halves on the edge of the box and landed to Dave Tillson, who just lobbed it over Phil, who was racing out of his goal. It was a like a punch to the gut. We were crushed.

The goal was so bad too from our perspective... a long punt up the pitch, two headers and a lob over the goalkeeper. The wind played a large part in it too.

We didn't come close to getting a goal back and were absolutely devastated at full-time. It was the third time in four years that we lost a 'final', if you include the league decider against Dundalk the previous season. But this was the cruellest one of them all.

As I've said, the worst day of my League of Ireland career.

WE HAD BELIEVED the hype.

We were complacent.

The Dundalk loss the year before was a different story. They were a very experienced team with a history of winning things, whereas the Bohemians defeat was totally *wrong* from our point of view.

Complacency is not really something you sense before a match. But afterwards, it was obvious that's what cost us.

Ultimately, we went into the game thinking we had it won.

We didn't do what we were supposed to and didn't work as hard as we should have. I suppose that's the brilliance and the beauty of sport. The underdog will always have a chance when the favourite takes their eye off the ball and think they have it, if they don't prepare properly and don't give their opponents respect.

If you think you can turn up at a final and have the cup won before you walk out on the pitch, you deserve what you get.

We underestimated Bohs and got the greatest kick up the backside ever that day.

Even now, if the City lads speak about the 1992 cup final, every one of us will agree… 'That was the worst day… EVER!'

Our over-confidence turned into tension and then jitters on the day when we started slow. We could have no complaints about losing. After missing out in a few big games, there was talk that we were always going to the bridesmaids, never the bride.

Were we bottlers?

There were definitely questions about our mentality.

Noel O'Mahony, our manager, was furious.

He questioned if we were capable of producing the performances required on a big stage. We were being called a 'nearly team'.

I wondered myself if we were ever going to win anything.

It felt like a year's worth of work and effort, the whole season… GONE.

Into dust.

THERE WAS ALWAYS drama with Cork City, nothing was ever straightforward and that proved especially true the following season.

From the start, the 1992/93 campaign was unpredictable, a real roller-coaster.

We had a bit of nightmare start. City were meant to move into a new stadium in Bishopstown, but, of course, it wasn't ready for the start of the season. There was a hold up over safety concerns about the main stand, and it went on for months. Turner's Cross wasn't ready either.

So, we had to play our first few matches down in Cobh at St Colman's Park. It wasn't ideal by any means, but it was no excuse for our performance in our first home match of the season. Bohemians came down to Cork, full of confidence after the FAI Cup final win.

And they battered us.

4-1. After the game, there was absolute mayhem in our dressing-room.

All hell broke loose.

Fellas were accusing each other of not pulling their weight.

Punches were thrown, lads were flaking each other out. It was bedlam.

Noel, who was under savage pressure, eventually managed to calm everybody down. We were a very tight knit group, but we used to argue all the time. There would be fights at training occasionally.

Nowadays, lads might have a scuffle or a shoving match. But we had actual flake outs during training. Saturday morning was tougher and more physical for us than most games. We would have seven-a-side training and they were tough going because no one wanted to lose. The City players went hell for leather.

If you lost, the abuse and slagging would be merciless. Some lads had a temper, others would get thick, but once they walked away and it cooled down, everyone was fine. That was a particularly memorable dust-up after the Bohs defeat though. It took a lot to calm things down. A lot of frustration had built up, from the cup final loss and the few other near-misses.

Players we were desperate to win, and we all feared standards were slipping.

WE PUT THINGS right the following week against St Patrick's Athletic and went on a winning run over the next month. We beat Waterford, Drogheda, Derry City away and Bray Wanderers.

The 1992/93 League of Ireland season turned out to be unpredictable, exciting and just incredible. It's hard to think of another season like it before or since.

The run-in was amazing.

For long spells we were top. Bohemians were neck-and-neck with us, and so were Shelbourne.

The lead at the top of the table rotated between the three teams all the way through the season. The difference between winning and even drawing a game could mean being first in the table or third. There was so little margin for error.

Going into the final month of the season all three teams were on 36 points.

We played Bohs at Dalymount Park in the first week of April. If we won, we would go top with Shels, who beat Limerick on the same day, with two games to go. The winners between us and Bohs would be in pole position to win the league; the losing side would surely be out of the title race.

They beat us 2-0. Anto Whelan and Pat Fenlon scored the goals.

Bohs were a real bogey team for us at that time and that looked to be it.

They opened up a lead on us – it was still two points for a win at the time – and we dropped into third place with two games to go.

On television and radio reports, in the newspapers, the talk was that City had gone, that we were done for... blew it again!

Winning the league was out of our control and it looked like we were the bridesmaids once more. Noel O'Mahony was stepping down at the end of the season too.

We were never going to win a big trophy.

CHAPTER 10

GOING INTO THE final two games of the season, the title was completely in Bohemians' control. If Shelbourne won their remaining games, and we won our remaining games, it wouldn't matter.

As long as Bohs won their matches, they'd be champions.

At this point, we had gone from St Colman's Park out to our own ground in Bishopstown. Using Cobh's stadium wasn't popular with City fans. But Bishopstown certainly wasn't any better.

There was a lot of criticism aimed at the club, which was justified. Bishopstown was essentially a mucky field with no stands. We used to have to tog out in the ESB club behind it. They had a complex and we had nowhere else to get ready.

So, both teams got changed in the ESB club and walked across a farmer's field that was between the complex and Bishopstown stadium. When you think about it now, it's absurd, that two teams had to walk across a field to play a League of Ireland match, but that's just the way it was. We were still in the title race, but our facilities were anything but championship-level.

WE PLAYED DERRY City on a Wednesday afternoon, our second last game of the season. If we didn't win this game, then we stood no chance whatsoever of catching Bohs. Derry were going for Europe if they could get third.

We were the better team and controlled the game from the start without making a breakthrough, despite having a few efforts on goal.

Eventually, Johnny Glynn put us ahead with about 20 minutes to go. We dropped off then, trying to hold onto our lead. Derry started to push forward. We became quite nervous and rushed. With about four minutes left in the match, they scored.

It was another punch to the gut for us. It looked like our season was gone.

A couple of City fans behind the dug-out turned on Noel and the players. They started hurling abuse.

We made some changes and went for it. Paul Bannon switched from centre-back to centre-forward alongside Pat Morley and me. At that point, we were just hoping for one chance, one favourable bounce of the ball. The game went into injury time and we got the ball into the box. Paul had a shot which was saved by the Derry goalkeeper. Gerry McCabe followed up and his shot was saved, too.

The rebound landed to me, two yards out… the last kick of the game.

I knocked it over the line.

The City fans went mental. I was mobbed by the lads.

Derry were out on their feet.

The full-time whistle went… 2-1. We had won.

Now, at the time, we didn't realise how significant the goal would be. We were over the moon because the win meant we still had a chance of qualifying for Europe. We still had a chance of winning the league as well, but the odds were against us and massively in favour of Bohemians.

On the last day of the season we played Limerick at Bishopstown and comfortably beat them 3-0. We were on 40 points. That would prove to be the most straightforward part of the day. Shelbourne were playing Derry at Tolka Park and they got a late goal to win it. They also finished on 40 points.

Bohemians were away to Dundalk and only needed a point to win the title. Dundalk weren't as strong as they had been; they were in mid-table. There was no question that Bohs would beat them and win the league. When the full-time whistle went in our game, we were coming off the pitch expecting to hear that Bohs had wrapped it up.

But word was going around that their bus had broken down on the way up to Dundalk. Kick-off had been delayed by 90 minutes. And they were losing 1-0. Tom McNulty, who had scored the goal that lost us the league on the last day two years previously, had scored for Dundalk. We were in shock.

If Bohs lost, we were back in it as the league would be decided by a three-way play-off between ourselves, Bohs and Shelbourne.

WE RAN ACROSS the mucky farmer's field to the ESB club, still in our gear from the match.

The City players and coaching staff stood in the car park and turned on the commentary of the match.

There were loads of City supporters there too; no one was leaving or going home until the Bohs match finished. We listened to the commentary from a car radio.

There were guys with pocket radios to their ears.

Some of the City lads were too anxious to listen and went into the dressing-rooms. Others were glued to it.

Dundalk held on beat Bohs. All three teams finished on 40 points. Bohs had the best goal difference. But goal difference wasn't used to decide the league at the time. It was going to a three-team play-off.

We were back in it! The lads celebrated like we won the league.

The relief was incredible, we had gone into the day hoping to try to do enough to finish second and maybe qualify for Europe. No one could have predicted that it would work out as it did.

I don't think there have been many three-team play-offs to win a league title anywhere. The format was like a mini-tournament. Teams would play each other twice, and the side with the most points would be champions.

It sounded relatively simple in theory, but again, nothing about that season was straightforward. The play-offs took over a month to complete.

WE WON THE first game at home to Bohemians.

Pat Morley got the goal. It was a big win for us psychologically. Bohs had been our bogey team all season. We fully deserved to win on the day though.

Our next play-off match was away to Shelbourne at Tolka Park.

We lost 1-0.

Shels scored while we had a player down injured, and Morley was sent off for arguing with the referee. I think it was his first red card at any level of football. Noel and the players were up in arms over it.

We drew our next two games... 1-1 with Shels at home, and 0-0 away to Bohs. We thought that was it for us again. Bohs were playing Shels in the last game of the round-robin. The winner was going to be league champions.

We were out of it. *Again.*

GERRY MCCABE WAS going back to Scotland on the Monday. So, we decided to have a party on the Saturday for him, the same day Bohs played Shels for the league title.

As far as we were concerned, the season was over. We were gone, *again*, and had missed out on the title. *Again.*

So, the team met in Cork that Saturday and we ended up down in Kinsale.

We were socialising all day and into the evening, having great craic... 20 of us, oblivious to the Bohs-Shels game.

We were done, the season was over... the title gone.

At around nine o'clock, some fella walked into The Spaniard, the pub we were in. He approached us. 'Lads, the game in Dublin is nil-all.'

We were all in good form at this stage of the evening.

'What?

'What does that mean?'

None of us ever expected that match to be a draw. If it stayed 0-0 though, we were back in the hunt. We actually thought Bohs would beat Shels.

It was then a repeat of the last day of the regular season.

We all ended up in the car park again, outside the pub and someone put on their car radio. We huddled around and listened to the commentary of the final 10 minutes of the match.

When the full-time whistle went, they could probably hear us in Dublin celebrating.

We were all jumping around, hugging each other outside this little pub... 'We're back in it... We're back in it!'

It then dawned on us... *What do we do now?*

Do we play everyone again... TWICE?

No one knew what was going to happen.

The league hadn't planned for this.

WHEN WE WENT to training on the Tuesday night, the league still hadn't made a decision.

Either way, Noel had a training plan for us.

He ran us non-stop for an hour.

We ran and ran… *and ran.*

We didn't see a football once.

The whole time, he was going to us… 'We won't f**king waste this opportunity!'

We were all fuming, absolutely furious.

What are we doing this running for?

We were fit as fiddles. It was May, at the end of the longest season the League of Ireland had ever had!

The next day, the league decided the three teams would play each other just once, and the matches would be staged at neutral venues.

We were first up.

We played Bohemians on a Wednesday night at Turner's Cross, which was classed as a neutral venue because we hadn't played there all year. It was probably a stretch to call it 'neutral', but we weren't complaining.

There were 6,000 fans at the game and most of them were supporting City. Pat Morley scored a great goal and we beat them 1-0.

Bohs, meanwhile, were peeved.

Eamonn Greg, their manager at the time, a gentleman, claimed that they should have originally won the league because of their superior goal difference.

But that wasn't in the rules, and goal difference as a tie-breaker didn't come in until a few years later.

Shelbourne and Bohs were due to meet the following Wednesday. Which meant that, if we beat Shels at the RDS on the Saturday, we would be champions.

It was a cup final for us.

If we won, we'd be league champions and qualify for Europe, or as it was renamed that year… the Champions League.

It had also been 19 years since a Cork team won the League of Ireland, when Cork Celtic won the title. For Shelbourne, it was more like a semi-final – they still had to play Bohs on the Wednesday.

They were going for the double after winning the FAI Cup final against Dundalk the previous weekend.

We took a big crowd up with us, but it could have been massive. On the same day, the Cork hurlers were playing in the National League final. In Cork city, hurling is very strong, and a lot of the hurling heads also followed the soccer team. The support was split, but there were still plenty of City fans at the match.

I started on the bench. Noel went with Paul Bannon and Pat Morley up front. I was City's record goalscorer at the time; I had started almost every game over the previous few years.

But you have to quickly put your own disappointment aside. The only thing that mattered was winning the title. It turned into an incredible match, full of goals and drama. It was the most entertaining game of the season for supporters, but nerve-wrecking for anyone involved.

We took the lead through Pat Morley.

Shels equalised.

After half-time, Shels had a player sent-off, Kevin Brady, and within a minute we scored to go ahead. Dave Barry got a lovely goal. I came on as a substitute then.

Yet again though, Shels pegged us back. They got another goal with about a half an hour to go. A draw was a good result for them. It left them with the chance to win the league against Bohs on the Wednesday. They dropped off us and looked to hold onto the draw.

It was our 38th game of the season. Both teams were running on empty.

Yet we were such a resilient team, with incredible team spirit, and so battle-hardened. We dug deep again and scored with about 15 minutes to go. Paul Bannon got the goal... Pat got a touch on it as it was going in.

We held on.

CHAMPIONS AT LAST.

At full-time, there was a pitch invasion, as the City fans ran on and celebrated with us.

Noel was almost in tears.

The players were hugging each other.

Everyone was celebrating.

We were no longer the bridesmaid team, the nearly men.

The club wasn't even 10 years old and we had become the best side in Ireland after a gruelling, testing season.

IN IRISH FOOTBALL, it's easy at times to think you're operating in a small bubble.

It wasn't glamorous at all.

We spent most of our lives going up and down the country roads for matches. Four-hour journeys each way.

No decent dressing-rooms to change in.

Poor facilities. Muddy pitches.

Playing in all weathers.

Sometimes it felt like we were an afterthought for the wider public. Cork were flying in gaelic football and hurling, so those teams brought the crowds out and got the coverage.

This was during the Jack Charlton era, when the Ireland team were on top of the world and football the main sport in the country.

It felt that the League of Ireland was impervious to the rise in popularity for the sport as a whole though. We were still playing in the same rundown stadiums. The league hadn't moved on since I joined in 1985.

Yet, it was special to see the reaction of the Cork public when we got back to the county, to see the effect sport can have on a community.

When we returned to Cork on the Sunday, there were fans waiting for us at Kent Station. We got off the train and made our way through. Everyone was cheering for us. The Cork hurlers won the league too.

The whole city was celebrating.

You could feel the buzz around the place as we made our way back into the city centre. It was brilliant to see all the Cork people so happy and behind the team.

On the Monday, we had an open-top bus parade from Kent Station to Patrick Street. There were thousands out in the streets, all decked out in green and white, cheering for us and singing.

When we reached the stage, Deccie Daly, our captain, introduced each member of the team and coaching staff one by one. Everyone got a big cheer.

We felt loved.

Appreciated.

Respected by our own, which is what matters most of all.

PART FOUR

600 and Counting

CHAPTER 11

NOEL O'MAHONY STEPPED down as manager after we won the league.

I think the Cork City chairman Pat O'Donovan had more or less agreed with Noel that he was gone. And then the play-offs happened.

And then the second play-offs happened.

Noel wasn't an old man by any means, he was 53 or 54 at the time, but there was a feeling that the team needed to push on.

We had some brilliant players in the team. And I think, tactically, Noel was a bit behind in that regard at that point. We needed to expand a bit.

Noel was steeped in Cork soccer since winning the league as a player with Cork Hibernians. He instilled a hardness, a resilience in the team.

We were a Cork team in every sense, a tough side. And Noel played a massive part in that. In his second spell as Cork City manager, he oversaw us getting into Europe, drawing against Bayern Munich. And, in his last game, we won the league. It was a fitting, but bittersweet end for him. Noel was given a testimonial dinner by the club. O'Donovan already had Noel's replacement lined up... Damien Richardson. Rico was a Dub. He had played for Shamrock Rovers and came to us from Gillingham, where he had been a big player with them before taking over as manager. We were his first club back in Ireland.

He was similar to Noel in that he was very aggressive. But he was a much more positive manager.

Noel could be quite negative. If we got a draw away from home, he was happy with that. Even if it was a draw away to a team bottom of the table, it didn't matter. Win at home, draw away and you'd be grand – that was how Noel saw it.

A lot of us thought it was wrong to just accept a draw away from home. The team had matured and improved, we were champions. We felt that we were well capable of winning matches… home or away.

Damien was the opposite of Noel in that regard. We played to beat everyone. He brought in more coaching, but Rico's biggest impact was psychological. He would tell us we were better than everyone else and it worked because the team knew they were good, we believed it. It was exactly what we needed to hear.

Rico had a massively positive effect on the team.

DAMIEN'S FIRST MATCH as manager was also our first game in the European Cup, or the Champions League as it was renamed.

We drew Cwmbran Town, who had won the Welsh league.

A few days before the European game, Rico signed a striker, Tommy Gaynor. Tommy was one of the most talented players ever in Ireland. He was six foot two or three, a gifted player. For a big man, he wasn't great in the air, but his technique was brilliant, and he had fantastic control. Tommy was being released by Nottingham Forest. Damien came in for him and gave him a one-month contract to help see us through the first round of Europe.

Gaynor was worth two players; he was head and shoulders above everyone, but he was also getting paid massive money. The story at the time was that he was getting £400 a week. Now, £400 a week in 1993 was huge money in the League of Ireland, especially for City, who paid poorly. A lot of the local players were on £40 or £50 pounds a week. But Rico obviously felt it was worth it if it meant getting through to the next round in the Champions League.

Europe was worth big money to the club.

WE PLAYED AWAY to Cwmbran Town away in the first leg in Cardiff; the match was staged at a university complex. There were only about 3,000 fans there, but we brought 1,000 City supporters over for the game.

It was the first time Wales had a team in the European Cup. It was expected to be our first win in European competition – but we went in at half-time 3-0 down.

We dominated possession but before we knew it, they had scored three goals in the first half an hour. We got our act together in the second-half.

I didn't start but I came on for the last half an hour and scored – my first goal in Europe and City's first in the European Cup, but I couldn't really celebrate because we had to get play restarted! I then set-up the second goal for Anthony Buckley. We had a load of chances to win the match or draw it but, nevertheless, the second-half goals gave us a chance to turn the tie around at home. It finished 3-2 and we got out of jail.

Two weeks later, at Turner's Cross, the place was heaving, absolutely packed to the rafters. At that point, European games had to be played in all-seater grounds. But there were fans standing and sitting on walls to try get a view of the game.

It was a blisteringly hot day at the start of September. It was the first day we wore the horrendous-looking candy rock strip too, which had just been brought in.

Again, they scored early and frustrated us. We were 4-2 down on aggregate The crowd in the Shed end were very vocal and it looked like we were going out.

In the last 15 minutes, we scored twice. Pat Morley and Johnny Glynn got the goals; Glynn's goal came five minutes from the end. We won the match and scraped through on away goals. We were the better team, no doubt, but it was touch and go at times and we nearly blew it. It was the first time in 14 years that a League of Ireland club had won a European Cup match. Before us, only Dundalk, Waterford and Bohemians had won a game in the tournament. A European victory was absolutely nothing to turn your nose up at, no matter how it came. But it was a close call.

In the league, we hit the ground running and it became a two-horse race between ourselves and Shamrock Rovers, who were managed by Ray Treacy.

After about 10 games, we had left everyone else behind us. We were playing some great stuff. We weren't distracted by the excitement of Europe as we had been in previous seasons. And then we were drawn against Galatasaray, the Turkish double winners, who had seven or eight internationals in their squad.

It turned into one of the most eventful, incredible two-legged ties for a League of Ireland side ever.

WE DIDN'T KNOW a lot about Galatasaray as a team because Turkish football didn't have the pedigree of other nations in Europe at that time. Galatasaray were rich, they had German owners and had bought a player, Kubilay Türkyilmaz, for over one million pounds from Bologna that summer.

But Turkish football was well down the list of European countries when it came to pedigree. They were like a grade three country for football – Ireland beat them twice in qualifying for Euro '92 – 5-0 at home and 3-1 away.

When we got them in the draw, people were saying to us, 'Oh, Jesus, Turkey. That's a dangerous place!' It was incredibly hostile, extremely rough.

But that's what helped make it such a great trip.

Turkey was probably the best European trip we ever had, even better than Bayern Munich. To this day, I have never experienced an atmosphere at a game like the one that we had in Istanbul. It was a totally unique experience, bordering on surreal, from the moment we arrived.

WE HAD A man with us, named Jerry Harris. Jerry was our kitman, a brilliant guy who stuck with Cork City and Cork football back to the days of Cork United; he'd been close with Noel O'Mahony.

Every time we went on a European trip, Jerry would get crates of Guinness to bring with us. We would bring around 20 or 30. This was the norm, as there was a massive drinking culture in the league at the time.

On the day we arrived at the hotel, Manchester City were there. They were over for a friendly game against Fenerbahçe. They were sitting on the steps of the hotel as we arrived, about to go to training.

A few of us knew Niall Quinn, the Ireland centre-forward, who played for them. Quinny and the Man City lads were stunned when we pulled up in the bus.

Jerry got off and asked the lads to bring in a crate each. We began unloading the crates of Guinness and made our way past them into the hotel. All the Man City lads were looking at us, open-mouthed, wondering… *Are they not here to play a Champions League match?*

Quinny was laughing, going, 'Ah, stop it, lads!'

GALATASARAY HAD A handful of Turkish internationals in their squad, a Swiss international, and a Swedish international. They were a very good team.

In the UEFA Cup the previous season, they beat Roma and they were always pretty formidable at home. I don't think any European team had beaten them in

Turkey. It was only when we went over that we realised exactly why they were so strong at home. The intimidation was absolutely savage, although not before the match.

They couldn't have been nicer to us before the game. We were brought on a tour around some sights in Istanbul. We went on a cruise up the Bosporus, and had lunch overlooking the Black Sea. We were also brought through the Grand Bazaar, the huge market in the city.

We all had our Cork City gear on, so the street traders in the market knew who we were. They all started clapping for us. But they were chanting… '5-0… 5-0… 5-0.'

The newspapers that morning said Galatasaray were going to beat us by that number of goals… 5-0. We were expected to lose heavily.

Galatasaray aides were with us. They were helpful and nice to us. We were no threat to them, so it was good PR for the club.

We were told that, if we had been a high-profile team, we would have never been given that treatment. We didn't take offence. We were on another 'holiday'.

THE ALI SAMI YEN Stadium was nicknamed 'Hell' by the Galatasaray supporters. It was a bowl-shaped ground, with two high tiers and was a sea of yellow and red on the night. The noise was astonishing.

On the night, the attendance was around 30,000 – there were 20,000 in the ground when we arrived two hours before the game. The atmosphere was electric, the noise, the singing.

Their supporters never stopped from the time we went out for the warm-up.

They were chanting and chanting… and chanting.

It was relentless.

At the time, we didn't know a lot about Galatasaray, other than the club was rich and paying big money for players. Some of their players went on to have great careers. Hakan Şükür was their centre-forward. He went on to score a load of goals for the Turkish national team and played all over Europe. They had a guy called Kubilay Türkyilmaz, who was of Turkish descent but declared for Switzerland and scored a lot of goals for them.

Tugay Kerimoğlu, who went on to play for Blackburn Rovers in the Premier League, was in midfield. He was such a gifted player. And they had all of these other lads who played international football for Turkey.

Some of them were in the national team 10 years later when Turkey finished third at the World Cup. At that point though, they were unknown to a lot of people in western Europe.

WE HAD OUR chances in the first-half.

For such a talented team, they were a little bit loose at the back. After five minutes, Anthony Buckley had a shot saved and he had another effort on goal a few minutes later. We had a goal ruled out for offside, too.

Tommy Gaynor rounded the goalkeeper and put the ball into the net, but it wasn't given. It was something of a marginal call.

You could see why the Irish international team would go to places like Turkey or in eastern Europe at this time and they would get a raw deal from the referee. The refs weren't going by the same rules because the intimidation was incredible.

But Galatasaray still dominated the game. They scored a good goal before half-time. Kubilay collected the ball outside our penalty area from a free-kick, took a few touches and buried it past Phil Harrington in goal.

The crowd erupted. The noise deafening.

They made a sound I had never heard before or since after a goal.

It was like a wail… a deafening howl.

I could feel the hair stand up on the back of my neck.

It was just electric.

We did well to reach half-time only 1-0 down.

THEY UPPED THE intensity in the second-half, and got a second goal, which may have been marginally offside. But there was no way the referee was going to rule this one out.

Tugay nonchalantly played a 35-yard pass with the outside of his boot over our defence to Kubilay. He controlled it and laid it back across the box for Arif Erdem to score.

Again… deafening noise.

More… HOWLING!

The supporters let off fire-crackers and flares. It looked like the stands were on fire. The noise and the colour was stunning. At this point, also, the crowd were baying for blood. They wanted to see five or six, or seven goals.

Galatasaray were absolutely battering us.

Kubilay and Şükür both had shots that smashed off the crossbar – one of the shots was so hard the crossbar rattled for a good 30 seconds after impact – and Phil Harrington was forced to make a couple of fantastic saves.

I have no doubt that if they had got a third goal, they would have won 5-0, or 6-0.

But, defensively, they were a bit loose, quite casual, and we were getting a few half-chances on the counter attack.

On the few occasions we did break forward, it looked a bit like we were causing them problems. So, strangely, because they were so dominant, we always felt that there was a chance. And we got it just after an hour of play.

Phil took a goal-kick, cleared it up the pitch and the ball landed to Dave Barry about 10 yards from their penalty area. Dave went past one player, jumped over another tackle in the box and was forced slightly wide. He swung his leg and crossed the ball back for Pat Morley, who was in the centre on the six-yard line.

Falko Götz, their German midfielder, stuck his leg out trying to cut the pass out and deflected the ball into the net.

2-1. We had an away goal.

The change of mood in the ground was the most incredible I ever experienced at a match.

For the first time since about two hours before the game, when most of the crowd arrived, the supporters stopped singing. It was like a switch had been flicked. And another, entirely different noise.

They began... HISSING... all 30,000 of them.

Galatasaray didn't want the ball, none of them. They were passing the ball sideways and backwards, looking for someone else to take responsibility.

The crowd were now completely on their backs. All of Galatasaray's fluid play went out the window, their intensity dropped... they were rattled.

As the game went on, they started getting very frustrated. There were a few dives looking for penalties and free-kicks, gesturing to the referee. Şükür had one or two half-chances. We were camped on the edge of our box, just chasing them down and clearing the ball when we got it.

But we hung on.

WHEN THE FINAL whistle went, we all started celebrating. Some of the lads were so exhausted, they dropped to the ground.

It was an unbelievable result. An away goal, in that atmosphere, against such an accomplished team.

We were all celebrating, hugging each other.

The lads were going, 'This is amazing… 2-1… and they have to come back to our place. We got out of jail here'.

Galatasaray looked totally deflated – the crowd were absolutely raging. The whole atmosphere was extremely hostile. The hatred was astonishing. It was vicious.

The entrance to their dressing-rooms, which were underground, was down a dark, narrow tunnel behind one of the goals. There were police officers lining the way. They were very aggressive towards us as we made our way down the steps and into the tunnel.

Pushing and shoving us. Mouthing at us. It was intimidating.

We couldn't leave the dressing-room for an hour after the match. We had to wait until the crowd had all left.

When we eventually got outside, one of the windows of our bus had been smashed. The Turks had won the game, but it didn't feel like that. Galatasaray expected to win by five or six goals. No one associated with the club was happy about the result.

The club had given us two aides who were helping us around. They had been very helpful and friendly.

But when we were all getting on the bus celebrating, high-fiving each other, you could see the anger in the aides' eyes. They did not want to be on our bus, but they had an obligation to bring us back to our hotel.

They couldn't speak with the rage. It smacked of viciousness. It was incredible, because they had been so nice to us. We had never experienced anything like this.

The City lads couldn't wait to get back to the hotel, to get ready and go out. This was why we were in Europe, amongst other things… for the night out after the game. This was what we lived for, especially after such a positive result.

But we were advised not to leave our hotel.

They told us it wouldn't be safe if we went out and if we were identified. If any Galatasaray supporters saw us, they wouldn't be clapping for us as they had been in the market.

So, we spent the night in the hotel bar.

It turned out that the staff in the bar were Besiktas and Fenerbahce supporters.

They were all delighted for us.

It wasn't a bad night at all.

OUT OF ALL the European games in which Cork City played, Galatasaray at home was the first time that we all agreed... 'You know what... we have a chance against these fellas!'

They were the first big team we thought we could beat. We were going to each other... 'We really have a chance against these lads'.

They were obviously better than us. But they were loose at the back and wouldn't like playing at Bishopstown.

No one liked playing at Bishopstown.

It was a bog.

Turner's Cross wasn't great at the time, but it had at least been a pitch, it had a decent surface. At Bishopstown, there was a field and a stand around it. They then put up a fence, goalposts and a dug-out.

We had to play the match on a Wednesday afternoon because there were no floodlights installed. It was on the outskirts of Cork, about four miles from the city centre. Bishopstown didn't have a car park. There was no by-pass near the ground, so it wasn't convenient for people coming out.

The move to the ground was deeply unpopular with City supporters, and there were a lot of arguments about it. It was miles out for people who lived in the city. The idea was to develop it into a modern facility, but that never happened.

The stand had to pass an inspection. The FAI were talking about potentially moving the match to Dalymount Park in Dublin, if the stand wasn't fit for purpose.

The pitch, which was incredibly heavy already, was made worse by it being a wet, windy day. The conditions were horrible, which helped us though.

BEFORE THE MATCH, the Galatasaray players came out and had a look around the ground. They had never seen anything like this.

They weren't used to playing in the rain and wind, on such a bumpy surface. Bishopstown was a million miles from anything they would have ever expected, or experienced.

Galatasaray had arrived in their own private plane and now they were getting ready in the ESB centre because we had no changing rooms.

We could see them walking around the pitch, in their yellow jackets, red slacks and shoes. They were looking at the surface with a mixture of disgust and bewilderment, getting muck on their nice, clean shoes.

Obviously, none of us could speak Turkish, but it looked like they were saying to each other… *The absolute state of this place!!!*

And they thought their ground was 'Hell'.

We could see they really didn't fancy it; it was written all over their faces and in their body language.

Even more, we were thinking… *This is our big chance!*

There were 7,000 at the match, and a few more standing outside the far fence trying to get a look. Around 500 or so Galatasaray supporters travelled over and, in fairness, they made a fair bit of noise.

The atmosphere wasn't as hostile for the Turkish players in Bishopstown as it had been in Istanbul for us, of course. Nothing could be.

But it was still brilliant in its own way, and we could really sense the excitement. We heard there were around 40 Turkish media personnel over too. It felt like a massive game – even if RTÉ didn't show the game live, only on a highlights show that night.

It was the biggest match in Cork City's history given what was at stake. Cork football was on the big stage, against a good European team, with our destiny in our own hands and a real chance to cause a massive upset. Considering where we had been just a few years previously – all the different iterations of Cork teams over the years – this was a proud moment for everyone associated with the club and football in Cork.

Although, that's not something you reflect on before kick-off, with the rain coming down, the wind whipping across the ground and the Galatasaray players up to their knees in muck on the pitch.

It was a very tight game.

We had a couple of half-chances in the first-half and troubled them on set-pieces – we were quite unlucky with one header, and Declan Hyde had a shot that was deflected over.

It was tit-for-tat.

We certainty didn't have our backs to the wall as we would have in other European games. We got stuck in amongst them. Galatasaray were very technical and were trying to play out from the back and through midfield.

But it just didn't work in Bishopstown. The pitch made it difficult.

The ball bobbled and bounced, and scuffed off the surface.

We were able to close them down and get tackles in, disrupt them. We got to half-time at 0-0 and we were all buzzing. We now genuinely believed Galatasaray were there for the taking.

I'll never forget that half-time. In the changing room we were all saying, 'Right lads… we need to go for this in the second-half.

'This lot can be taken!'

One goal from us! And we'd be through on away goals.

But Rico was saying, 'No, lads… we just need to keep everyone behind the ball'.

We were adamant though – Galatasaray were there for the taking. This great team, with all these international players, double-winners with one million pound players in their team, World Cup stars… they were there to be beaten by us, a team of part-time players, most of us getting 40 or 50 quid a week.

We had the chance to win it. We were all disagreeing with the manager.

'We need to go for this.'

'We need to put two up front.'

We were pleading.

Rico wouldn't agree to it.

DAMIEN'S LACK OF experience on the day possibly influenced his decision. He just didn't see the opportunity that was there for us.

In the second-half, we came out of the blocks raring to go again and caused them plenty of trouble for the first 20 minutes or so. We had half-chances where we could have scored. Dave Barry and Tommy Gaynor had decent efforts, and there were three or four times when the ball broke and on any other day, any one of them could have gone in.

Our best chance came after about an hour.

Fergus O'Donoghue launched the ball down the pitch. Tommy held off his marker and headed the ball onto Pat Morley, who got it down before it broke for Anthony Buckley. Buckley took it past the defender and into the box.

The goalkeeper raced off his line.

Anthony shot… with his left foot, at angle from about six yards or so.

The net shook and the crowd behind the goal let out a big cheer – we could see some of the umbrellas people were holding pitched up and down as supporters were celebrating.

The ball hit the side netting, though.

It was the closest we came on the day to scoring.

On another day, it may have gone in.

We had the ball in their half with a throw-in 15 minutes from the end. Dave Barry collected the ball and played a loose pass in midfield.

Galatasaray got to it first.

Şükür played it off to Tugay, who played a first-time pass with the outside of his boot down the middle of the pitch and in behind our defence for Kubilay to chase.

Kubilay was too fast, he was never going to miss. He raced onto the end of the pass, took a touch and finished past Phil Harrington with the outside of his boot.

It crushed us.

The Galatasaray players ran off and celebrated at the side of the pitch, and their supporters made a lot of noise. The celebrations weren't faked either.

They were delighted. The Turks knew they had gotten out of jail.

We were gutted.

Damien then made some substitutions and tried to change it. But the game was over. This was our chance. I always look back at that game and think… *We could have created a bit of history there.*

And then, Galatasaray drew Manchester United in the next round. It hit home even more. The hurt and disappointment doubled.

We missed out on the chance to play at Old Trafford and to bring Man United over to us for a competitive game.

There was a rumour at the time that Alex Ferguson asked Denis Irwin about us, in relation to Galatasaray and how Man United might get on. Denis apparently said something like, 'Well the lads back home did well against them… and sure they're only part-time. They wouldn't be great.'

The craic for us at the time with Man United fans around Cork was… 'You guys are lucky you didn't get us, we might have knocked you out!'

We never thought that Galatasaray would knock Man United out. United were a serious team at this stage; they had just won the Premiership and would win the double that season.

But Galatasaray *did* knock them out.

They had that famous game in Istanbul. The first leg ended 3-3 at Old Trafford and Galatasaray got a 0-0 draw at home… United were out.

Eric Cantona got sent-off and there was a scuffle going down the tunnel – Cantona and Bryan Robson were said to have been hit and punched by the police in the tunnel.

The Turks denied it, but we were watching it back home going, 'That definitely happened… that was them!'

We had witnessed how they behaved when we were in the stadium.

The Man United result really hammered home how well we had done against Galatasaray.

Unlike them, we actually managed to score in Istanbul, in that atmosphere with referees who did not want to help the away team at all!

But, again, the City players really felt we had missed a golden opportunity. The fans and the press thought we had been brilliant, that we had gone so close. Everyone thought we had been unlucky.

It was a typical Irish moral victory in many ways.

But, deep down, the City team felt that there had been a *real* chance, that we could have done them, that we could have done more in the game. Of course, there was an obvious talent gap between the teams, and they would only ever have needed one chance to beat us.

But Damien's lack of experience was also a factor. He was a very positive manager, but that was his first experience in Europe as a coach. At that point, we were an experienced team. We were a *serious* team in our right.

As a group, we had already been in Europe.

We had played good sides and, when you do, you get a sense sometimes… *You know what, there's a chance here!'*

Galatasaray was that big chance.

CHAPTER 12

IN THE LEAGUE, however, our performances went up a level or two under Damien. We were playing great football. Rico's approach suited us. We were a good team, and we knew it. Plus, Damien filled us with confidence and told us we were capable of beating anyone.

City were chasing Shamrock Rovers for most of the first half of the season. They had a very good side. Stephen Geoghegan was their top scorer. At one stage, we were 10 points behind them. We were beating them 2-0 at Bishopstown that December, but Rovers came back to draw the game.

The gap was closed, though, ahead of a match against them in February.

We played them in Bishopstown again on a Sunday afternoon. The weather was awful and the pitch even worse. There was a mud bath outside of each box, and a massive mud bath in the middle of the pitch. The pitch was so bad that the teams weren't allowed warm-up on it before the game.

If we had gone out on it, the pitch would have been completely wrecked and the game wouldn't have gone ahead. This didn't go down well with Ray Treacy though, the Shamrock Rovers manager.

Ray said that if both teams weren't allowed warm-up on the pitch, then the match should be called off. He didn't want to play it.

There was a fierce rivalry between Ray and Damien – they had played together at Shamrock Rovers.

And there was a competitive rivalry between Rovers and City because we were both going for the title. The referee overruled Ray, and the game went ahead.

Ray went nuts afterwards.

Bishopstown was packed for the match. I'd say there was about 7,000 or 8,000 there, our biggest crowd in the league that season, a phenomenal crowd. We beat them 2-1. Johnny Glynn scored the goals.

For one goal, the ball was knocked over the top. Alan O'Neill, the Rovers goalkeeper came rushing off his line. But the ball got stuck in the mud. Johnny ran onto it and chipped it over O'Neill's head. Something similar happened again for our second goal!

We went top of the table for the first time that season. We were level on points, and goal difference, with Rovers.

After that win, I genuinely thought we were going to win the league again. No one had retained the title since Rovers in 1987. But we all believed we were going to do it.

There were 10 games left, we were in great form and we had the experience to do it. We were a confident team.

IT STARTED TO slip away from us during the run-in, though.

City signed a centre-back on loan from Derby County called Justin Phillips; he joined us at Christmas. Justin was just a young lad, but he did very well for us. We had been giving away goals before he came in.

We were almost unbeatable with him in the side. He became a massive player for us. And then, with a few games to go, he did his cruciate.

We suffered a blip, dropped a few points and Rovers went ahead of us. They ended up winning the league with a game remaining. But the whole way through the season there had been nothing between us. It was so tight.

We were probably a better team than we had been the previous year when we won the league.

THE FOLLOWING SEASON we qualified for the UEFA Cup – which meant Cork City had played in all three European competitions just over 10 years after being founded.

We were drawn against Slavia Prague, the Czech team.

When you qualified for Europe, you would look forward to the draw all summer. It always happened during pre-season and it would create a buzz amongst the lads.

When we were drawn against Slavia Prague, to be honest, we weren't blown away by it. We didn't know anything about them. This was before the internet, and satellite TV was still in its early days.

We obviously knew they were good, but we had no information about them. The Czech Republic had only been formed a year earlier, after the split of Czechoslovakia. We hadn't heard about most of their players.

We soon found out how good they were.

When I look back through all the European games I played for City, Bayern Munich was the glamour tie.

Torpedo Moscow was a novelty, our first game in Europe.

Galatasaray was the most exciting because it was so intimidating and unique, and we pushed them so close.

Slavia Prague, however, without a doubt were the best football side we played against.

SLAVIA HAD FIVE or six Czech internationals in the team.

Patrik Berger and Vladimír Šmicer, who both went on to play for Liverpool, played for them. And they had a guy called Radek Bejbl, who went on to play for Atletico Madrid.

They were all young at the time, in their early twenties. It was only within 18 months of playing Cork City that people realised who they actually were or how good they were.

Slavia went on to a UEFA cup semi-final and they were beaten by AC Milan. Almost half of their team were in the Czech Republic side when they played against Germany in the final of the European Championships in 1996 at Wembley. They narrowly lost in extra time. The game between City and Slavia wasn't as close. The first leg was in Prague. It was a blistering hot day in early August. Slavia hit the post a few times and Phil Harrington help keep the score down.

We got away with losing 2-0.

I'll always remember when we got back to Cork, the headlines in the papers were saying that there was still a chance for us in the home leg.

There wasn't.

These guys had absolutely destroyed us.

We couldn't get near them.

Slavia should have scored a lot more goals in Prague. Their total football was phenomenal to watch, but exhausting to play against. They were beautiful players, and their pace, their movement were levels above anything we had seen.

Ahead of the second leg at home, it was one of those occasions where we knew we had no chance. They were serious players.

The night before we played them in Bishopstown, we were training at the ground. There was a UEFA rule that allowed the travelling team to use the pitch the day before a game.

Some of us were all sitting in the stand watching Slavia doing a crossing and shooting session. We were blown away by how good they were.

Slavia beat us 4-0 the next day.

They were 3-0 up at half-time and they could have scored at least another four or five if they wanted to. They were a class team.

Berger just looked magical. You could see this guy was absolutely phenomenal, Šmicer too – 10 years later, he won the Champions League with Liverpool and scored in the final.

They battered us 6-0 across the two legs.

We could do nothing about it.

IN THE LEAGUE of Ireland that season, we took off like a train.

At the half-way point, we were into the League Cup final and top of the table. It didn't look like we'd be caught.

We played Sligo Rovers away a week before Christmas on a Saturday night. We lost the game, but it was a tough match, and we were still top of the table.

After the game, Rico came into the dressing-room and dropped a bombshell. He told us he had resigned as manager. He was walking out on the club.

All the City players were absolutely shell-shocked.

We were stunned.

We begged Damien to stay.

But he was stubborn.

He wouldn't listen.

There had been a massive disagreement between Rico and the board. It was over money.

Rico felt we weren't getting backed properly by the club. O'Donovan and the board had put the money into developing Bishopstown. City weren't ever big spenders, but Rico said we were falling behind other teams.

Whatever it was, Rico leaving absolutely decimated the team. And to make matters worse, he took over as Cobh Ramblers manager not long after leaving us. Cobh were *nowhere*.

Rico said it was a matter of principle, but it just felt like a kick in the teeth to us. And I think, with hindsight, if Damien was to look back, he wouldn't do it again, he would have stayed until the end of the season.

We had thought we were almost invincible.

Rico had built us up that way. We were so good at that point, we'd win games 4-1, 5-1... blow teams away. This was the City team at its absolute peak. Pat Morley and myself up front were scoring almost every week.

Back then, teams used to play back-to-back fixtures. You'd play two games against the same team home and away in consecutive fixtures. We beat Monaghan 5-0 away, and then 6-0 back in Cork the following game. In between that, we beat Bohemians 4-0 in the League Cup. We were a flamboyant team. We played with a real swagger, we were all attacking and going for it.

Rico leaving just devastated the team.

NOEL O'MAHONY came back as manager. Noel had been great for us, he helped mould the side we became, and we won the league under him.

We won the League Cup against Dundalk, but otherwise nothing went right. I don't think we won a league match for six weeks.

We had 36 points when Rico left. Seven weeks later, we had 37 points.

The whole team just collapsed.

Noel couldn't get a kick out of us.

He wanted us to get behind the ball again, to play for a draw away from home. The City lads just didn't buy into it.

We had moved on as a team.

We had gone to another level.

To be fair to Noel though, it probably had nothing really to do with him or his approach. The team was just stunned after Rico left.

After being top at Christmas, we plummeted down the table and finished seventh.

THE FOLLOWING SEASON was the worst period I ever experienced at Cork City.

We hit rock bottom.

Rico leaving was a big blow, and then the club hit the skids financially.

Pat O'Donovan, our chairman and owner, was looking to develop Bishopstown, but was having trouble with planning permission. He owned a lot of land and he was trying to sell sites for houses.

I don't doubt that he was trying to do the right thing, but he was also a businessman and he was trying to run his business too. Which was fair enough. He was hoping to get the land around Bishopstown developed.

O'Donovan also ran into a bit of a personal battle with the FAI. He was quoted as saying something to the FAI to the effect of... 'At least I own my own ground, ye own nothing'.

He had assets, but the club ran into cashflow problems. He didn't get a lot of support from the FAI. I suppose they tried to bring him down to size. The FAI started making things awkward for him.

The club went into receivership, the company which owned Cork City was liquidated. We were homeless, and out of Bishopstown before eventually returning to Turner's Cross.

The condition of the club was mirrored on the pitch.

We descended into a rabble.

Rob Hindmarch, an English guy, took over as player-manager. Hindmarch was 6'4", a big strapping old style centre-back. He was absolutely brilliant in the air, but slow as a duck. He had played for Wolves, Derby County and Sunderland in England. I think Cork City was his first job in management.

Straight away, Hindmarch started bringing over a load of English players. We went from the period between 1988 to '95 with a strong Cork base, a strong local base of players, to more English lads than Cork fellas in the team.

The issue wasn't that they were from the UK. We had Scottish and Welsh lads in the team before. Hindmarch's players weren't great quality. With the exception of Dave Hill, they were all poor, well below the standard that was needed.

And their hearts weren't in it.

The local players were all part-time. The UK lads were technically full-time, without training full-time.

So, what do you do then when you don't train during the day?

You go out at night.

They had no interest in playing and only wanted a social life.

The manager didn't understand the league either. There has always been an idea in Irish football that English managers are going to be saviours.

But nine times out of 10, they're a complete waste of time.

They don't understand the country or the League of Ireland – the *level* of the league. I'm not sure if they come over thinking we're non-league but whatever their preconceived notions, they never seem to get what the league is about. They invariably bring over lots of English players who think the same.

So, we ended up with a load of bad English players, while three of our best players – Dave Barry, Declan Daly and Liam Murphy – all had season-long injuries.

CORK CITY PLAYED a match one day and had six lads from the UK playing for us.

I was captain on the day. We were in the bottom half of the table.

I remember looking around the dressing-room and thinking… *This is all wrong… we have fallen so far!*

The culture of the club had gone. We were in complete freefall.

After competing for trophies for years and playing in Europe with a solid core of local players, almost overnight City went back to where we were in the 80s – down in the bottom half of the table, out of Europe, scrapping around, in financial trouble, and looking to bring in outsiders for a quick fix.

It was the worst year of my playing career.

The demise of the club was well underway.

Cork City was on its knees and on the threshold of going under.

CHAPTER 13

EVENTUALLY, A NEW board came in.

They prevented the club from going bust.

The new owners were local men, business fellas, all decent people who effectively saved the club. They were led by a new chairman, Terry Dunne. He was a Dubliner, a real soccer man, who lived in Tralee.

They god rid of Hindmarch and brought in Dave Barry to be manager, with Liam Murphy as assistant – and Dave finished out the end of the season.

They also changed our kits from green and white, to red and white.

We were back at Tuner's Cross too. But on the pitch, we were fighting relegation.

DAVE WAS COMING to the end of his playing career. He had been a brilliant player for City. With Liam as his assistant, they helped us stay up, and survive. The 18-month or so period between Richardson leaving and Dave taking over was horrendous, the worst I experienced at the club. And then Cork City received another blow when Pat Morley decided to leave.

Pat went to Shelbourne. We were in turmoil as a club.

Pat was at the peak of his career and Shels were a big team at the time. They had already signed Stephen Geoghegan to play up front and were flush with money. There was talk of them paying players £250, £300 a week and giving £10,000 as a signing on fee. In the League of Ireland in the mid-90s, £10,000 was absolutely colossal money. It would have paid off a fair chunk of anyone's mortgage.

Whereas, at Cork, lads were on around £50, £70 a week. We weren't full-time. We all had day jobs, which paid the mortgage. Football money paid for our social occasions.

Pat was working for Adidas at the time and a lot of his work was in Dublin.

It looked to be a brilliant move for him personally.

But the City lads were hurt. Pat and Dave had a bit of a barney.

Dave was trying to rebuild the club and Pat had his mind made up, he wanted to get out and join Shels. Dave couldn't accept that Pat would leave us.

Pat was one of our own and he was leaving us at our lowest point, when we were so down on confidence and good players.

There was an element of anger too... *He's leaving us for that shower in Dublin!*

It felt significant. Cork fellas *never* left Cork.

If they did, they signed for teams in the UK. They certainly didn't go to Dublin. It wasn't part of the culture. Money never came into it for the City players. We all had offers to leave – Dermot Keely asked me to join Dundalk around the same time – but we always stayed. It was different in Dublin, where players weren't associated with just one club. I remember chatting to Paul Doolin, who was a tough player, but a brilliant one. He played for everyone – Bohemians, Shelbourne, Dundalk, Derry City, Portadown, Shamrock Rovers.

We had won the league, and Paul said to me, 'Is that all you've won? You have an awful habit of losing!' He was referring to the finals Cork lost.

'Hang on a minute, Paul,' I replied. ' We are one club. You've been with eight clubs. I congratulate you on what you won, but you won it because you went around to any club that paid the most money.'

NOWADAYS, PLAYERS ARE professionals. They go where the money is. But at that time, for us, it was almost an extension of the GAA culture. We were playing for our local team, and the thought of playing for someone else, especially a team in Dublin, was just alien to us.

Noel O'Mahony drummed that into us. He was *all* about Cork.

Pat, to be fair to him, knew Cork City were poor at the time. And he felt he had to do what was best for himself. Which was fair enough, and financially he got a great deal.

However, the move caused a lot of anger among the City fans towards him that lingered for some time. It was a massive blow to lose someone like him and a tough time for the club. The end of an era.

CITY WERE MOSTLY mid-table during the following season, 1996/97. Dave was getting things back on track, and we had a lot of young fellas coming through. The likes of Ollie Cahill, Mark Herrick, Derek Coughlan and Colm O'Brien all came into the team and we were building again without ever challenging.

At the end of the season, we won a few games in-a-row and crept into fourth place. Out of nothing really, we qualified for Europe. We were in the Intertoto Cup. Which was brilliant, because it guaranteed us four matches.

We were drawn in a group with German team FC Köln, Maccabi Petah Tikva from Israel, Standard Liège from Belgium, and a Swiss side called FC Aarau.

In three of our four games, we were unbeaten.

We drew 0-0 with Standard Liège in our first game at Turner's Cross.

There was a joke at the time that the Intertoto Cup should be called the 'Inter two-bob cup'. It had a bit of a bad reputation. The winner qualified for the UEFA Cup and there were a lot of games involved. But we were delighted to be in it.

We then drew 0-0 away with Maccabi, which was an amazing trip. We went to Bethlehem and Jerusalem, and saw all the sights. Köln then beat us in Cork – Toni Polster, the Austrian striker, scored both goals. We drew 0-0 with the Swiss team in our final game. We didn't score a goal in the group, but it was a nice experience, fantastic for us. We even managed to finish above the Swiss.

CITY FINISHED THIRD in the League of Ireland that season, but were way back from Shelbourne, who finished second, and St Patrick's Athletic, who won the league under Pat Dolan. But that season was remembered for our cup run.

We had never won the FAI Cup. Bohemians deservedly beat us in the final in 1992 when we were massive favourites, and we lost to Derry in '89 when they won the treble.

I was 33 at the time and was starting to think I'd never get the chance to win it.

City had a very difficult run in 1998, and we were on the road a lot. We beat Bohemians at Dalymount. It looked like we were about to get past Derry City, but they scored late at Turner's Cross. That meant we had a replay at the Brandywell.

I always liked playing at the Brandywell. Although it was never an easy game, it was a brilliant trip. We went up and beat them 1-0.

Sligo were up next in the quarter-finals. They were very strong at the time, on a run of about 15 or 16 games unbeaten. They were favourites for the match at Turner's Cross. We battered them; it finished 2-0.

Athlone Town at St Mel's Park was our semi-final. It was fitting for me personally, going back to Athlone, where I played my football with the Athlone B team over a decade earlier. We beat them 3-1. We were back in the final.

It just so happened that Shelbourne were going to be our opponents. Shels were *the* team at the time. They had brilliant players like Stephen Geoghegan and Pat Fenlon. Pat Morley was now there, and Damien Richardson was their manager.

For us to come up against two figures who had been such a big part of our team, who we had such history with… well we couldn't have written it, really.

SHELBOURNE WERE BIG favourites for the final. They narrowly lost out on the League of Ireland title to St Patrick's Athletic the week before, but had won the previous two FAI Cup finals, the first team since the great Shamrock Rovers team of the 80s to retain the cup. Shels were odds-on to beat us.

The final was at Dalymount Park, which had open terraces at the time. City fans took up most of the ground. Shels were flying, but they didn't have a big following even though the game was held just down the road from them.

It was a hot summer's day in May and the pitch was rock hard, it hadn't even been watered. The ball was bouncing all over the place. It was a low-quality match, a tight game.

I didn't start but I came on with about a half an hour left and almost scored. The game ended goalless though.

The replay was set for the following Saturday.

All week, the talk was that Shels would beat us, that they couldn't be as bad as they had been again, that they were suffering a hangover from losing the league, it was still in their system… all of this type of talk. If anything, they were bigger favourites than the first game. But we felt the exact opposite.

We were all believing… *We'll do these!*

It wasn't the same confidence as we had in 1992, when we blew it against Bohemians. Shelbourne were the team winning trophies, paying big wages, a side with some of top players in the country – and they had Rico, our former manager. We just really fancied ourselves ahead of the replay.

Dave Barry made a few changes for the game and he brought me back into the team.

Ahead of the match, we stayed in Bray because it was out of the way for us. It was an evening game, so we were hanging around the hotel that day.

It was another scorching hot day.

I remember Arsenal were playing Newcastle in the FA Cup final. I had been a fanatical Arsenal supporter since I was young fella. I was rooming with Philip Long and he asked me to go downstairs to watch the final. I didn't go, because I didn't want to lose out on sleep. I wanted to rest ahead of our game.

I don't care how Arsenal do. We've a game to win tonight.

I knew I was playing in the final. I was 33. This was possibly my last chance to win the cup. Arsenal were going for a double, something that would have meant a lot to me. When I was younger, it would have been the end of the world to me if they lost.

But it was just irrelevant to me now.

Ever since that day, following Arsenal didn't matter as much to me. Arsenal winning or losing never had the same emotional effect on me.

They won the double, but, ultimately, I had no affiliation to them.

Cork City was my team.

I WAS EXTREMELY focused ahead of the final. We all were. This was our chance to prove a lot of people wrong.

City had almost gone bust two years previously. The club was a mess.

We scraped our way back up the table, got back into Europe, were back near the top of the league and had the chance to win the cup.

It had been 25 years since a team from Cork had won the FAI Cup.

It only added to the motivation that we were up against Pat and Damien, who had left us, and Shels, the club with the most money in the country.

It was a tight game, but a good game, very competitive.

Noel Mooney was in goal for us; he had taken over as number one keeper from Phil Harrington. Noel was a very good shot-stopper, and he made a few decent saves. There weren't a lot of goalscoring chances in the match, but it was a better game, both teams created more than in the previous game. Ollie Cahill had a great chance for us before half-time – he came close when he tried to lob the Shels goalkeeper.

And then, about 70 minutes in, we had a corner.

Kelvin Flanagan whipped it towards the back post. Derek Coughlan, our centre-back, lost his marker and headed the ball into the net. 1-0.

The funny thing about the goal was that we actually practiced it. Dave Barry was very much a true Cork person, a very passionate guy. But he wasn't really into tactics. Not many in the League of Ireland were at that time, I suppose, other than Pat Dolan – we used to always hear that Pat was *big* into tactics.

We would never practice set-pieces or anything like that. We just went out and played.

But that week we practiced this corner, where Derek would peel around to the back of the six-yard box and Kelvin would whip it towards the back post.

We practiced it about 10 times that week.

The one time we practice a set-piece, it worked out for us.

It was the exact goal Derek scored that day.

PAT MORLEY CAME on for Shelbourne with 10 minutes to go. He shouldn't have been brought on though.

Pat started brilliantly for Shels when he joined them from us. He and Stephen Geoghegan were on fire, absolutely electric together and were scoring loads of goals.

But Pat suffered a cruciate injury, a terrible blow at the time, and was out for about a year. He wasn't ready to play against us, yet Richardson had him on the bench. And then he brought Pat on when they were chasing a goal. He was just back from his injury and had barely kicked a ball.

Morley went up front and was up against Declan Daly, our captain. Deccie and Pat would have been very friendly, they knew each other for years.

Deccie said to him, 'Pat, don't come near me. You're not right. You can't take a challenge'. And he was right.

Pat shouldn't have been on the pitch, he wasn't ready.

Richardson was wrong to bring him on.

I think he was trying to rattle us.

It didn't work though.

WHEN THE FINAL whistle went, it was a weird feeling, surreal.

I had been in the league over 12 years and it looked like I was never going to win the FAI Cup, that I was going to go through my career without doing it. That Cork City were never going to win it.

It was strange as well that we managed to do it against Shels with Pat and Rico on their side.

Pat missed out on winning the cup with all his buddies, the team and players he had spent years with. The City lads had no problem with him.

He was still one of us. Pat came out with us in Dublin that night.

He got an incredible offer from Shels, and it made sense for him to leave at the time. I think deep down, a lot of us knew he was right to go, that it was a great move for him. Shels were top dogs.

It just didn't work out for Pat, as it should have.

It was different with Damien. We bought into his management; he was very good. We were playing great stuff, top of the table, absolutely flying. And he left us over a stupid argument with the chairman. He obviously had his reasons.

But, to us, Rico walked out on us and we felt he let us down.

I suppose we felt… *Why didn't he stay to the end of the year… Win the league and then move on?* Rico leaving set us back so far and no one forgot it.

Pat re-joined us a few months later, and Damien left Shels.

THE FOLLOWING NIGHT we went back to Cork. It was a Sunday night, a beautiful summer's evening.

Like in 1993 when we won the league, it felt like the whole city was celebrating.

We got back to Kent Station on the six or seven o'clock train. Nearly 10,000 people turned out to welcome us back.

We went down Patrick Street on an open-top bus, and there were people on each side of the street cheering and waving. We stopped half-way down, at the old Guinness house, where there were speeches made.

It was a glorious experience.

CHAPTER 14

CORK CITY STARTED the next season, 1998-99, with a game against CSKA Kiev in the UEFA Cup Winner's Cup, with the first leg at Turner's Cross.

I'm not sure whether they underestimated us, or whatever, but we went two up within about a half an hour. Kelvin Flanagan scored a penalty, and Derek Coughlin scored our second with a header.

We were flying.

The atmosphere in Turner's Cross was electric. It was going brilliant, and we were relatively comfortable in the game, until about 15 seconds from the end.

There were 93 minutes on the clock when they scored.

It was bittersweet. Of course, we were buzzing to record a win in Europe. It was brilliant.

But we were gutted when the goal went in because it was an away goal and we knew they weren't going to be as complacent in the second leg. And they weren't.

CSKA got their act together and beat us 2-0 in Kiev two weeks later. I didn't start in either game. I came off the bench with a few minutes left in both matches.

At that point, I was a veteran in the City squad, the club's longest-serving player. I knew I was getting close to the end of my playing career and started to think about going into coaching.

I did a couple of coaching courses that Brian Kerr was running as Technical Director of the FAI. Noel O'Reilly, his long-time assistant, was involved too.

Noel was a great guy and the two were very good coaches. They were passionate about Irish football. The coaching courses were a great foundation for me and they gave me the idea that, maybe when I finished playing, I would move into coaching. I was always into that side of the game and had it in the back of my head. The courses were the next step and over the next while I ended up earning my coaching badges.

IN THE LEAGUE that season, we flew out of the traps. We won eight games in-a-row and didn't lose a game until we played St Patrick's Athletic in Inchicore.

Like ourselves, they had a brilliant start.

We were both very good sides and within 10 matches of the start of the season, we were both out of sight. It was between us and Pat's for the title.

They went top after beating us, but we were relentless and kept winning. We played Pat's again in January at Turner's Cross. We were a point ahead with the chance to go four points clear. The match was played on a Saturday afternoon, live on RTÈ, and every ticket was sold out a few days beforehand.

The place was heaving. There must have been about 11,000 at it, a massive crowd for the League of Ireland at that time.

Pat Morley and myself were up front. We were one of the best teams in the country again, going for the title against our nearest rivals.

It felt like old times.

Often, when there's a League of Ireland game on TV, the quality can suffer, teams might freeze a bit on the big stage. But this was an excellent game.

We battered Pat's in the first-half and went one up... Morley scored.

The Shed end at Turner's Cross was bouncing and the crowd really drove us on. It should have been two- or three-nil at half-time, but Ollie Cahill and I hit the post with shots.

In the second-half, the game slipped away from us briefly and Pat's scored twice. They were going for their third title in four years. Liam Buckley had taken over as manager from Pat Dolan, who was now the club's CEO. But Dolan still had the same presence on the sideline.

We had experienced players who had won trophies, but maybe their winning experience helped them more. We pushed to get an equaliser, the goal that would have kept us top of the table.

But unfortunately, Morley missed a chance at the very end.

We were deflated.

Pat's went two points clear of us, but there still wasn't a lot between the teams. We continued to be neck-and-neck for the rest of the season, even on goal difference.

Roll on to our third game against St Pat's… we went to play them in Inchicore. It was the third last game of the season – we were level on points and the winner would undoubtedly be champions.

Richmond Park was bursting at the seams, jam-packed and we brought up a massive crowd for the game.

City supporters took up half of the stand behind the far goal and all of the Camac stand.

The game was live on RTÉ again, but it wasn't a classic.

It was a very tight match, very physical with lots of fouls and not much football played. Again, there was nothing between the sides. With about half an hour to go, Kelvin Flanagan was sent-off after a second booking. It was very harsh. The referee was fussy and was handing out cards to everyone.

Kelvin's red was incredibly tough to take.

About 10 minutes later, Paul Osam scored for Pat's. They had a corner – and they had obviously worked on it, because it went to the back post, a few players made runs, caught us out and Ozo headed it in.

They beat us 1-0.

We were disgusted. There were two games to go; we beat Galway United and hammered Shamrock Rovers 3-0 at home. We did our part and needed Pat's to drop points. They were up against Shelbourne in their next match.

It was a Wednesday night, and there was torrential rain in Dublin. The pitch was waterlogged. The word was coming through to us that the match could be called off.

However, the league was saying it couldn't be postponed because the final match of the year was on the Sunday and the season needed to be wrapped up.

We were thinking… *Maybe Shels could do them on a bad pitch?*

But they had dropped off from the previous seasons – Rico had gone, Pat Morley was back with us and they weren't at their best.

Pat's narrowly beat them 2-1.

They then beat Bray Wanderers on the final day to win the league. We lost it by three points – due to our results against Pat's.

The difference across the season was that they beat us three times. Pat's dropped points against other teams. Most of the points we dropped were against Pat's.

We finished with 70 points from 33 games, miles ahead of every other team, our best season in years, but still finished second.

IN THE LATE 90s, Shelbourne were the team to beat, so it was an achievement for ourselves and Pat's to be challenging them, beating them to cups and league titles.

Shels had all of the money at the time. They signed up all the big players.

They brought over big teams like Manchester United, Celtic and Leeds United for games. Shels were selling tickets for £40 or £50 for these matches at Tolka Park.

Ollie Byrne ran the club; he was Shels through and through, and he had all the contacts. Ollie would do anything for the club.

Shamrock Rovers were the team everyone wanted to beat when I came into the league in the mid-80s; Shels were that in the 90s.

Rovers were homeless after been kicked out of Milltown at the end of the 80s. They were in turmoil and spiralling at this point, doing the rounds of the different grounds in Dublin. Rovers were just trying to survive.

Bohemians were always there or thereabouts but were never known to pay big money. Derry City could do anything. They had runs where they were doing great and then they would nearly go bankrupt… and they would come back again.

Pat's were well run by Pat Dolan, they were very professional by League of Ireland standards. Dolan was very good for the club.

But there was no standout team

BUT THE STANDARDS in the League of Ireland were the same as the time when I joined.

Of course, there had been some brilliant players and we came up against some great teams. But the standards on the pitch remained relatively the same.

The crowds fluctuated. There were lean periods and times where we could have thousands at games.

However, football experienced a boom in Ireland in the 90s. The national team reached two World Cup finals and the game spread into rural areas where it was never popular before.

The money flowed into the English Premiership across the water.

Rugby became professional.

And the GAA became more marketable than it had been, in direct response to the increase in popularity of soccer. Meanwhile, the League of Ireland stood still, as it had for the previous decades.

The Celtic Tiger and the sports boom didn't reach us.

We were still getting changed in the same clubhouses, playing in the same stadiums. Most were, at best, dated. The worst were dilapidated.

Some pitches were still mud baths during the winter.

We were a fit team, but there was no thought given to diet or anything like that. You just ate whatever you wanted and there was an ignorance towards physical conditioning.

A pre-match meal would be chops and chips, or chips and steaks, or chips and chicken. Chips with everything, really. And pints after matches.

Or maybe we wouldn't eat at all. There were plenty of times we went into games and had eaten nothing... having come straight from work.

But this was the case across the whole league.

It wasn't very different, diet-wise, in English football until Arsene Wenger came along.

WE PLAYED IFK Gothenburg in the UEFA Cup the following season.

They beat us 3-0 away.

Gothenburg were an established team, they had beaten Manchester United, Barcelona and Rangers in European games in the 90s.

We managed to restore some pride and beat them 1-0 back at Turner's Cross in the second leg. Pat Morley scored.

We played good football in the league that season, scored a lot of goals, and ended up finishing second again, this time behind Shelbourne.

Dave Barry stepped down then.

He had stabilised and helped rejuvenate the club after we were in the doldrums. He had helped turn things around, he brought Patsy Freyne and Pat Morley back.

But Dave felt his time was up – not winning the league hurt him.

The crowd were probably on his back a little too. We won the FAI Cup and we had been close to challenging for the league, but we hadn't won it. Dave probably felt he was getting more stick from the crowd than he deserved. He had given it four years as manager and had enough.

Colin Murphy was appointed manager in pre-season. He was an English coach, but he was on a different level to Rob Hindmarch, our last English coach.

Murphy was a proper manager, he had managerial skills and a presence. He only lasted about a week, 10 days at most, with us though.

Peter Taylor took over as Leicester City manager, replacing Martin O'Neill, who had gone to Celtic. Taylor and Murphy knew each other well.

So, Taylor came for him. Murphy left us to become 'Football co-ordinator' – a Director of Football role – at Leicester in the Premiership.

A few months later, he took Damien Delaney, who was a young lad and had just got into the City squad, with him to Leicester.

We were left without a manager, so it was a bit chaotic. The club appointed Derek Mountfield to replace him. Mountfield had a brilliant playing career. He was part of the Everton team that won a load of trophies under Howard Kendall in the 80s. He was a centre-back in the team with Kevin Sheedy and Gary Lineker. He won the FA Cup, the Cup Winners Cup and the English First Division with Everton. I think he was the only member of that team that never got an international cap, but he had been a very good player.

Derek was a gentleman too.

But he was absolutely, totally out of his depth as a manager.

Like Rob Hindmarch, he was a player trying to be a manager. He had no managerial skills at all, it seemed to me.

There was significant change in the Cork City boardroom that led to Mountfield getting the job. Brian Lennox joined the board and told them that he wanted to take over the club. The old board didn't stand in his way; they were prepared to hand over the club for nothing, knowing we'd be lucky to break even in the League of Ireland.

Brian became the sole owner and he appointed Mountfield.

Brian later admitted he got it wrong appointing him. There were other managers at the time in contention for the position. But Mountfield overwhelmed Brian because of his playing career, which has nothing to do with being a manager. I think he had briefly managed Scarborough in the old English Division Three before he came to Cork.

He lasted until January with us.

A 4-0 DEFEAT to St Pat's at Turner's Cross in January 2001 finished off Derek Mountfield. It was one of the worst days in Cork City's history.

At this point, I was more or less finished as a player. I knew I wasn't good enough anymore.

Liam Murphy was still assistant-manager, Patsy Freyne was still there and playing. But I was on the bench, training away and helping out in the background.

I was on the bench for that Pat's match when we were 3-0 down at half-time. The City team hadn't tried a leg. They put no effort in. It reached the point where it had become almost comical with Mountfield. He was so far out of his depth and everyone knew it.

The players certainly knew it.

Derek just had no presence.

He was like a fish out of water.

It was just wrong.

I was absolutely furious watching the first-half.

It's harsh to ever accuse players of not trying. But that's how it looked. It was the easiest game Pat's ever had. I was raging.

There were times at Cork City where we had good teams and bad teams. We had great times and hard times. But even when we were bad, when the club was in turmoil, there was still a culture of running through walls for the team.

Here, on this day, fellas had decided not to bother their backsides.

At half-time in the dressing-room, Derek stood up and started mumbling about how we had to be better in the second-half.

I slumped in my seat. I just couldn't listen to it anymore. I stood up.

'Derek, will you please shut up?'

I tore into the team.

'We never knelt down to any team, never gave anyone any easy game. Pat's have come down to Cork and they're laughing at us. It's embarrassing... a disgrace. Some people should be ashamed of themselves.'

I was fuming.

It had been building for months.

I actually felt sorry for Derek. He just didn't get it. He was a nice man, a gentleman, but not a manager. Derek tried to be everything to everyone – manager, player, physio and, worst of all, he was trying to be friends with everyone. You can't be friends with everyone as manager.

There was a lot of ill-discipline in the group; a lot of players that needed to be sorted out. He couldn't handle it.

The next day, the board sacked him.

DEREK RANG ME and thanked me for my efforts. He asked me would I come for a drink with him before he went home to England; he was inviting one or two of the other senior guys too.

I said I would.

Liam Murphy, who had been appointed manager until the end of the season, then rang me and asked me was I going? He said that Derek had invited the entire team.

'The team that got beaten 4-0 yesterday?' I asked.

'Yeah, he's going to have a bit of a going away party for everyone tonight before he flies home tomorrow.'

I couldn't believe it.

'There's no way I'm going to that!'

I rang Patsy and told him. He didn't realise the whole team would be there either, he thought it was just the senior players. He said he wasn't going to go in that case either.

I called Derek back and said, 'I thought tonight was going to be a drink for a few people around you. I didn't realise you had invited the team.'

'No, I don't want to finish on bad terms with everyone. I just wanted to have a drink with everyone.'

'Derek, thanks very much but I won't be part of that,' I said.

'I can't accept that performance yesterday. And at the moment I can't see some of the lads from yesterday, because I don't feel like they put the effort in.'

I didn't go, either did Patsy or Liam.

We were then accused by some of being instrumental in getting Derek the sack. Whereas it was the exact opposite – we were the ones trying to help him.

The boys had a rocking night by all accounts. They got loads of free drinks and were there until two in the morning.

The lads all knew I was fuming!

In fairness, they all probably thought... *Your day is gone... You're finished!* Which was fair enough. I'd been at the club a long time, into my third decade.

But I had been through so much with Cork City.

I couldn't just stand by and accept players not trying hard for the club.

I SHOULD HAVE retired then. Liam asked me to stay on and help out, so I finished out the season. I didn't really play though. I came off the bench mostly, making maybe 10 or 12 substitute appearances.

I was one of the last of the core Cork City group still there.

Pat was still around and was trying to beat my goals record. I had ended up with 129 league goals for City. With about seven or eight games to go, he reached 129 goals for the club. He was bursting his backside to try to beat the record! It became a joke at training with boys saying, 'You're not going to get ahead of Caulfield!'

And he didn't!

We finished on the same goals for the club, although I played a lot more games for City.

As a player though at that point, I was gone. I was never sentimental about it.

I didn't shed any tears or have any regrets. When your time comes, there's nothing you can do. I wasn't as quick as I once was, and I wasn't as fit as I once was. It was time for me to walk away.

I've always been practical.

I was lucky to play 650 competitive games (over 450 league) for Cork City. And we had some brilliant times.

The Cork City team from the late-80s and early-90s, the team that first got into Europe and went on to win the league, were all close.

There was me, Deccie Daly, Phil Harrington, the late Paul Bannon, Fergus O'Donoghue, Stephen Napier, Liam Murphy, Dave Barry, Pat Morley and Patsy Freyne. Anthony Buckley and Cormac Cotter too, Philip Long...Mick Conroy.

It was a great social life for us. After matches, we would be all out together. Our partners all socialised together too.

There was no dual carriageway, so every match we went to, we were driving through every village and town. Trips to Dublin coud take four hours up and four hours back. We were together so much. On the bus trips, we would pass the time playing cards, some might read the newspaper.

Often, we would just talk about the match or whatever; about players, get someone to take a pop off a certain opposition player.

On the way home, we'd usually stop in Durrow in Laois for a pint. It was our release. You played a match, and the few pints after was your night out. We never missed work though, we always showed up the next morning.

We used to hear stories about Dublin teams, and their trips to play in Galway or Cork. It was like a holiday to them, because they only made that trip once or twice a year.

Cork City were on the road every second weekend.

It was part of our routine.

We lived to train three times a week, play the match at the weekend and have our night out. It was the culture throughout the league.

When we were on our run to winning the FAI Cup in 1998, in the home game against Derry City, they scored a late equaliser in Turner's Cross to make it 1-1.

The match kicked off at two o'clock on a Sunday afternoon and was wrapped up by four.

By half four, we were all down the pub.

The replay was in Derry on the Tuesday. So, we had to go to Derry after work on the Monday for the game.

We were down in the pub on the corner of Turner's Cross, drinking pints all evening. At about eight, Dave Barry got up and said, 'I'll see you tomorrow lads, don't be late'. We were meeting the following day at half six at the Silver Springs Hotel. Dave was the manager.

But he still didn't say to us, 'Lads, you need to go home now... put down the pints!'

We all had seven or eight pints in us and left soon after; back home, had a bit of food and into bed for work the next day.

We worked all day, met at the hotel and drove up to Derry, got there at one or two in the morning and went straight to bed.

The following night, we beat Derry 1-0.

Now, considering our preparation for the game, I can only assume that the Derry team were drinking the whole way back to Derry!

THAT CORK CITY team were all so close.

We were almost inseparable – training together through the week, the match on the Sunday and the night out.

This was our life for mostly 10 years.

We were all living and working in Cork and most of the lads were from Cork. We bought into it and felt like we were representing the county and the city.

We were all ready for a scrap too, everyone was desperate to win for each other. It helped us on the pitch, no doubt about it.

I would speak to lads from other League of Ireland teams, and they all would say they absolutely hated us. They hated coming to play in Cork.

We demanded a lot from each other, too.

Our Saturday morning training sessions could be brutal. We had a mentality that successful sportspeople have – when you're on the pitch, you demand the most from each other, you expect each other to play to a certain level and put in the effort.

If we had a go at one other, no one would get offended. Because when we came off the pitch, it was back to normal.

It's a mentality that's different nowadays; sometimes people will get offended if a teammate has a go at them.

But in our time, that was just how it was.

PART FIVE

Time to Boss

CHAPTER 15

I KNEW MY time as a player in the League of Ireland had come to an end in 2001. I wasn't sentimental about it and I certainly had no regrets. My day was done. I was finished. I was almost 37 and knew the time was right to walk away.

And I honestly can't say I missed it.

I had my time, and it was brilliant, but it was time to do something else.

I went straight into coaching Avondale United in the Munster Senior League. My routine was the same; training during the week and matches at the weekend. It wasn't an easy job to start with, but I was very clear in what I wanted to do.

Avondale were a very big club in Cork but had experienced a few horrendous years. They had fallen from the very top of the Premier Division to the bottom of the First Division. Avondale had a lot of lads who were playing soccer during the winter but they would walk away once the GAA season kicked off.

I had to put a stop to it.

IN AMATEUR FOOTBALL you have to get the players, it's the biggest thing. I took over with two games of the season to go and after the last game I went into the dressing-room and explained myself.

'Look lads, if any of you are playing GAA… you're gone!' I was bullish.

I'm sure some of them thought… *He's saying that now, but he'll want us back next year.* But this was how it had to be.

And, if they were playing gaelic, we didn't take them back.

The main difference between being with Cork City and Avondale United was that I went from being a player, where I was in a bubble and only had to look after myself, to being responsible for everything.

I was player-manager. And like any new manager, I made plenty of mistakes. But I had a confidence in myself. I was determined to put a structure in place. By this point, I was working for Diageo, and on the road selling for them as a Business Development Manager. I was used to dealing with people, and I suppose you pick up different skill-sets from your experiences.

I was very hands-on in training. I loved the coaching side of it. Being on the field, particularly in the first year when we were in the lower division, I was able to get a lot of goals because, at that level, I was probably a step ahead of many players. But I soon found myself preferring not to play. I didn't really want to. I wanted to just manage the team and it was easier to just do that.

From the start, I set about getting the best amateur players from within the county. I drove around, met them all and got as many on board as I could.

One of the players I had in my mind was John Cotter.

John had huge potential when he was younger, and was highly rated by Cork City. He played a few games for the club when he was 20 or 21. But, for whatever reason, he never kicked on, maybe he wasn't given enough opportunities.

John left City before I finished with them.

I had him in mind when I took the Avondale job as someone who could do well for us. I heard he was playing with a local junior team, way down the leagues. I couldn't get a hold of him though. This was before everyone had a mobile phone.

Finally, I spotted him at a City match that summer – the first season of summer football in the League of Ireland – and I asked him to join us.

He was with me from that day all the way through.

THERE WAS NO messing in the team. If you were going to play for us, you had to train. You had to pay your membership too. I would meet fellas, trying to get them to sign, but I would always say, 'If you join us, you have to pay your membership'.

Some would say, 'Ah yeah, but sure John Cotter, Noel Hartigan… they don't pay theirs!'

'No… everyone pays!' I told them. 'Even Noel, who scored the winner for

Cork City in the 1999 League Cup final against Shamrock Rovers... yeah, even he pays his membership fee.'

Before every match, the captain collected the subs money in the dressing-room... home and away. Or lads didn't play.

We introduced discipline and order.

Out of nowhere, in my first full season, Avondale won the division and got promoted. The following year, we then won the Premier Division. We were the first team to ever win the two Munster Senior League divisions back-to-back. From bottom of the First Division to the top of the Premier Division in two seasons; it was brilliant, a phenomenal experience.

When you have a successful team, it becomes a lot easier to get the right fellas in, because they will always turn up and it helps move the wrong ones out... the fellas who don't want to put the effort in.

I started to get a few lads from University College Cork too. The UCC lads would traditionally have gone to College Corinthians, because they were formed by ex-UCC people. But we started getting a few of them into Avondale.

Of course, I made a few bad signings. But, generally, I was getting players that were good quality, dedicated lads. They were probably a level below the standard required for Cork City, but they were very good in the Munster Senior League.

We had a few fellas who had played for Cork reserves and possibly didn't get the break.

ROCKMOUNT WERE OUR big rivals.

They were the top dogs in Cork at the time and won the Intermediate Cup – the biggest cup for teams at our level – in 2004.

Rockmount were well known because Roy Keane played for them before he joined Cobh Ramblers. His brothers played for them too. Roy's brother Denis was a very good player.

Avondale and Rockmount became the two top teams and it became a serious rivalry. They were a northside club, we were from the southside.

Rockmount were managed by Billy Cronin. He was probably one of the greatest non-league managers ever in Ireland. He didn't care about the League of Ireland, he was all about non-league football and Rockmount was his team. The two teams, the two sets of players, we were almost at war in our games against each other. The teams didn't communicate with each other if they saw each other out – it was that serious. The managers were at each other's throats.

I remember Lisa Fallon, who later came to work with us at Cork City and then went on to work with the Northern Ireland team and Chelsea, talking to me about the rivalry. Lisa is from Dublin and was a radio sports reporter. She ended up living in Cork. Lisa started writing soccer reports for the *Evening Echo* and covering our games.

'I used to love reporting on your matches with Rockmount,' she once told me. 'The two sides were so aggressive!' It was true.

Billy and I couldn't bear to lose to one other, and neither could the players. I laugh now when I look back, and when I meet Billy now we joke about it.

But back then we were very aggressive to each other at games, it was that intense!

IT WAS ALWAYS between Avondale and Rockmount for trophies.

Rockmount were a very aggressive, defensively strong team. We were evenly matched.

The league games between us would be on a knife-edge because it felt like it would decide the title.

It was a *real* rivalry in the city.

We'd never have a player with us who would go and join them. And we wouldn't go and try to take one of their players.

The quality of football was very good too, the highest level for non-league.

I was able to take a loss and move on, but it was difficult when it was to a rival like Rockmount. It proved to be a great learning experience for me because you had to take your beating, dust yourself down and try to improve.

Rockmount, as I've said, won the Intermediate Cup in 2004. We won two in-a-row then in 2006 and '07. They won it in '08. In the 2006 final, we played Blarney United in front of 3,000 people at Turner's Cross in an all-Cork final. Blarney had come out of junior football and had 2,5000 supporters at the match. The previous year, 2005, we had lost four finals.

We came second in the league and Cork City beat us in the Munster Cup final. But we got over the line against Blarney, beating them 1-0 thanks to an Eoin O'Driscoll goal.

It was the first time Avondale had won the cup since 1978.

The following year, we battered Cherry Orchard 5-1 in Dublin and we got to the final again where we played Bangor Celtic, another Dublin team. The final was in Turner's Cross again, and again we won 1-0. John Cotter got the winner in the last minute. Bangor had been the better team, to be fair, but we took our chances.

In 2009, the league went down to the final game of the season, an evening game against Rockmount at their place.

It was nearly impossible to win away to them. It was an intimidating game, with a very tight pitch, crowded all the way around.

I had already made up my mind that I was leaving after the match.

I had done seven years as manager. But I was thinking to myself ahead of the game... *Jesus, if we lose tonight, I can't leave.*

If Rockmount won, they would win the league.

If we won, or it was a draw, we would win it.

We drew the game and took the title.

I stepped down as manager then.

IN MY SEVEN years with Avondale we won 14 trophies.

It was a great time for the club, and I loved it. It was a great learning curve for me as a manager.

I came out of the job thinking... *This is great, I'll take a break and I can relax now.*

I wasn't at home more than a month after resigning and my head was done. My wife Gráinne and my daughters Aideen and Sinéad were saying to me, 'What are you doing? You're at home annoying us'.

I was there in the evenings watching television, watching rubbish I never would have watched before in my life. I was, for probably the first time in my life, absolutely bored. I had nothing to do.

Football and sport had been my life... training at least three times a week and having a match at the weekend.

I ended up taking a year out. But I was bored out of my head.

I was doing my UEFA A licence badge, and nearly had it done – back then, there was no Pro Licence, so I was almost at the top level for coaching qualifications.

And then, out of the blue, an old Diageo colleague of mine, Noel Healy, asked me to get involved with UCC's soccer team.

I met with the head of UCC alumni, Kieran Nestor and John McCarthy, two lovely fellas. They offered me the chance to take over as manager of the university football team.

I had my reservations.

I had given so much to Avondale that I wasn't interested in managing another Munster Senior League team. I was loyal. I didn't want to manage against Avondale.

But the big competition for UCC was the Collingwood Cup, which was for the university teams in Ireland. That was the main focus, rather than the league.

There was also a bit of reverse snobbery on my part towards UCC, which was common enough around the area. There was this stigma about their team... *Ah UCC, sure they're all soft college fellas... They have an easy life.*

I was also thinking... *I can't be looking after them.*

When I look back now, it was completely wrong to think that.

I took the offer, and Noel came on board as joint manager.

There was a uniqueness to the UCC job because they were just students, they didn't work full-time and were all eager to be involved. In hindsight, it was great for me as a manager.

With Avondale and UCC, I got experience of working with two different types of people.

The UCC job helped me to deal with young fellas coming out of underage football. But, like with Avondale, it was about setting firm ground rules.

In other teams, the players could play for their local teams at the weekend and then for their college team in the cup. We had fellas on the team who played with Avondale or Rockmount.

At the start, we'd some saying... 'Oh, I'll only play for you in the Collingwood'. *No chance.*

If you weren't going to play for us in the Munster Senior League, we wouldn't pick you for the Collingwood Cup.

I had the team for four or five months before the cup, playing week-in and week-out. In other college teams, they would only bring most of their players together for the college games or the Collingwood.

We had a set team and stuck to it.

There were Cork City players in UCC that I couldn't pick for the Collingwood because they didn't play for us every Sunday in the Munster Senior League. They would have made us a better team, no doubt, and they wanted to play for us.

But I couldn't pick them and that's how it was.

IN THE COLLINGWOOD Cup, UCC caused a big shock by beating UCD in the semi-finals – they had League of Ireland players in their team and had won the tournament the previous year.

In the final, we played NUI Galway.

The game went to extra time and we got the winner from Dingle's Luke Burgess. I was especially pleased for the team, they were a good group and I had become protective about them.

I wasn't as aggressive as I had been managing Avondale, but I was on the sideline defending the students because everyone we came up against hated them. Opposition lads would give them dog's abuse, curse at them, leave elbows in. They got a rough time.

I strongly defended them because I saw a different side to the lads. They were just young fellas. They were all ordinary fellas, most of them didn't come from privileged backgrounds.

They weren't streetwise though. They were naive and were coming up against hardened players, who didn't respect them and wanted to kick and hit them, push them around.

Even the referees were against us.

I always felt the refs picked on the UCC players. They'd book our lads for cursing. Whereas, if a senior player for Rockmount or Avondale cursed at a referee, nothing would be said.

We were an easy target.

I used to tell the UCC lads... 'You need to be harder... don't let teams bully you!'

To my surprise, they got tougher.

We had some hardy players.

The Collingwood Cup was the only thing UCC were interested in when I took over. They didn't care about anything else. But I was telling them... 'There's no point training all year, lads, playing in the senior league and waiting for one week of the year'.

In the Collingwood, which was played across a few days, if you lost the first game you were out. So, I got them to change focus.

The Munster Senior League became our number one priority, and the Collingwood number two.

We got relegated from the Premier Division the year we won the Collingwood Cup, but got promoted straight back up. We then started to beat Avondale and Rockmount. John Cotter had taken over as Avondale manager and they were flying. But we were more than able to give them a game.

Noel took over UCC after me and they have since won a few Premier Division titles.

They are probably now the main team in the Munster Senior League, taking over from Avondale and Rockmount.

It was strange. I had been Avondale manager for seven years, but I found I had as much of an allegiance to UCC and that team.

I loved the UCC experience.

CHAPTER 16

I REMAINED A supporter of Cork City in my years away from the club.

I loved 2005 especially, watching City win the league on the last night against Derry City. Damien Richardson was the manager again and the team were doing very well. Rico benefitted from the team that Pat Dolan had built. Pat brought in a lot of good players before he left after there was a disagreement with Brian Lennox, the chairman.

I would bring my daughters along to games at Turner's Cross in the hope that they would take an interest.

But they had no interest at all!

I really enjoyed going to the games as a supporter. It was great, there was no pressure on me and the team was doing well. I was at the 2007 FAI Cup final in the RDS when City beat Longford. Rico left soon after.

Lennox sold the club to a private equity fund called Arkaga and that's when the trouble started for Cork City. They were throwing money at players, doubling players' wages and looking to go fully professional. I think they even proposed building a new 20,000-seat stadium.

It all sounded great, but it was ultimately too good to be true.

Some of the stuff was off the wall.

Neal Horgan, who played with me towards the end of my career, wrote a few years later in a book about that season, that there was a striker at City who had a 'clean sheet bonus' in his contract. This was madness and, ultimately, it couldn't last.

Arkaga, despite saying they had a long-term plan for the club, pulled out. They upped and left, and the club went into examinership in August 2008.

City were heavily in debt. A month later, the great economic crash happened in Ireland and around the world.

The club struggled to pay players' wages. Tom Coughlan, a local guy, took over, appointed Roddy Collins as manager, and the club got out of examinership.

But it soon went pear-shaped again.

The High Court issued a winding-up order in 2009.

Cork City was about to go bust.

Celtic came over for a friendly and the money raised helped keep the club going. But the situation continued to get worse.

The Cork City supporters group FORAS – Friends Of the Rebel Army Society – took over and the club entered the First Division in 2010 under a new company name.

They won the First Division in 2011 and got promoted back to the Premier Division.

AS THIS WAS going on, I was looking on as a supporter, working away and managing Avondale United and then UCC.

I had been offered the Cork City manager's job on two occasions over the previous couple of years. The first time was in or around 2007, when I was at Avondale. But I couldn't give up my job to take it.

It was too much of a risk.

When the FORAS people took over the club in 2010, they rang me late one night and offered me the job. I think they thought I was definitely going to take it.

But, within 10 seconds of them ringing, I said, 'No, I can't do it!'

They were shocked.

I had changed jobs about two months beforehand and I was on the road a lot. I couldn't commit to it.

I was disappointed because, if the offer had come a few months earlier, before I changed jobs, I would have taken it.

I certainty wanted to be manager of Cork City.

But managing in the League of Ireland is risky. You could be sacked within six months or mightn't even get paid. It was an uncertain life. In my head it was clear at that time – I couldn't give up a full-time job for a League of Ireland manager's job, not when I had a family to support.

Tommy Dunne was appointed, and the club was saved when FORAS took over.

I continued to manage UCC.

I thought my chance of ever managing City was gone.

In August 2013, Tommy was sacked and Stuart Ashton was put in charge until the end of the season. City were looking for a new manager and even advertised it online.

I was still a regular at matches but hadn't been approached about the job. I found that strange, because the club had approached me twice before.

The night before the deadline to apply for the job, I rang the FORAS chairman Mick Ring. I told Mick I was interested and the first thing he said was, 'Sure, you don't have the badges!' They assumed I didn't have my coaching badges. That's why I didn't hear a thing.

I joked to him, 'You see me at matches every week, did any of you think to ask?'

I had done my coaching badges at the end of the 90s when Brian Kerr was FAI Technical Director at the time and Noel O'Reilly his assistant... they were brilliant people, particularly Noel, who was a gem of a person.

They were absolutely brilliant football people, who loved the game and were deeply invested in the game in Ireland. They knew their stuff. People now talk about systems in football – we were taught three or four different systems on the courses, how to set sides up. They brought in outside coaches too. Andy Roxburgh, who had been Scotland manager and was a UEFA Technical Director, came in to speak to us, as did Mick McCarthy, who was Ireland manager at the time.

When the Cork job came up, the only problem was I didn't have a pro licence. So, if I got the job, I would have to complete the pro licence course within my first two seasons as manager.

Mick Ring said, 'Well, Jesus, you better get your application in then'.

I applied and kept working away, waiting to hear back.

The league finished up. St Patrick's Athletic under Liam Buckley won the title and Cork City finished in mid-table, in sixth.

I went for an interview over the October Bank Holiday weekend. Pat Lyons, who later became chairman and was vice-chairman at the time, was there with Timmy Murphy, the CEO, and Mick Ring.

I was meant to give a presentation, to show them my ideas for the team and the club.

But Pat said, 'John, we don't really need to see your presentation. Talk to us about what you could and would do, and what you can't do'.

I was there for about an hour and a half.

'I know every player in Cork, from underage and non-league, junior and intermediate and college players, all the way to League of Ireland. I can develop players and bring them through.' That I could promise them.

However, the club was in bits. They were in debt and crowds were down to an average of 1,000 at matches.

FORAS had saved the club, but Cork City was treading water.

It didn't faze me. Without wanting to sound arrogant, I felt I was ready for it.

When I left the interview, I found out that Glenn Roeder, who had managed West Ham United and Newcastle United in the Premier League, had also been interviewed for the job.

Martin Russell, who had managed UCD, was also in the running.

I heard that they were leaning towards Roeder. They felt I wasn't experienced enough, or they wanted a big name.

But Pat Lyons had spoken up… 'No, John is the man for the job!'

THE FOLLOWING THURSDAY, after I got home from UCC training, I received a call from the FORAS board.

'We want to talk to you about your position.'

I told them I couldn't, I was flying over to London the following morning to join a few friends and go to an Arsenal game.

'Well, can you meet now?'

This was about half nine at night. I had been working all day and then took training. I had driven home to West Cork from the city so I went back in to meet them in the Cork Airport Hotel.

'We want to offer you the job,' I was quickly told.

I was delighted, of course.

And then they showed me the contract.

I took a look and said, 'Ah lads… I'm on way more money than that where I'm working now. I need more to be able to do it.'

They said they didn't have any more money.

I suggested we draw up a bonus scheme to try and make it work.

They said, 'Ok, no problem'.

They probably didn't think I'd any chance of reaching the targets!

It wasn't about the money for me though, I wasn't motivated by it. But I was leaving a good job and needed to minimise the risk as much as possible. I was going to be on a lot less than I was with Diageo, and also less than Tommy Dunne before me at Cork City.

We shook hands on a two-year deal that night, in principle.

I met with them again on the Monday and then rang my boss in Diageo.

He said, 'We need you to work until December!' The pre-Christmas months are the busiest time for the drinks business.

So, I said I would, and I combined both jobs until the end of the year, even though my contract with City wasn't due to start until January 1.

It was a big risk, I knew that from the start. I was giving up a good job with a big company. Some people told me I was mad to give it up for a job in football.

And there was a nervousness from home.

I had a family to support and, of course, Gráinne and our daughters were worried.

'What if it doesn't go right?'

'What if you're sacked after a few months?'

Football management is a job where you're always going to get sacked at some point. It is inevitable.

There's no manager who goes through his career without being let go. But my wife understood this was something I wanted to do. I was giving up a great job to take on a position with such little security.

But I felt it was now or never for me to be Cork City manager.

It was my last chance. I told myself… *I'm going to put my life into this!*

I WAS VERY clear in what I wanted to do with the club.

I wanted to get the crowds back to Turner's Cross. I wanted to make it a fortress again.

I wanted to get people from all over the county... West Cork, North Cork, East Cork, all around the county and the city, to rally behind the team.

I wanted to make the Cross a great place for City fans, but a nightmare for away teams. The crowds had dropped off dramatically, down to on average 1,000 people per match. I even noticed myself, when going to games, that the buzz wasn't there. In Cork, if a team isn't doing well, they won't be in the news, they won't get the following.

That was the main thing in my head. I wanted to get the crowds back.

I wanted to make City a competitive team, to ensure there were never any easy games. I felt once supporters saw that we had a passionate team that gave everything and worked extremely hard, then they would be back.

Fortunately, there was a massively positive reaction to me getting the job.

It was lovely to see, but it was maybe a bit over the top! Because people probably felt I was going to sort things out straightaway, and instantly make the club successful again.

It wasn't going to be that easy. Pre-season that year was very difficult. We only had five players on the books and signed up for the next year. The club weren't paying full-time, just part-time contracts.

So, the players were only contracted until the end of each season.

Their contracts only started back in March, when the league season commenced. A lot of the players had to go on the dole during the off-season, or try and get jobs for Christmas. It was tough for them, and obviously not ideal for me as a manager, but that's just the way the League of Ireland was in the years after the crash.

There were some great players at the club, however.

We had Mark McNulty, who was a very good goalkeeper. Darren Dennehy and Dan Murray at centre-back. Dan was a very good footballer. They were both good organisers, two strong boys.

We had Colin Healy in the middle of the park, who was tremendous on and off the pitch, a great guy. Billy Denehy joined us after Shamrock Rovers released him.

Did we expect him to be as good as he was? Probably not.

Billy, who was Darren's brother, was a revelation for us on the left-wing, exceptional, teams couldn't handle him. He finished the season with 16 goals.

Gearóid Morrissey was one of the five players contracted to the club.

I brought Liam Kearney back for his third spell at the club. Liam had been with Avondale. I brought Darren Murphy, another Cork lad, back from England; he had been with Stevenage and Woking.

I also brought in Mark O'Sullivan, a centre-forward, from Avondale.

Michael McSweeney and Josh O'Shea, two lads I had at UCC, joined us too. There was a great Cork nucleus to the squad.

We also managed to get what looked like a big coup when Anthony Elding became available. Anthony was an English centre-forward who had been all over; he played for Leeds United and in the lower leagues in England. He then went to Sligo and was extremely prolific.

Anthony had scored the winning goal in the cup final for Sligo Rovers a few weeks earlier when they beat Drogheda. But there was a dispute over a new contract. He wasn't happy and became available.

I met him and he agreed to join us. Now, the move didn't go well for him, but it was a coup for the club.

All of a sudden, we went from being nowhere to signing the player who scored the winner in the cup final. That got a lot of publicity and showed that we meant business for the new season, that we were going to be competitive again.

But, still, trying to put together a squad for January was tough and so was pre-season. There was no messing about, it was really hard training. We trained every day and made no apologies about it.

The lads were brilliant, they all bought into it. We got them in full-time training every morning, even though they weren't going to be paid until the start of the season.

I brought John Cotter in as my assistant. Billy Woods, Phil Harrington and Lisa Fallon would join the coaching team too. Mick Ring, who was on the panel for my interview, became our kit man.

We brought in a system of play and worked on our strengths.

THE FIRST GAME of the season was against St Pat's, who were league champions. It was at Turner's Cross. Ahead of the match, it was probably the most nervous I had ever been in my career.

I had played in cup finals, massive games for league titles, European matches and the rest. But I never felt a nervousness like this before.

REBELHEART • JOHN CAULFIELD

All eyes were on me.

All the pressure on my back.

I had a lot of goodwill from the Cork public, of course. But that wasn't going to do me much good if we got off to a bad start.

We had a good pre-season, but there was still a question hanging over us... What *level* were we at?

No one knew.

And we were coming up against a serious team. Pat's had Christy Fagan, Greg Bolger, Kenny Browne... Keith Fahey.

Turner's Cross was absolutely packed for the game – over 5,000 people on a wet, drizzly night at the start of March.

It was a cracking atmosphere.

We could taste the excitement.

It was just how I hoped it would be – the crowd back, everyone behind the team and us in a massive game.

And then Gary Buckley scored for us after about 15 minutes. Turner's Cross was absolutely rocking. Fagan equalised for them in the second-half before Johnny Dunleavy was sent-off for us, a second yellow card.

St Pat's probably thought they were going to win it from there. But we stuck at it... it finished 1-1.

It was a very positive result.

I came off the pitch thinking... *We'll be all right this season.*

I didn't know where we would finish or how the rest of the season would go. But the performance against Pat's, with the big crowd at the Cross humming and fully behind us, showed me that we were going to give every team a game.

That first year was just a total roller-coaster.

The team bought into what we wanted to do straightaway. There was a brilliant attitude within the group but also great craic, a genuine camaraderie. There were no big-time players, no big hero. Just a good bunch of lads with a great bond. There was a very strong Cork flavour to the team – it stank of Corkness!

Straightaway we brought together a very competitive, hardcore team with a lot of talent. The crowds kept coming to games and, in a very short period, I knew we'd be more than okay. The team was going to give everything, and we'd see where it got us.

I knew we weren't ever going to be overrun. Mark O'Sullivan up front won every ball, he was unbelievable. Billy Dennehy was a whippet down the wing.

We were defensively strong too. Dunleavy was very good that first year.

Some people might say that in that first year we were quite direct, but we were a dangerous, exciting team.

In training and behind the scenes at the club, I wanted to make sure everything was right for the players... the training gear, the food at the club for them. We had financial limitations, of course, but we did our best to work within our means.

There was a hallway in the old ground at Bishopstown that I got partitioned and turned into another room. We called it the 'first-team room'. We put a television in, and I managed to get a dartboard and pool table from people for nothing. We wanted to create a space for the first-team players to relax, like you would have in English football.

It also would be a place for any fella in the underage team to aspire to get to. We put a bootroom in too.

It was simple stuff but important.

I had been in teams with Cork when we were successful and when we were rubbish. Team spirit was massive. And it wasn't like the City lads could build team spirit in the pub like it was for teams in my day in the League of Ireland!

All these little things helped, and we went on a run after the Pat's match and didn't lose until May. We beat Derry City away and Bray Wanderers at home. We got a great win over Shamrock Rovers at Turner's Cross and kept going.

In the opening nine games of the season we were unbeaten and went top of the league.

CHAPTER 17

IN OUR TENTH game of the season, we travelled to Oriel Park to play Dundalk, who had come from nowhere the previous season to challenge St Pat's and missed out on the league title.

Stephen Kenny was their manager.

Kenny had been at Longford Town, Bohemians, Derry City, Dunfermline in Scotland and Shamrock Rovers. I had never come across him in football – he didn't play in the league and went into management fairly young.

He was successful with Longford and Derry – he won a cup with Derry. It didn't work in Scotland, and the Rovers experience had been a bit of a nightmare and he was sacked. Kenny then took over at Dundalk. They were a good side. Richie Towell, Chris Shields, Stephen O'Donnell and Daryl Horgan, who had left us, all played for them.

All of a sudden, they put themselves in the picture.

He was one of the most experienced managers on the circuit, along with Liam Buckley. He deserved my fullest respect, and he got it! We'd often chat at matches too. At that point, it was hard to imagine the rivalry that would very quickly develop between our two teams.

I WAS ALWAYS meticulous in my preparation for training and matches. But I went against my better judgement that day. The bus to Dundalk left late, after we were told we'd be there with plenty of time to spare.

On the road to Dundalk, just outside Dublin, there was gridlock. A pipe had burst. The road was backed up.

We were 25 minutes late for the match.

Dundalk battered us.

4-0.

But, after the delay, we were beaten before we stepped on the pitch.

The lads hadn't eaten before the game, because we'd been stuck on the bus for four hours.

I was furious with myself.

The following week we travelled up the road again, this time to play St Pat's in Richmond Park.

It was pouring rain, the pitch was soaked.

We were playing in difficult conditions against the league champions and they were beating us 2-1.

Rob Lehane, a young lad, came off the bench and equalised for us to make it 2-2. It looked like we were going to get a point, which would've been a very good result. And then, with the last kick of the game, in injury time, Conan Byrne scored for Pat's to win it.

We were out on our feet, sick to lose it like that.

All of sudden, we went from top of the table and unbeaten to fourth place, and two defeats in-a-row.

Questions were being asked.

I can still see the headlines and articles that were written after it... *The bubble has burst... And Cork are gone.*

It was as if people were thinking... *Ah sure, they started grand, but this is their real level now... They've come back down to earth.*

It wasn't like that amongst the group though.

The Dundalk loss was a write-off. It was bad preparation which I took the blame for. But against St Pat's, we played very well. We were unlucky, beaten by a last minute goal in a game where there was nothing between the teams.

To write us off after that was just wrong.

Of course, we were disappointed we lost, but the team was full of good lads. They dusted themselves down and went back to training hard.

We then went on another run.

We beat Derry the following week and just started to pick up steam again.

I remember we played Athlone Town, who were bottom of the league, in our last home match of the season before the summer break.

Turner's Cross was packed, and the crowd were right behind the team. But Athlone were making it difficult for us. We were dominating but could not score against them.

And then Mark O'Sullivan popped up with an unbelievable header from about 15 yards out into the top corner of the net.

1-0.

The crowds were back, we were getting 4,500, 5,000 at matches and we could all feel the buzz around the place.

In our last match before the summer break, we went up to Dublin to play Shamrock Rovers. We beat them 3-0 earlier in the season at the Cross, so there was talk of them putting it right against us.

We won 2-0 in Tallaght Stadium.

Brian Lenihan, who would leave us for Hull City later that summer, did brilliantly well to set up a goal for Mark. Gearóid Morrisey got the second. The City lads rushed back to Cork because they were off for a week's holiday during the break.

We got them back in for a week's training ahead of our first match after the break, at home to Limerick at Turner's Cross. It was a beautiful summer's Friday evening, the crowd was heaving.

We came into the game with five wins in-a-row, but Limerick were doing well too, they'd won three matches on the trot.

We hammered them 3-0.

And news came through that Dundalk had drawn with Derry and dropped points. We were two points behind Dundalk with a game in hand.

It was a bit surreal.

From being nowhere at the start of the season and having little expected of us, we were right in the mix for the title, 17 games in.

People had written us off, expecting the wheels to fall off, but we just kept going.

In August, we dropped points against Dundalk, Bray Wanderers and Athlone Town. It looked like we were out of it, that Dundalk were going to run away with it.

At one point, we were eight points behind them.

And then we won six games in-a-row. Mark McNulty saved a penalty with three minutes to go against Sligo Rovers. Dan Murray won another game for us in the last minute with a header against Shamrock Rovers. Colin Healy scored with a fantastic overhead kick versus St Pat's.

That's how the run-in went.

We looked gone and kept coming back and winning. There was nothing in the games, usually one goal, but we kept finding a way.

Dundalk started dropping points too.

OUR LAST HOME game of the year was against Bohemians, with over 6,000 packed into the Cross.

It was brilliant.

The rain was whipping down, a blustery night in October. But the atmosphere was electric.

My goal at the start of the year was to get the fans back, to bring the passion back and give them a team to get behind. And we had achieved that.

After a few minutes, the Shed end started cheering.

Bray had taken the lead against Dundalk and word had spread around the ground.

If we won, we'd go top.

It was a tough game, and I could feel the tension in the air. Billy Dennehy scored for us in stoppage time at the end of the first-half. In the second-half, there was a nervousness in the ground, but we stuck at it. Bohs had two players sent off, the second one in stoppage time at the end of the game.

We hung on and won.

Dundalk drew their match, so we were top by a point going into the final game of the season. And our last match of the season was away to Dundalk.

The winner would be champions, although a draw would do it for us.

It was pure fantasy... Roy of the Rovers stuff.

We had a mix of experienced players, like Dan Murray, who had gone away and come back, and Colin Healy, who had been there before and been with the club during some tough times. And we had players like Mark O'Sullivan, who had been playing in non-league for Avondale, Gearóid Morrisey and Michael

McSweeney, a lad from UCC who came into the team at the end of the season after an injury to Darren Dennehy.

It was all so new, it was like an adventure.

There was a brilliant atmosphere around the city too. The crowds were great, there was nothing but positive publicity and everyone was just happy that the club was doing well.

No matter what happened, we had got the crowds back, got the team competitive again and qualified for Europe.

But, of course, we were desperate to win the league.

CITY HAD BEEN involved in a few final day title deciders. The club beat Derry on the final day in 2005 to win the league, the last time we claimed the title. And I was involved in one back in 1991 against Dundalk, which we lost at Turner's Cross.

Dundalk were going for their first league title since 1995.

After 32 games, it came down to one match.

They had the best home record in the league that year. We had the best away record. It was all set up to be one of the great nights in League of Ireland history.

The match was at Oriel Park, on an artificial surface. Dundalk were a great side, they won games on grass too, but the pitch was an advantage. And, at that stage, it was in terrible condition. The surface was worn and there were parts of the pitch where the ball didn't bounce right.

Now, it might sound like sour grapes to ever bring that up. But there's a huge difference between playing on grass and an artificial surface, and it was something we'd have to overcome.

There were nerves ahead of the game, of course. But everything about the build-up was magical.

ORIEL PARK WAS packed.

There were about 5,500 at the game and we brought up around a thousand supporters. The place was heaving.

Dundalk is a great football town, very passionate.

Oriel Park though wasn't fit to cater for a crowd of that size, as we would find out. Health and safety concerns were certainly overlooked.

The match was on a knife-edge from the start.

Dundalk had more possession than us, but we came the closest to scoring. Mark O'Sullivan had a chance. John O'Flynn cut the ball back to him at the far post and he missed it from 12 yards out. Eight or nine times out of 10 that season, Mark would have scored it; he was disgusted with himself.

Just before half-time, we got a free-kick on the edge of their box. Billy Dennehy took it and his shot hit the bottom of the post and rebounded out.

Peter Cherrie, the Dundalk goalkeeper, was beaten; he hadn't even moved.

It was 0-0 at half-time, so we were 45 minutes away from winning the title because a draw did us. We never played for a draw though, and always went out to win. It was the only way we knew how to play.

A few minutes into the second-half, Dundalk scored. The ball was crossed in and bounced up and hit Stephen O'Donnell on the hand.

The Cork City coaching staff and substitutes were all screaming from the sideline for hand-ball. Brian Kerr on commentary for RTÉ said that it was a clear hand-ball.

But the referee let play go on.

O'Donnell buried it.

1-0 to them.

In fairness to the referee, it was one of those decisions that you get sometimes and other times you don't. Unfortunately for us, it went against us that night.

Dundalk were dominant after that. We were under the cosh and it looked like they would get a second. McNulty made a great save.

But we were still only a goal away from winning the league.

In the last 15 minutes – between the nervousness of the Dundalk crowd and our lads not giving up – we got back into it.

Rob Lehane came on as a substitute and – I can still see this now – he had a glancing header from about 10 yards out. When he headed it, from where we were standing, we thought it was in.

We were ready to jump up and celebrate. But the ball grazed the post.

A few minutes later, Brian Gartland scored for them and that was it.

Over.

Dundalk were champions.

The treatment of the Cork supporters made the night much worse. They were cramped into a part of the ground in Oriel Park that was totally unsuitable and were searched twice going into the game.

My family was in the ground too, a lot of the players' families were. There was a large bunch of women and kids there. We left that night – when they were eventually allowed to leave the ground – with a bad taste in our mouths.

We had to hang around outside the ground afterwards for quite a while to make sure our supporters got on buses back to Cork, and make sure the players met up with their families.

It was an upsetting and unsettling night for the City supporters.

The way our supporters were treated was beyond hostile. They felt unsafe.

We wrote to the FAI a month later, saying it was a disgrace the way our supporters were treated. But I think they threw a blind eye because it was the first time Dundalk had won the league in almost 20 years.

In hindsight, it was probably best that Cork City didn't win that night.

It wouldn't have been a pleasant night had we won.

There might have been big trouble.

THAT NIGHT IN Dundalk was horrible, but it had still been like a fairytale season for Cork City.

The previous November, when I took the job, we had five players on the books, the club was massively in debt and there wasn't a single person who thought we'd be challenging for the title.

I'm an optimistic man by nature, and even I didn't think we would be where we finished the season.

I believed that if we got the right players, with the right attitude and ability, and trained hard, then anything was possible with a bit of luck.

But no one could have seen at the start where we would end up.

Dundalk had been in a bad state a few years before too, but they had a year's head start on us and were challenging St Pat's for the title the season before. Their results against us won them the title, otherwise there was nothing between us.

City came from nowhere.

The club was miles ahead of where we thought we would be. And we had Europe to look forward to.

I got over the disappointment of losing out on the league very quickly. As soon as the FAI Cup final was done the following week – St Pat's beat Derry City 2-0 – it was straight into getting our squad ready for the new year.

THE PROCESS OF trying to sign players, to entice them, to beat off other clubs, is always very difficult.

We had a Cork team to the core, which is what we needed in order to be successful. We were trying to bring in players from outside who would make a difference, however.

Karl Sheppard was one such player.

He had been let go by Shamrock Rovers and he was a bit panicky because he didn't have a lot of options, bar some interest from a few clubs outside of Dublin.

He was a significant signing for us though, as he had a big reputation in the league and was also a very influential player, despite having a poor enough season with Rovers.

We lost Gearóid Morrissey, who signed for Cambridge United in League Two in England. Gearóid was a loss and we needed to replace him.

And that's where Liam Miller came in. Liam was a big signing for us; it was a massive story at the time. Mark McNulty rang me to say Liam was in Australia and he was thinking of coming home because his kids were young. He wanted to settle back in Cork.

We were in Europe for the first time and we were trying to build a better team. And Liam looked to be a perfect fit… Cork lad, back home, and we wouldn't have to sell the appeal of the club to get him.

Liam had played for Celtic and Manchester United and Ireland. He had been playing with a team in Melbourne.

There was talk that Liam was on mega money for City, but that wasn't true at all. When I met him to try do a deal, I told him straight out, 'Liam, we've no money!'

The club was still in debt and were paying it off. Our budget was slightly bigger than the previous season because we had the European games, but we couldn't break the bank for anyone.

Liam didn't mind though. He wanted to come home to Cork for his kids and family, and settle there. He was also great friends with Mark McNulty; they were both from Ballincollig.

Liam was the most down to earth, ordinary guy you could meet.

He was so pleasant and unassuming that it was actually hard to imagine that he played for Celtic and United.

Alan Bennett joined us too. Benno was another local guy; he had been part of the City team that won the league title in 2005 before he left for Reading. Like Liam, he had won a few caps for Ireland.

Benno was with AFC Wimbledon. He was club captain, and he wanted to wait until the English season was over to join us. I told him we needed him straightaway – we managed to get him for the start of the season.

Benno was a brilliant leader. He never roared and shouted… he led by example. He had a good presence about him. And he was a brilliant defender, always in the right position, and a great organiser.

We also signed Ross Gaynor, who could play at full-back and on the wing, from Sligo Rovers, and Steven Beattie and Kevin O'Connor.

Ahead of the new season, there were questions about Cork.

Would we be as good again the next season?

Were we 'one-season' wonders?

What was our true level?

I wasn't overly concerned.

On paper, our team was certainly better going into the second season.

That year, however, became probably the biggest learning curve and exacting experience I ever had as a manager.

CHAPTER 18

AT THE START of the 2015 season, it was clear that the title would be between Cork City and Dundalk.

St Pat's fell down the table; we heard there was hassle and internal problems that season within the club.

Shamrock Rovers never raised their game or challenged.

It quickly became a two-horse race, but even then, we were chasing Dundalk throughout the year. They went to another level and were pulling away from us. We went into the summer break five points behind them. They had a game in hand.

IN THE EUROPA League, we drew KR Reykjavik, an Icelandic team. It was Cork City's first European match in seven years.

I had played in 22 European games for City. This was my first as manager.

The coaching staff did a lot of analysis and preparation for the match, as we always did. We left no stone unturned because the European games are massive for Irish clubs. Advancing to the next round was worth over €200,000 to us. Whereas, the League of Ireland winners would only get €100,000, and the runners-up €50,000. The European games could make or break a season.

On paper, we thought we had the better team and the experience to come through the tie. But we knew it would be an even game.

The first leg was at Turner's Cross, and we took the lead. Alan Bennett scored a header after about 20 minutes. They got one back about 10 minutes later.

They had the away goal.

There wasn't a lot between the teams, but we made too many errors, and it ended 1-1. City had to score a week later in Iceland to go through. And we made the perfect start. Mark O'Sullivan scored after about 15 minutes to give us the lead, a lobbed shot over the goalkeeper.

It got even better for us then just before half-time, after KR Reykjavik had a player sent-off. It looked like we would go through. And then, 15 minutes from the end, they scored from a set-piece. The game went to extra time and they scored again – a soft, sloppy goal. Reykjavik went on to win 2-1 on the night, 3-2 on aggregate.

It was desperately disappointing for us and a revealing game.

In extra time we looked dead. Our team looked old. We had six players on the pitch in extra time who were over 30. All of the guys were brilliant players, and some had been with the 2005 team that won the league. And on paper we had a great team, better than Reykjavik.

But in extra time, we hadn't the legs to win it.

Losing in Europe was a big wake-up call. Our lads weren't as good as they used to be. It was a similar story in the league that season. Dundalk went to another level and pulled away from us. They were younger, quicker and stronger.

They just had more energy and were more dynamic. The reason we went out of Europe was the same reason we couldn't catch Dundalk. We only lost four games in the league, but two of them were against Dundalk. They won the league with three or four games to go and were 11 points clear.

We reached the FAI Cup final, where we also played Dundalk.

But that season showed me that we weren't as good on the pitch as we looked on paper.

There were also some problems within the squad.

IN OUR FIRST season, we had an unbelievably tight group, everyone was together, on the same page. The lads would run through a wall for one another.

In the second year though, some guys become more individualistic and began thinking more about themselves. There were ego problems between a number of players.

Dan Murray had been a big player for City and won the league with the club in 2005. But, in that second season, he was the only player who worked full-time and was coming towards the end of his career. He wasn't happy about not playing and became very frustrated.

I had issues with Billy Dennehy and Ross Gaynor. Billy had been disciplined a few times.

In the Europa League first leg against Reykjavik, Billy and Mark O'Sullivan had to be separated on the pitch.

In amateur football, it was easy to do something in a situation like that. If you've a problem with a fella, he's out. *Simple.*

In professional football, you just can't do that as there are contracts involved. We offered Billy – who had been brilliant for us on the pitch, our top scorer the previous season – the option to leave.

He was a big earner at the club but the only team who came in for him was Limerick, who couldn't afford him. The PFAI came down to meet us and wanted to resolve the problem.

Ultimately though, there was nothing we could do until the end of the season.

He had a contract and if a player on a contract decided not to leave, we were stuck with him. There were a few other players not getting on with each other. There was also probably a bit of resentment towards Liam Miller; some were probably thinking he was earning big money, but he wasn't.

Liam had wanted to come home to Cork with his family – that was it, it wasn't for money. And, as I've said, he was just a lovely young fella, always quiet, genuine, unassuming.

But maybe some stuff had been written, or people just assumed he must have been paid a fortune. So, there was maybe a little jealousy that turned into resentment, because everyone expected him to be the main man.

Liam played well for City, but he didn't play as well as we knew he could.

Whatever it was, that attitude towards him wasn't right, and it was symptomatic of a lot of the problems we had that year. We had a couple of fellas who were not working out and, ultimately, I found their presence disruptive to what I was trying to do.

Half-way through the season, I was thinking to myself… *We need to do a bit of surgery on this team.*

CORK CITY WENT on a run in the FAI Cup. We hammered St Pat's 4-0, beat Derry City after a replay, and got Bray Wanderers in the semi-finals. Danny Morrissey got the only goal of the game for us and we went through to the final at the Aviva Stadium, where we would play Dundalk.

I was relieved. There was a lot of pressure on me at the time. Expectations were high. We were second in the table again, but we weren't going to catch Dundalk.

My contract was due to finish at the end of the season. I wanted a new one, of course, which would give us the chance to push the club on. But to be honest, I wasn't sure if the club was going to offer me another deal.

It was an unstable time. I was getting a bit of stick from some supporters. I felt we had better players than the previous year when we came from nowhere to finish second. But I think some people thought we were going to be better than we were, given the signings we had made.

Maybe we should have been, but the problem was that Dundalk raised the bar again and got better. They had the money to bring in more players and, ultimately, that season in the league we were not good enough.

We needed to revamp the squad to catch them.

I ended up agreeing on a new two-year deal with the board. It gave me the chance to make the changes I needed to the squad and I set about doing it.

DURING THE WEEK of the Cup final, the squad had a meeting about our plans for the match. We were going to stay two nights in Dublin, with the players' partners joining them on the second night, the Sunday. Everything was paid for. We also got the players suits for the final.

So, we were just going through a list of stuff, thinking everything was grand.

As a management team, we'd agreed that there were a few unsettled lads in the group, but we'd also agreed to deal with that problem after the final. It was one week. Cork City's first FAI Cup final since 2007. *Let's see if we can pull off a shock here.*

Because, in a cup final, there's always a chance that the best team might have a bad day. So, there was an excited mood within the group.

I WAS ABOUT to finish up the team meeting on the Monday before the final.

I was checking my list to see if everything was sorted.

And I said, 'Oh, and by the way lads... the tickets, each player will get three free tickets for the final'.

I thought that was it. The meeting wrapped up... everything sorted.

And then, out of the blue, Ross Gaynor said, 'Dundalk are getting six free tickets!'

Now, I'm not a mean person, but the tickets were only a tenner.

It was on the tip to my tongue to say... *Well, if you won the league by 11 points, you would have had six free tickets, too!*

I was thrown a bit.

I said, 'Well, look lads, there are three free tickets per player. And they are only a tenner each!'

Ross said, 'We should get six tickets!'

'Look lads,' I told them. 'I'll see what I can do, but I would say there won't be any more tickets.' I then said we were looking after them for the final – we'd got them their suits, two nights in Dublin... the best of everything.

All of a sudden, it went from what was a very positive meeting to one in which I was trying to defuse a bomb. That is the thing about management, you think everything is rosy in the garden one minute, then next... you're dealing with a big problem.

'Hold on lads... do you not want to stay the second night?' I asked them.

And some players went, 'No, no, no... we do!'

'If you don't want to stay on the Sunday, you can go back on the bus,' I informed them, getting my back up. 'It's no problem!'

I left and went to my office, absolutely fuming.

I called the management team in. They were furious, too.

We parked it, and went and took training.

After training, there was a knock at the door. It was Dan Murray.

The meeting shouldn't have ended as it did. I was disappointed that Dan, as our most senior player, hadn't stood up and put Ross in his place.

In my time as manager, Dan had been treated well at City, and there were never any problems over money in his relationship with the club.

I had huge admiration for him, and remained very disappointed.

Ross Gaynor's comments didn't bother me as much. He was usually complaining about the food, or the gear or something... and he wasn't from Cork.

In this instance, it was tickets. I found Ross difficult if he was ever dropped, even though on this occasion he was playing in the final because Steven Beattie was cup-tied after we signed him from Sligo Rovers.

With Dan though, his issue was that he hadn't been playing. He was gutted that he wasn't going to start the cup final.

I had told him, 'It doesn't matter… it's done and dusted'.

IN THE CUP final, we went out and gave it everything, we played reasonably well, and the game went to extra time.

Dundalk were stronger though and eventually scored. Richie Towell got the goal in the second half of extra time. Dundalk won the double.

I remember saying to John Cotter after it, 'If we had won, it would have been totally wrong'.

We didn't deserve it.

We had fellas in the team who wouldn't talk to each other.

There was a distinct lack of team spirit – some fellas didn't give a damn about the other lads in the team.

It was the exact opposite to how it was meant to be, how it was when I was a player for Cork City. And how it was in my first season as manager.

When you win a few games, players will always be happy – those who play anyway. But, when you lose a game or two, players will blame the manager, usually, not themselves. I think that's partly what happened after we lost in Europe.

I got a lot of stick. The players got stick.

Some stood up and were leaders, like Alan Bennett.

But some looked for scapegoats.

After the match, we had our meal in the hotel in Stillorgan before the players went into town. Before they left, I had made up my mind to tell the lads whom I was deciding to let go for the following season, that I had made that decision about them.

I said to John Cotter, 'I'm going to meet the boys now, the fellas that we're letting go… I'm going to tell now them'.

'Now?' Cotts asked.

I said, 'Right now!'

Cotts asked if it would be better to wait until the morning.

'No… I'm telling them now.'

It was one of those times when you realise what you are about to do is right. I went around and I told seven of the lads. And I thanked each one of them. That season, we finished second again, played in Europe for the first time in eight years and reached the cup final, but internal team matters had created that toxic environment.

It was the biggest learning curve I ever had in management.

I WAS VERY active with transfers the following pre-season. We had to go and reinvent a new team for 2016.

I wanted to get players signed who would be young and hungry, to make us a more dynamic team. And, of course, I wanted them to have the right attitude and be ambitious.

We lost lads whom I felt we would not miss. But we also lost some others, lads I enjoyed working with… like Liam Kearney, John O'Flynn and Liam Miller.

I had a chat with Liam, and he thought the season went okay for him, but he didn't reach the heights we were maybe expecting. It's possible that, after a few years in Australia, where the pace was slower because it was much warmer, he found it tough to adjust to the more intense nature of football in Ireland. He left us for a club called Wilmington Hammerheads in North Carolina. I had some contacts in the United States and helped set it up.

Back in Cork, the pressure was on me; we couldn't get this wrong.

We needed to rebuild and bring in, not only the right players, but the right people to join the group.

I signed Kenny Browne and Greg Bolger from St Pat's, two top players, and Gearóid Morrisey came back to us after his year with Cambridge United. Straight away, we had freshened up our midfield and added more legs, more dynamism.

We signed Eoghan O'Connell on loan from Celtic to play at the back. Eoghan, who is a cousin of Munster and Ireland rugby legend Paul O'Connell, was a good kid and hard as nails. I had played with his dad at Avondale. It was up front where we made the biggest change, though.

I had a hunch about Stephen Dooley, a winger who had been playing for Derry City. In the two games he came on against us, we beat Derry in both, but he nearly changed the course of both games.

I liked him a lot, and thought he was underrated by many people in the league.

On my Pro Licence course, I asked Peter Hutton, who had been Derry manager, about Dooley. Peter said he was a great player. Yet, Derry had let Dooley go at the end of the season. I got in touch, and he would barely talk on the phone; he seemed quite shy.

'I'd like to sign you for Cork City,' I told him.

I asked if he would come and meet me in Sligo to chat about the move. He lived in Portstewart, outside Coleraine, at the top of the country.

We met and I told him about the club, and what we saw for him if he joined us. I couldn't get a word out of him, he was really quiet, an introvert. He told me he would go home and think about it, and get back in touch.

I said, 'Grand, I'll give you a ring tomorrow!'

He said, 'No, give me a few days.'

A week went by and I heard nothing. I thought... *I better do something here.*

I rang Dooley and said I was going to drive up to meet him at his house. I left West Cork and drove to Portstewart – from one end of the country to the other. It was lashing rain the whole way up, pouring down.

I got stuck in traffic in Dungannon and was delayed by an hour, eventually arriving at half six. His mother and father were there too. Dooley lived in an estate by the beach, with his parents. He came from a good family.

His mother said to me, 'You must like him if you drove this far for him'.

I said, 'Well, I want to sign him'.'

'He won't be signing today,' his father then informed me.

They were thinking hard still and wouldn't give me an answer – even after me driving from the other end of the country. I had forms with me. As I was about to leave, I said, 'Sign that form, and I'll ring you on Monday. If you don't want to sign, tear up your copy... and I'll tear up mine'.

Stephen rang me on the Monday and said, 'I think I'll join you'.

It was worth it. He turned out to be a genius.

I had done a lot of work to revamp the squad, but we still needed a goalscorer.

PART SIX

City and The Town

CHAPTER 19

ABOUT 10 DAYS after the cup final, I was in Dublin and met Gavin Dykes. Gavin and I went to school together in Sligo; he was a few years younger than me, and he had been a player in the league and a coach.

He said to me, 'You should sign Seáni Maguire… you'd love him!'

I said, 'Seáni Maguire?

'Not sure,' I continued. 'He hasn't kicked a ball.'

Maguire had been let go by Dundalk, he wasn't even on the bench for the cup final. Before that, he had been with West Ham, Accrington Stanley and Sligo Rovers. He had been highly rated – he was still only 21, but his career was fizzling out.

And, hand on heart, I hadn't really considered signing him.

He just wasn't on my radar.

Gavin was adamant though.

'I'm telling you John… you'd love him. He's a good finisher.' Other than ability, of course, what I look for in a player is someone with passion, someone who has a bit of decency and respect, and also a good attitude.

Someone who has a *bit* about them. So, when Gavin said that I'd 'love' Maguire as a player, it got me thinking, because Gavin knew me.

I had seen Seáni playing with Sligo. Obviously he hadn't got anywhere with Dundalk, but he did okay with Accrington. I watched him a few times and just thought, *He's not really done anything...* and I didn't think he looked in great condition.

But I had nothing to lose by having a chat with him, so I rang Seáni and met him in Portlaoise.

I quickly noticed that he had no confidence whatsoever.

He was on the ground, blaming himself for how it went with Dundalk.

Seáni Maguire never blamed Dundalk or Stephen Kenny, or anyone at the club – which was just as well because, if he had, I would've got up and walked out. To me, it was pretty simple as to why he didn't play when he was there – Dundalk had David McMillan and Ciaran Kilduff up front, and they were scoring goals.

Seáni wasn't as good as them at that time.

We spoke for about an hour. He told me about his time in England, with West Ham and the money he had earned – he blew his chance over there, he admitted.

But there was a decency about him.

He wasn't a headbanger and there was no ego about him.

Some people have unbelievable egos, it blinds them. Seáni though, was just a really nice young fella.

I said to him, 'Look, you have a think about it... and I'll have a think'. I never offered to sign him. I just wanted to meet, to get a read on him.

I always liked to meet a player before signing him, because you need to see what they're like... find out more about where are they from, their family life... get a sense of their personality, and so on. I needed to know that they would fit into the group.

Seáni really impressed me as a person.

As I was driving back down to Cork, I was thinking... *Will he be good enough?* I was halfway home, when I rang him.

He was back home in Kilkenny.

I said, 'Come down to Cork tomorrow and I'll show you around!'

That was another thing I was adamant on – if you were going to sign for us, you had to come down to Cork first. It allowed me to sell the place to players, to show our link with UCC and the Mardyke arena. If a player was talking to another club, he might think... *Jesus, they've a good set up down here.*

And if they weren't going to make the effort to come down, then they weren't serious about joining us.

SEÁNI CAME DOWN the following day, and we did the tour.

I was straight with him.

'I'm looking for a centre-forward.

'There's a position there if you're good enough.

'But look, Seáni... I'm not going to lie to you... I don't know if you're good enough.

'I haven't seen a lot of you.

'And from what I have seen, you haven't done enough. But to be fair to you, you said things aren't right, you said you want to come to the right place.

'So, here's an opportunity.'

He asked me, 'Do you think I'll play? You've got Mark'.

'Mark O'Sullivan is 33,' I said.

'He has been absolutely brilliant for me, I've managed him for 10 years. But he's getting to the stage of his career where he won't play every game.

'And we need more if we're going to progress. He's still a very good player, but if you can't offer me more than Mark, you're no good to me.

'The position is yours... if you're good enough.'

I knew by him that he had no other offer – you didn't need to be a genius to know that. He had been forgotten about, which happens all the time in football, lads just drift out of the game.

I offered him €200 a week to sign for us.

'Is that all you can give me?'

'Sure, no one wants you.'

'I know, but I was on €700 a week at Dundalk.'

'Fair enough, but they're not signing you, are they?'

There was a pause.

The lad's confidence was on the floor and I didn't want to make it any worse.

I said, 'Ok, I'll tell you what, I'll give you €250 a week... and we'll put you in accommodation'. He said, 'okay.'

'For you, it's not about the money!' I told him.

'You're 21 years of age, you're a young fella. For you, it's all about the football and playing. Don't worry about money. If you get into my first-team and you're banging in goals, I'll give you a new contract. No problem. But, right now, you haven't done anything... you know that yourself.'

We shook hands on a deal.

I told John Cotter we had signed him.

'We'll take a chance on him.'

Seáni came down the following week and signed the deal.

There were no bonfires in Cork when he joined us. There was no reaction at all, really.

No one in Cork really knew who he was.

I was still unsure about how it would go. But I had being a striker myself. I knew if his confidence was down, I could get around him and if he had the right attitude to push himself, get himself fit, then he'd have a chance.

I also liked that he didn't blame anyone else.

We came back for pre-season in January, five weeks later. After three days of training, Cotts said to me about Seáni, 'He's some player!'

Whether it was the fact that he gained a bit of confidence from me signing him, I don't know. But ever since then, Seáni has never looked back.

In the League of Ireland, it is very hard to build a team, because the turnover of players is massive. But we had made it work to our advantage and going into the 2016 season, we had reinvented the team.

We brought in a lot of new players, but Seáni took us to the next level.

IN THE FIRST game of the 2016 season, we played Dundalk in the President's Cup at Turner's Cross.

We won 2-0. Gavan Holohan and Seáni scored for us.

The game was significant for City for a couple of reasons. It was the first time we beat Dundalk during my time as manager. And, Seáni scored against the team that had let him go a few months beforehand.

And I think Dundalk realised... *These guys are going to be a serious team.*

As I've said, before I took over at Cork City, I wouldn't have known Stephen Kenny, our paths had never crossed. He started coaching with Longford Town when he was young and he did very well everywhere he had been, other than at Shamrock Rovers.

I think Stephen felt hard done by at the end of his Rovers' exit, and he was. Rovers were based in Tallaght, he was from Tallaght and he had said it was the club where he wanted to be.

I don't know what happened behind the scenes – I wasn't even a manager in the league at the time.

He then went to Dundalk and, a bit like me with Cork, he took over at a club with huge history which was on its knees. And he brought them up the table. He was building his team and I think, with Dundalk, he wanted to prove Rovers wrong.

I think he wanted to win, and win and win, and show them how wrong they were. Dundalk were in position to dominate when the St Patrick's Athletic team of 2013 and '14 disintegrated quickly.

We were second to them in 2014, when no one really thought we would do anything. But we stuck around and, going into 2016, we had improved our team.

When we beat them in the President's Cup, you could see then that we were probably getting a little too close for comfort… in Stephen's books. As the season went on, and he kept scoring, the Seáni thing probably annoyed him too.

At matches in 2014 and '15, when we played Dundalk, Stephen and I would have had a chat before and after games.

Now, we weren't friends, we would never have gone for a pint and we were very different people, different personalities. But there was a respect there.

After Dundalk beat us in the FAI Cup final in 2015, when they won the double, I went into their dressing-room at the Aviva Stadium and congratulated them. They were the better team, so it was the right thing to do.

From the President's Cup game in 2016 on though, there was barely any communication between Stephen and myself, bar shaking hands before and after games.

We became a thorn in the side of Dundalk.

It's fair to say, I believe, that Stephen liked me a lot more when they were beating us all the time.

I FELT WE had a great team going into the 2016 season. And there was a buzz about Cork City.

You could feel it around the city and the county.

The crowds were back, we were in Europe and new sponsors had come on board because we were doing well. The club had been in debt, but we turned the whole thing around. Off the pitch, we were improving too.

I effectively ran the club from a football point of view. Before I arrived, we had one underage team and a team starting in the under-19 league. I put the academy structure in place.

We liaised with the Mardyke Arena and with UCC, improving the facilities available to us. We were a good news story around Cork, and we were in the media a lot.

Straightaway that season, we started winning and winning well.

Within a couple of games, people could see we were a *serious* team. We were winning games 2-0 and 3-0. Whereas in the previous two years, we were always winning by the odd goal.

And again, it became pretty clear very quickly that it would be between ourselves and Dundalk for the league title.

Our first match against Dundalk in the league that season came four games in, the day after St Patrick's Day, at Oriel Park.

We beat them 1-0.

Seáni scored from a penalty.

It was a brilliant victory and one that proved that the win over them in the President's Cup wasn't a fluke.

Seáni had started the season extremely well. He scored twice on the opening night against Bohemians, and had four goals in the first four games of the season. The previous year, with Dundalk, he wasn't even part of their match-day squad for the FAI Cup final.

It remained neck and neck between us and Dundalk for the whole season. We played them at Turner's Cross in June, before our European campaign started, and we beat them 1-0 again, in front of a sell-out home crowd. Stephen Dooley scored the goal.

Two of our off-season signings scored the goals in both wins over Dundalk.

The gap between the teams was a lot closer, no doubt.

We got past Linfield in the Europa League – a 1-0 away win and a 1-1 draw at home.

The City team was building up a head of steam and we came back from the summer break to play the Swedish cup winners, BK Häcken. They had a couple of international players and the standard of football over there, plus the set-up and facilities, was above anything we had here in Ireland.

Häcken had a great all-seater stadium in Gothenburg that held about 7,000 people, with corporate boxes also around the ground.

It was a different level than in Ireland. But there was nothing between us on the pitch.

Seáni scored for us, before they equalised late in the game. It finished 1-1 and we got the away goal, we were in control of the tie.

Häcken were absolutely distraught after it.

They fully expected to beat us.

Ahead of the second leg though, I think they thought… *Ah well, Cork did okay… But we'll beat them over there.*

Turner's Cross was absolutely packed for the game. It wasn't a backs-to-the-wall job for us. We went hell for leather and there was nothing between the two teams.

We won 1-0. Kevin O'Connor got the goal.

It was a major surprise to most people. But we fully deserved to win. We had developed into a very good team. It always looked like we could score. I would say we were at our top at that stage.

We were then drawn against Belgium side Genk.

IN EUROPEAN FOOTBALL, there are levels.

We played the Icelandic team KR Reykjavík the previous year, and they were on a similar level to the League of Ireland, in terms of their ability and the set-up.

Swedish football, and Häcken, was a level above again – all-seater stands, private boxes, great facilities.

And you then go up another level altogether in Belgian football. Genk had a 21,000 all-seater stadium and some top-class players, including Wilfred Ndidi, who joined Leicester City for €20million a few months after we played them. Leon Bailey, a winger, joined Bayer Leverkusen for €20million. Leandro Trossard, who later signed for Brighton in the Premier League, was also in the team. There was a guy named Mbwana Samatta, who went on to play for Aston Villa in the Premier League. And Neeskens Kebano, who signed for Fulham.

Unfortunately for us, they didn't sell their best players until after we played them. Genk were much better than us when we played them in the away leg. Bailey scored for them after about a half an hour.

But we were dangerous, and they were almost hanging on at full-time. Seáni missed a one-on-one and we had our moments. We were very unlucky not to get a draw.

Brian Kerr was doing commentary on the game for TV and he said it was the best away performance he'd ever seen in Europe by a League of Ireland team. And this was in the same year Dundalk went on their European run and reached the Champions League play-off stage.

They eventually qualified for the group stages of the Europa League, while we went under the radar.

We were in the third round of Europe, something which Cork City had never done before. Financially, it was huge for us, worth a quarter of a million euro alone every time we won. If we qualified for the group stages, that went up to half a million euros with an opportunity for more. It also opened doors for more sponsorship, because we were getting so much coverage in Cork.

Every Thursday night for six weeks in-a-row, we had a European game.

The media coverage of the team was wall-to-wall in Cork.

In the county, even the most ardent GAA supporter who couldn't care less about soccer or Cork City was following the team because of the exposure the European games brought. We were the talk of the county and city, and there was a real buzz behind the team.

If we had snatched a draw in the first leg, we would have had a real chance in the second leg. If you can get an away goal, it allows you to play on the counter attack – which is what we were very good at.

Whereas we went back to Cork, and to a full house of supporters, who all wanted us to attack.

I was trying to tell the players… *Listen, let's sit in and play on the counter attack.* But the natural reaction, with the crowd behind us, was to go for it and get at them.

The problem for us was Genk were on that *other* level.

They taught us a lesson. They knew they got out of jail in the first leg. There was a sense they felt… *This shower are better than we thought.*

These boys were on a completely different level. Ndidi in the middle of the park was incredible, as was Bailey on the wing, who destroyed young Michael McSweeney, catching him out for their two goals. Michael didn't do anything wrong, he was just up against a top player.

Alan Bennett got a goal back for us, but they beat us 2-1.

It was still a great run for us. We were competitive in every single game, we never had our backs-to-the-wall and were dangerous in every match.

Dundalk went on their run too, and so we were overlooked a little. When they qualified for the Europa League group stages, Dundalk were calling off games, so we got ahead of them in the table.

They had games in hand though, and it boiled down to the match between us with five games to go. The entire season came down to this match, but we were hamstrung going into the game.

Cork City and Dundalk were all-go during September and October that year.

With the fixture pile-up, Dundalk were getting games moved around because of their run in the Europa League.

Seven of their last 10 games that season were at home. But that wasn't an issue for me.

There was an international break at the start of October, and our match away to Galway United was moved from the Friday to the Saturday night.

We were thrown a curve ball when Seáni was called up to the Ireland under-21 squad for a dead rubber Euros qualifier against Serbia on the Friday – a day before our match against Galway. We had to play Dundalk on the Tuesday in what was effectively a title decider. Ireland couldn't qualify for the tournament, but Noel King wanted Seáni in the squad. Kevin O'Connor was called up too.

Normally, if a team had two players called up to an international squad, the upcoming league game would be pushed back to another date. The FAI, however, insisted there was no rule saying you could call the match off- that it was up to the clubs. We were late into the season, and Dundalk were still in Europe, everyone was playing games, so there was no scope to call the game off.

Fran Gavin, who was competitions director for the FAI, passed it off as Noel King's problem.

So, I got in touch with Noel and asked him to leave Seáni out of the squad because we needed him for the Dundalk game.

Noel said it was his decision to call him up and he wanted him in the squad.

I said, 'C'mon, it's only a dead rubber game… there's nothing at stake!'

'Ah no, we're still playing for seeding for the next qualifying campaign,' Noel replied, which was a load of nonsense in my mind.

I tried my best, but he wouldn't budge. I was very angry about it.

Seáni didn't want to go to the match, he wanted to pull out of the squad. I told him not to, because that would have ruled him out of our games. And could you imagine if he pulled out and people said, 'Oh he wouldn't play for his country!'

Seáni had been in the Ireland under-21 squad during that campaign but didn't start a single game.

Noel King had the best goalscorer in the country at the time in the Ireland squad and he was picking lads from the English non-league ahead of him. Seáni used to be brought on with a few minutes to go.

After pushing for him and going against us, Noel left Seáni on the bench against Serbia. Ireland lost the match 3-1 at the RSC in Waterford – Seáni came on as a sub with 20 minutes to go, when he should and could have been left off.

I knew Noel a long time – he played in the League of Ireland for Dundalk, Shamrock Rovers, Bohemians and Derry City. He had been a manager in the league too, so he would've known where I was coming from wanting to pull Seáni from the squad.

But he didn't budge. It was beyond frustrating.

The whole episode left a sour taste in my mouth.

THIS WAS HOW it was a few days before the two best teams in the country were due to play in a title decider live on television.

We collected Seáni and Kevin after the game in Waterford and drove to Galway to play on the Saturday.

We won 5-0. Seáni scored twice.

On the same night, Dundalk lost 3-0 to Sligo Rovers.

They were only a point ahead of us going into the game on the Tuesday night at Oriel Park. The winner of the game would, in effect, be almost certain to go on and win the league.

Daryl Horgan scored twice for Dundalk in the first-half.

We got back into it and Mark O'Sullivan scored in the second-half, but they hung on and won it.

Dundalk went four points clear of us and, with three games to go that was it, the league was over.

Seáni and Kevin had played their third game in five days.

Both were physically wrecked for the Dundalk match. Seáni could barely tie his laces. He was our key guy, our goalscorer and the whole thing with Ireland had been such a hindrance.

It cost us.

It was the worst possible preparation for what proved to be the title decider.

Dundalk went on and won it again for the third year in-a-row. It was galling for the lads.

We were gutted because we really felt we'd win the league. We had beaten Dundalk three times that season – in the President's Cup and twice in the league, home and away.

We felt we had the measure of them.

With the pace we had up front, we were a completely different animal than the team we had been the previous year.

It was a hard one to take.

But, as the FAI Cup would prove, there was nothing between the two teams.

WE WERE DRAWN against Shamrock Rovers in Tallaght in the quarter-finals of the cup.

It was a tough draw on paper. Rovers were doing well that season – they ended up finishing in fourth place.

But we battered them. We won 5-0. Seáni got a hat-trick.

To go to Tallaght and humiliate Rovers just shows how good we were at that time. It was a massive win. Next up was St Pat's in Inchicore. We beat them 3-1. Alan Bennett scored and Seáni got two goals.

After a replay, Dundalk got past Derry City in the other semi-final.

For the second year in-a-row, it was Cork City versus Dundalk in the FAI Cup final. And for the third time in three years, we were playing each other in a decisive end of season game, after our title decider in 2014.

We had lost the other three games against them, so we were desperate to win it. Dundalk, meanwhile, were going for their second double in-a-row.

Dundalk were still playing in the Europa League at the time. On the Thursday before the FAI Cup final, they played Zenit St Petersburg away. There was some talk they wanted the final to be pushed back.

But because the match was at the Aviva Stadium, the FAI said it couldn't be moved because there was an Ireland rugby game at the ground the following week. Dundalk flew back from St Petersburg after their match, and stayed the two days in Dublin, so I'm not sure exactly why they needed the game moved back.

We prepared slightly differently than the year before for the final. For a start, we weren't staying in Dublin for two nights like in 2015. We had a different bunch of players though, there was a great attitude and, as a result, our preparation was better. There was no one looking to stir it up and complain about the number of free tickets they were getting.

We had 'The Last Supper' on the Thursday night, the first time we introduced it.

The players were feeling the pressure. There was talk of us being the nearly-men – just as there had been in my time as a player before City started winning trophies. This was the talk, even though some of our best players hadn't even been involved the previous year or in the title decider in 2014.

Our team on the day was Mark McNulty in goal.

Steven Beattie, Alan Bennett, Kenny Browne and Kevin O'Connor in defence.

Greg Bolger, Garry Buckley and Gearóid Morrissey were in midfield.

Up front we had Karl Sheppard, Stephen Dooley and Seáni Maguire.

And our subs were Colin Healy, Mark O'Sullivan, Chiedozie Ogbene, Gavin Holohan, Michael McSweeney, Ian Turner and Matt Connor.

We were a dangerous team.

CHAPTER 20

THE AVIVA HAD over 26,000 at the game – our fans took up the whole South Stand behind the goal. There were no local matches in Cork that day, so clubs from all over the city and county took buses full of supporters up to the match. I said to the lads before the game, 'Look at our crowd out there, they've all got up at six this morning to make their way up here to support you!'

It meant a lot to us.

It was a very tight, cagey game. There weren't a lot of chances, but we had the better openings.

McNulty made a brilliant save from David McMillan when he was through on goal. Chiedozie Ogbene had a chance for us near the end to win it after Seáni squared it to him in the box, but Gary Rogers saved his shot.

There was nothing between the teams again and the game went to extra time, where there was still no separating us. There were a couple of half-chances for each team, but it looked set to go to penalties.

We got a throw-in near Dundalk's goal in stoppage time in extra time.

It was going to be the last action of the match. There were 40 seconds left on the clock and that was it… it was going to penalties.

Beattie took the throw and got a good distance on it.

Two Dundalk players went to attack it, but Mark O'Sullivan headed it on. The ball bounced outside the six-yard box and landed with Seáni.

The ball bounced up. Seáni swivelled and turned.

Brian Gartland came across and got his body in the way.

Seáni swung and shot with his left foot, but he didn't get a clean connection. The ball hit off Gartland's leg and deflected the other way.

Rogers was rooted to the line.

The ball rolled over the line… into the far corner. He had scored. The Cork fans erupted. Flares went off. It was a haze of red and green smoke.

We were celebrating on the bench.

The City players mobbed Seáni.

The Dundalk players were on their knees. We thought that was it, the last kick of the game. But the match went on beyond the one minute of stoppage time and Dundalk got a free-kick in our half.

Three minutes into stoppage time. Rogers came up for it and Horgan knocked it into the box. Their header went over the bar and the ref, finally, blew the whistle. The Cork end exploded again. The Dundalk players collapsed onto the ground.

The lads spilled off our bench and started celebrating with the players on the pitch. I went sprinting down the sideline as fast as I could towards the City supporters. The passion, the joy… the relief!

IT IS DIFFICULT to overstate the significance of that moment.

Cork City came from nowhere three years earlier, when there were five players on the books and the club in debt.

We got the crowds back, got the passion back and rebuilt the squad twice.

We missed out in 2014 and '15. Got back in Europe.

But we were written off and overlooked.

We kept coming back, kept looking for ways to improve. There was serious pressure on us because we were missing the big trophy, the big day, that would show how far we had come. And finally, we got it.

Here we were, winning the FAI Cup for just the third time in the club's history, the first time in nine years.

The Cork end was packed, there was brilliant team spirit in the squad, and we won it in the most dramatic, memorable way possible.

It was fairytale stuff.

Not only that, but we also stopped Dundalk, the team that some were saying was the best to ever play in the League of Ireland, from winning a double-double.

There was tension around the match. At this point, the rivalry between Cork City and Dundalk, between Stephen Kenny and myself, between the two squads and the two sets of supporters, was massive.

There was a mutual respect, but it had developed into a grudge match.

Stephen didn't come into our dressing-room to congratulate us, as I had with Dundalk the previous year.

The two teams were incredibly well-matched. It took until the very last minute for us to be separated. It was amazing that it was Seáni who was the one to score the goal too.

He came to us when he was at his lowest point for confidence. It was like a light bulb lit up in his head when he came to us and he realised... *I need to get things going, get this right.*

Seáni probably just ended up in the right place at the right time, and that was it. The cup final goal against Dundalk was his 29th goal of the season.

Only for it actually happened, it would have been too good of a story to be true.

Alan Bennett at the back was phenomenal for us that day, a warhorse, as was Colin Healy coming off the bench. It was Colin's final game for the club. He had been absolutely brilliant for us and had a great career. I was so thrilled for him in particular.

ON THE DAY after the final, we went down the Grand Parade in Cork with the cup. It was a beautiful night, and there were about 8,000 supporters out to welcome us back.

It was what we dreamed of and what I dreamed of when I came back to manage the team. I didn't know how and when we'd get to this point, but it was the dream.

This was the pinnacle of what I wanted to achieve with the club. It took three years, but we got there... and now we wanted to stay there!

I had given my life for this.

The job affects everyone and everything around you... your family, your health, your face, your weight... even your hair!

When I was a player, if the team lost, the players got blamed. But, when I was a manager, the culture had changed, and it was always the manager's fault. Even though, after you prepare the team you can't affect it once the players go on the pitch. Ultimately, it's up to them to carry it out.

The pressure is always there. I was gone from home almost 24/7.

I had a grey head of hair on me!

I had always been involved in football and on the road, but the difference now was I that was in the public eye. There are two local newspapers, three radio stations and a national newspaper based in Cork. It's all-consuming.

But, when you win, when things come together, it becomes addictive.

The tension and pressure and stress gives way to relief, and then contentment and happiness. For the week or two after we won the cup, we brought the trophy around the city and county, into schools and clubs to show the kids in Cork. And it was just brilliant, magical.

Seeing the kids wearing the City gear and their faces lighting up when we'd bring the cup in was special.

Even down in West Cork, where I live, and there's no big affiliation with soccer – in the heart of GAA country – they were behind us and the kids were wearing the City gear.

Seeing how happy Cork people were made it all the more special.

The joy and relief of winning a trophy doesn't last long for a manager, however. In the League of Ireland, it is always hard to build and manage success because the turnover of players is massive. The two weeks after the season ends are, without doubt, the most stressful time.

In some League of Ireland clubs, the manager only coaches the team. But I had responsibility for working within the budget, signing players and letting them go, while overseeing the entire football operation of the club.

Dundalk were a super team but were privately owned. They could pay more and, ultimately, money dictates the players you get.

We were fan-owned by FORAS and I was a great believer in the group. But we were operating at a financial level well below Dundalk.

So, there was no time to relax that pre-season, especially as Seáni Maguire was out of contract. He was free to go. Charlton Athletic and Swindon Town were in for him – two English League One teams.

I met him a few days after the FAI Cup final. There was a lot of pressure on him to leave. His agent was trying to push through a move.

I said to Seáni, 'You've been brilliant. If you want to go to Charlton or Swindon, and your agent wants you to go… he's getting a few bob, then that's fine.

'The only thing I'd say to you is that if you get 25 goals next year for us, then there'll be Championship teams after you.

'You might even be in the Premier League.'

He said, 'Do you think so?'

'You're a goalscorer. Anyone would take you… Burnley, Newcastle… teams in the Championship or even the Premier League if you're scoring goals.'

I tried my best to convince him, but I thought he would go, and I would have wished him well.

Yet, the next day, Seáni rang me.

'I'm going to stay!'

I WAS THRILLED.

It's unusual for a player to turn down a move to England. But I genuinely believed he was better than Swindon or Charlton.

He was more than that if he really wanted it.

Seáni signed a new contract and we put in a release clause of €150,000. We knew we'd lose him eventually, but to have him for the new season was fantastic.

The only setback we that pre-season was losing Kenny Browne, who left us on the eve of the season starting, to join Waterford. He had been brilliant for us, one of the best centre-backs in the country, but he wanted to go back home. Luckily, we signed Ryan Delaney, a Wexford lad, from Burton Albion on loan and he developed a great partnership with Alan Bennett. It was like they'd been playing together for 10 years.

Greg Bolger was quite close to Kenny and I got worried that he would leave, so I made a move for Conor McCormack, who was with Derry City. Michael O'Neill, who managed him at Shamrock Rovers, told me Conor was a brilliant player and he was always very busy when we played Derry. He was a tenacious player, hard as nails.

I'd heard there had been a little bit of unrest in Derry. A number of players under contract were on the move. So, I rang Conor and we met a few days later. He was a great guy and I knew he'd fit in. He agreed to join us.

We also signed Jimmy Keohane from Sligo Rovers. Jimmy was a very intelligent fella and he could play almost anywhere – right-back, left-back, right wing, left wing and in the centre of the park. No matter where I played him, he did a job for me.

And Shane Griffin, a left-back, joined us on loan from Reading.

For the second year in-a-row, we managed to improve the team pre-season. And, once again, Seáni was incredible.

After he signed a new deal, I recommended that he work with a strength and conditioning coach, and focus on his speed over five yards. As a striker, you cannot work enough on your pace – being quick over five and 10 yards, that's the key to a striker's game.

I told him, 'Strikers who have speed think they will always have it and when they lose it, they can't get it back. So, keep working on it. There's more in you'.

He did three or four 40-minute sessions a week.

When we came back for pre-season training in January, Seáni was half a stone lighter and was so good. It was like having two players.

Seáni had been brilliant the season before. But he was now twice as good. He went to a level where he was untouchable. He was a leader too, incredible in the dressing-room. He was never injured and never moaned. And he got a buzz from being the guy who was getting the goals.

Seáni was the top player in a team full of top players.

We took off like a train.

THERE WERE TIMES in the 2017 season when I'd be driving home to West Cork in the car going to myself… *I didn't even have to say anything to them!*

We were that good from the very first kick of the ball that year. We played Dundalk in the President's Cup at Turner's Cross and battered them 3-0.

Seáni Maguire, Kevin O'Connor and Karl Sheppard scored for us. We were on a roll.

In the first game of the league season, we played Finn Harps up in Donegal. The game shouldn't have gone ahead. The pitch passed three inspections, but it was like a bog, waterlogged.

We were bursting to play because we had travelled up and it was an overnight trip. There was a big crowd there; the match became a real scrap and there was genuine potential for an upset. But Seáni scored a beautiful goal for us.

We won 1-0.

Dundalk had a slow start to the season. It didn't matter though because we started like a house on fire and won our first five games.

We played Dundalk at Turner's Cross in the sixth game of the season on a Saturday afternoon. The Cross was absolutely packed, there was nearly 7,000 there and we would've got many more in if there was more space.

At half-time, we were two up, Karl Sheppard scored both. We just tore straight into them, didn't give them a second on the ball.

Conor McCormack shut down Patrick McEleney brilliantly in the middle of the park, something we identified during the week in our video analysis. Conor didn't give him a chance to play.

We were deadly when we broke forward then, so clinical.

For our first goal, Stephen Dooley, Seáni and Shep all linked up in a great counter-attack. Seáni and Shep then combined for the second goal. We ended up winning 2-1 and fully deserved it.

City were top of the table with six wins from six games, six points clear of Dundalk, with 15 goals in those games.

I joined Cork City as a player in 1986. I was there during the good times, the bad times, and the very bad times. I was there when we had great team spirit, and when we were on our knees. And I watched on as a supporter when the club had success and when Cork City almost went extinct.

I saw it all with the club.

It was quite clear, in 2017, that this was a special team, and it was a special time in the club's history.

Seáni got the glory, but it wasn't just him that made the difference for us. Our front three of Seáni, Karl Sheppard and Stephen Dooley were incredible. The movement and interplay were just brilliant, teams couldn't live with them.

Dooley was probably the most underrated of the trio and the most underrated player I managed. He was special, a total introvert but highly intelligent. He set up so many of Seáni's goals and probably went under the radar because of his quiet nature.

He was tough on himself at times. If he played nine perfect crosses but misplaced one, he'd be in the dressing-room afterwards worrying about that one bad cross.

Stephen was a player I never had a go at, ever. I would always put my arm around him and encourage him, try to make him see just how good he was. Because I honestly thought he was a genius on the pitch.

If Dooley had more arrogance, he could have played in the English Championship.

He was that good.

And that was the level we were at, too.

THE INTEREST IN Seáni never went away.

But, as I had said to him a few months earlier, this time it would be from a Championship club... not League One or Two.

Not long after the Dundalk game, in maybe the first or second week of April, Seáni's agent rang and said that Preston North End wanted to do a deal.

Peter Ridsdale, who was an advisor to the club's owner and had previously been Leeds United chairman, rang me and said they wanted to sign Seáni.

The English market is controlled by agents, so deals are usually done before you know it.

So, as far as we knew, personal terms had already been agreed between the player and the club.

It was a question of what the transfer fee would be.

Our hand was strengthened because we could block the deal – well, not completely block it, because you can't stop a player progressing to a higher level. The transfer release clause was €150,000, plus add-ons.

And the transfer market didn't open again until July 1.

We had some bargaining chips.

There were a few meetings with Ridsdale. Pat Lyons, the club chairman, and Seán Ó Conaill, the club's solicitor, were also there.

There were a few arguments with Ridsdale over the fee. He was a nice man, but, of course, he wanted to try and get the best deal for Preston.

Their opening offer was €100,000.

I said, 'No chance!'

City were looking for €200,000.

In the end, after some posturing and nonsense arguments, we agreed on €150,000, with another €25,000 after Seáni played 20 games for Preston. There was also a sell-clause where Cork would get 15 percent of his next transfer. It took 40 minutes to agree on the transfer fee, but it could have been settled in 40 seconds!

Afterwards, there were some people saying we should have got more money for Seáni given his form. But, at the end of the day, you're dealing with a person, a good person, who had put his trust in me and the club.

Seáni could have left for nothing at the end of 2016.

He cost us nothing and he was unbelievable from the day he signed for Cork City. He was on his third contract with us and had the chance to earn 15 times more with Preston and play at a higher level.

There was no way the club or I could stand in Seáni's way. It was about getting the best deal possible, which I felt we did. All that was left was to agree on was when Seáni would leave City for Preston. Ridsdale said, 'Well, we need him to join us the second week of July because we'll be over in Cork for pre-season'.

That wasn't going to work for us because we needed Seáni for the European games at the start of July.

In 2016, we had done incredibly well in Europe and reached the third round of the Europa League. We needed Seáni there for as long as we could keep him.

I had chatted to Seáni previously about this. I said to him, 'Realistically, Preston won't need you at the start of July... they'll be in pre-season and you'll be at your peak of fitness. They won't need you for a couple of weeks.

'But, when they're in Cork, you can go down and train with them for a week and keep playing games for us.' Seáni was fine with that.

I said to Ridsdale in the meeting, 'He can train with you guys that week Preston are in Cork. But he stays with us for the European games.'

We agreed that Seáni would join Preston on July 24, which was a Monday. Preston later came in for Kevin O'Connor, who was good friends with Seáni; they were in the Ireland under-21 squad together. We got one over them for Kevin, because there was no release clause in his contract. And we already had a left-back to replace him, Shane Griffin.

Kevin was a great lad, but it was easier to lose him because we had a ready-made replacement.

It wasn't that simple with Seáni, because he was irreplaceable.

So, as soon we shook hands on the deal, I thought to myself... *I need to bring some games forward.*

I wanted us to play as many games as possible for as long as we had Seáni.

CHAPTER 21

CORK CITY WON the first 12 games of the season.

Finn Harps 0, Cork City 1.

Cork City 4, Galway United 0.

Drogheda United 1, Cork City 4.

Seáni scored 11 goals in those 12 games.

He was phenomenal, unstoppable, just a level above every player in the league.

Cork City 2, Sligo Rovers 1.

Shamrock Rovers 1, Cork City 2.

Cork City 2, Dundalk 1.

Just like in the Dundalk match at Turner's Cross, we absolutely blew teams away. There was no arrogance in the players though.

The City lads were all lovely guys, honest, decent, hard-working fellas who gave it their all every day.

Limerick 0, Cork City 3.

Cork City 3, Derry City 0.

Bohemians 0, Cork City 2.

But it wasn't overconfidence.

They were battering teams every week. It was all 2, 3 and 4-0 wins.

Limerick 0, Cork City 3.

St Pat's 0, Cork City 3.

City were hammering everyone we came up against.

I remember sitting at matches and we'd be three-up with 10 minutes to go, and I'm going... *This is just great!*

I couldn't get enough games on the board before July, when we were due to lose Seáni. We needed to get as many points as possible to hold our lead over Dundalk.

Cork City 2, Bray Wanderers 1.

Cork City 5, Finn Harps 0.

In the 13th game of the season, we draw away to Galway United... 1-1.

It was frustrating for us because Galway got relegated that year.

They had a good team but would go and drop points against Bray Wanderers and UCD after giving us a game.

THE DIFFERENCE BETWEEN good players and very good players is consistency. And we were incredibly consistent through the season.

After the Galway result, City beat Drogheda United 5-0 at the Cross. We beat Sligo Rovers the following week 2-1 and then beat Shamrock Rovers 4-1 at home.

Gearóid Morrisey scored a fantastic goal that night, a wonderful strike from about 25 yards out. Gearóid was probably the most naturally talented and skilful player within the group. He played in the middle of the park and was strong with both feet, great in the air and tremendously fast over 10 and 15 yards.

The following week, we went to Oriel Park to play Dundalk for the last game before the mid-season break. We were 15 points clear. If we won the game, we'd be 18 points clear at the halfway mark of the season.

It was a beautiful summer's evening. The ground was packed, and we brought up a big crowd of supporters with us. Martin O'Neill and Roy Keane, the Ireland management team, were at the game, possibly scouting Seáni. Some people might have thought Cork were going to play for a draw in the match. But we never approached games like that.

We were confident and we felt we had Dundalk's number. In the last seven games between City and Dundalk, we won six.

Seáni came close with a shot after about 20 seconds; he hit the side netting. I remember there was still smoke from the flares on the pitch, Dundalk hadn't touched the ball, and we had already nearly scored.

We were that dangerous.

Our first goal was a classic City move from that season.

There was some intricate play between Dooley and Maguire at the edge of the box. Dools played it out wide for Sheppard, who squared it into the box. Seáni got free in the box, timed his run and finished it past Rogers. It was top class stuff from start to finish.

For our second, Johnny Dunleavy took a very clever, quick throw, firing it against Shep's back! He then curled a cross into the box. Seáni got away from his man and scored with a deft header.

In the last minute, the ball bounced free in the Dundalk box and Seáni slotted it away.

We had gone away to Dundalk and won 3-0.

Seáni got a hat-trick, his first for the club, against the team that let him go, the team who had been our nearest rivals.

It was incredible.

I was pinching myself afterwards, going back down the road to Cork, thinking to myself… *We're 18 points clear!*

Dundalk knew for sure coming off the pitch at Oriel Park that Cork City had gone to another level.

On our way back to Cork, we didn't have a care in the world. It was magical.

We were so far clear of Dundalk that it looked to everyone that we would certainly be champions.

The general feeling was that there was no way Dundalk would catch us. It would have taken a terrible collapse, but we all knew we needed to get as many points on the board as possible.

The City players knew that night that we would win the league, but not in an arrogant way, and it wasn't like we were going around saying it. We just knew no one could live with us.

We won the first 12 games of the 2017 season. After drawing the 13th game, we went and won the next eight league games.

After coming from nowhere in 2014, we were the best team in the country four years later. It was such a special time in the club's history.

Until Seáni left near the end of July, it was a dream. He continued to score goals for us after the mid-season break, including in Europe, which justified our insistence to hold onto him for the European games.

Cork City were drawn against FCI Levadia Tallinn, an Estonian team, in the Europa League. Getting through to the next round was worth €225,000 to the club and we went through in style. We beat Levadia 2-0 away in Tallinn – Garry Buckley and Steven Beattie scored the goals – and we hammered them 4-2 at the Cross a week later.

Seáni scored a hat-trick in the second leg, and Shep got the other goal. It was a great night.

In the next round, we were drawn against AEK Larnaca, a team from Cyprus, who had 12 Spanish players in their squad.

There was nothing between the two teams in the first leg at Turner's Cross, which was Seáni and Kevin's last home game for us. But Larnaca were technically good, and they also 'went down' at every opportunity to try and get something from the referee. It was a frustrating night for us, and then they scored from a corner, which was a sloppy goal from our perspective.

I felt confident we would score in the away leg, but it wasn't to be. It was another frustrating game for City. Larnaca scored in the first-half with another cheap goal – a shot was deflected, and their striker scored with a header. Again, they were buying cheap free-kicks, and made it difficult. A few decisions went against us too. It was also a stifling hot night.

Overall, Larnaca were better than us, but we hadn't played as well as we did in the competition the previous year against Genk.

It was Seáni and Kevin's last game for the club. In between the European games, Seáni equalled Pat Morley's record of scoring 20 goals for Cork City in a season. He scored our second goal against Bray Wanderers in a win at the Carlisle Grounds, a great header with eight minutes to go. He was sick not to break the record, but he got those 20 goals in just 21 games, an incredible ratio.

There were 400 or 500 Cork supporters at the match, everyone knew Seáni was going, and they gave him a great reception.

CITY HAD A bit of money after the transfers of Seáni and Kevin, and we did something I had never previously done as manager of the club – we paid a transfer fee for a player. All our deals were usually free transfers.

We signed Kieran Sadlier from Sligo Rovers. Sads was a talented guy, a forward with incredible technique, right and left foot, and deceptively good in the air. But he wasn't a centre-forward like Seáni, and we used to play him on the wings.

When Seáni left, we lost more than just his goals. He had a huge presence and was a leader. Seáni was vocal and he was the main guy in the dressing-room.

You can't just snap your fingers and find someone else like that. It was impossible to directly replace him.

Seáni was unique, there wasn't another player in the country like him.

Three months after he left us, Seáni made his debut for Ireland at senior level; he got a great reception when he came on against Moldova at the Aviva Stadium.

It would have been great if there had have been 'Cork City' beside his name when he was capped, rather than 'Preston North End'.

IN THE LEAGUE, our form dipped after Seáni left, which was inevitable. The team didn't reach the heights that it had with him, but that would have been the case for any side. It almost became a matter of seeing out the campaign, because it had been obvious since the summer that we would win the league. We won 21 of our first 22 league games. We were unbeaten for most of the season. The football we played, and our goalscoring, was phenomenal.

We won the league title with two games to go in the season.

Just like 12 years previously, we wrapped it up against Derry City at home. Turner's Cross wasn't at full capacity for the game because one of the stands had to be closed for repairs after it was damaged in a storm, but there were still 5,000 there and the supporters made a lot of noise and got right behind us. The game finished 0-0.

The supporters rushed onto the pitch, the players celebrated, and the Shed End chanted… 'CHAMPIONS OF IRELAND…

'CHAMPIONS OF IRELAND…

'WE KNOW WHAT WE ARE!'

The relief was immense. We led from the start and fully deserved it. Cork City had been the best team in the country that year, by a distance.

But, by the time we won the league, it was like some people had become bored of us. There was some criticism. We lost a couple of games and the narrative was… 'Cork City stumbled to win the league'… or… 'Oh, well you had Seáni Maguire.'

Yet we created history with our record for the first two-thirds of the season. We had been absolutely brilliant and had run away with the title. And Seáni wasn't even getting on the bench for Dundalk two years previously, remember. Nobody else wanted him when we signed him.

Some people also didn't take into account that we were a provincial team. And when a provincial club – a team from Derry, Sligo or Cork – wins the League of Ireland, it is a phenomenal achievement.

Firstly, regarding resources, on a practical level it is more expensive to run a club from outside of Dublin. Every second week, you are travelling up and down the country, and that's expensive – the cost of overnight stays, buses, food and all the rest.

Meanwhile, if you are a Dublin-based club, or near Dublin, the cost of buses, food, and overnight stays are minimal compared to a team from Cork or Derry, Sligo or Galway.

Shamrock Rovers, for example, would play St Patrick's Athletic, Bohemians or UCD in Dublin, and teams like Drogheda United, Bray Wanderers and Dundalk, are just a trip up the road.

Dundalk, who trained in Dublin City University, could be in Dublin within 50 minutes. It was just down the road. So, there were relatively few trips down the country or overnights or expenses. If we played Shamrock Rovers in Dublin, we would be home at three o'clock in the morning.

People didn't realise the amount of travelling there was for a team from the country.

There was also a much bigger media presence in Dublin, which can put teams under pressure because the coverage can be quite blinkered.

Cork City were only really seen when we came to play in Dublin. So, they would have a different opinion of us than someone who watched us every second week in Turner's Cross.

You'd see pundits talking about us, and I'd know that they were never at a City match in Turner's Cross. But they would have been at Dundalk matches, because it was only up the road from Dublin.

So, as a provincial team, there were factors that we were up against that the average supporter might not always appreciate or consider.

Ultimately though, that didn't matter.

Cork City came from nowhere back in 2014, and had finally won the title.

Not only that, but we also stopped Dundalk from winning. Some were proclaiming that they were the best team in League of Ireland history. Yet, here we were… champions.

If it wasn't for Cork City, Dundalk would have won four doubles in-a-row.

And, once again, they were waiting for us in the FAI Cup final.

THE FAI CUP was a different story for us as Seáni and Kevin didn't play in any rounds of the tournament.

I used that to try to motivate the players.

I would say, 'Lads, people haven't given you the credit you deserve. If you win the cup, they can say nothing about you. But if you lose, they'll point to Seáni Maguire leaving and say you weren't good enough without him'.

It was true.

We hadn't been given the credit we deserved for winning the FAI Cup in 2016. The talk all focused on Dundalk and how they were 'tired' from their games in the Europa League. And then in 2017, we weren't given the fullest credit we totally earned for winning the league. It came from certain sections of the 'League of Ireland' media, the pundits on television commentating on our games.

We'd be listening to the TV and hear… 'Oh, City are crawling over the finish line'. It irked our lads. Some people would say we were in Dundalk's shadow. But I would say we were a thorn in their side.

Cork City came from nowhere, with fewer resources, and won the trophies Dundalk would have won. That probably explains why Stephen Kenny took a few digs at us. He accused us earlier that season of 'manufacturing penalties'.

I thought that was an astonishing remark to make.

At that point in the season, we had scored 26 goals in 10 games and only one goal was a penalty. And, anyway, if you're attacking as well as we were, with mobile, skilful players like Seáni, Stephen Dooley and Karl Sheppard, you're going to get fouls in the penalty area.

Cork City had become an annoyance to Kenny.

Seáni's success probably annoyed him too, because it was a question everyone used to ask him. 'How did you let him go… and why didn't he do this for you?'

I didn't work any magic with Seáni. I just got into his head and he started to improve. It was the combination of right club and player at the right time.

Kenny was trying to throw stuff at us to knock us off our course though, to disrupt us. It became tit for tat between us, but a lot of the stuff was nonsense.

If I was 10 years younger, it would have been more heated and he would have got more of a reaction out of me. But I saw it as a sign that we were obviously doing something right.

It flared up again the week of the cup final with the Karl Sheppard stuff, but I tried to rise above it. We didn't let it knock us off course the week of the final, when it easily could have derailed us.

It was the biggest game in the club's history, a chance to make history, and we were absolutely desperate to get over the line, while proving some people wrong in the process.

WHEN KIERAN SADLIER picked up the ball and walked towards the penalty spot to take our final penalty in the shootout, my first thought was... *He never misses.*

And he didn't.

When Sads scored the penalty, I've never felt relief like it.

Cork City had won the double for the first time in the club's history.

My whole body, I could feel the adrenaline rushing right through me.

The relief... the relief was just incredible. It really did fell like a house had just fallen off my shoulders.

I was shaking with the nerves and the relief, all that tension had faded. And I was so thrilled for the players for what they had achieved. They worked their socks off from the start of pre-season in January to the last kick of the ball the following November.

They were a great group of players, worthy of being the first Cork City team to win the double.

I was thrilled for the supporters too, everyone who came up from Cork... all the families. It was just brilliant to give them a day out that they'd always remember... and a special season to remember!

I was delighted for the coaching staff... John Cotter, Lisa Fallon, Phil Harrington and Liam Kearney.

I couldn't have asked for better staff.

They were great people, brilliant at their jobs and fiercely loyal. Even if they disagreed with me sometimes, whatever was said stayed in the room.

It was only later that I could feel happy about everything we had achieved, particularly when we brought the cups back to Cork and around the schools and clubs… that was special.

I could never relax though.

In my entire time as Cork City manager, I don't think I could ever relax. The job was in my head 24/7. The job takes a toll on us all… us managers, on our mind and body, and on those around us. You carry the stress home, and the family are sometimes exposed to it. It never leaves you.

If we lost a game, my head would be wrecked for a day or two after it. Absolutely *wrecked*. I would take defeats personally, like it was my fault. Ultimately though, it wasn't.

There are so many aspects of the job you can't control.

But you can't get the same adrenaline rush from any other job. You can go work in a bank and have no worries when you log off.

As a football manager, or someone involved in sport, you almost just live for that adrenaline. People might say, 'The job has made you go grey or lose some of your hair, is it worth it?' Absolutely.

This was what it was all about for me.

This was my passion.

The pressure was always there, but the main difference after achieving success was that you stay on a high for the next while. The team had delivered, and the supporters were happy.

After winning the double, everywhere we went with the trophies, to the schools and the clubs, the kids were looking to get into photos with the cups and it was just brilliant to see how happy we had made people.

It was what I always wanted.

The club was in a very good place.

The passion was back.

We were winning trophies.

Everywhere in the city and the county, you could see people in Cork City jerseys. It was a fantastic time.

Yet, at the same time, that builds more pressure.

People get a taste for success and they want more, especially in Cork. So, coming towards the end of 2017, when the buzz died down a little and we were coming up to Christmas – before we went back to pre-season – I was saying to myself...*We must make sure we can go again!*

CHAPTER 22

BEFORE WE WON the double, my contract had been up. Cork City offered me a new deal, a two-year contract, about 10 days before the final.

I didn't sign it until after the game though because I would always be wondering… *Am I doing a good job? Do the board want me?*

If they didn't, I wouldn't stick around.

I very much felt that the board had to want me.

I had only ever done two-year contracts, because in football you can only do so much, and you only get so much time. I always felt that you do two years and then you assess it. This was a new cycle.

My fifth season as manager of Cork City. The only problem this time was that Seáni Maguire was gone and we were looking for a centre-forward.

Achille Campion, our French centre-forward, was a good guy, but he wasn't going to fill Seáni's shoes, even though he got us one of the most important goals in the club's history. I set about rebuilding the squad.

I had re-signed most of the players that I wanted to keep but I was still five or six short of where I wanted to be. I had a couple of deals lined up, but the other three top clubs had those players lined up as well. It's just how it always is.

The players are on holidays, and you're trying to bed things down so you can go on holidays in four weeks' time yourself!

Up until then in Irish football, only Dundalk paid 52-weeks. It was something we had never done; we had 42-week contracts, but we had started down that road and it gave us a bit more clout, even if it was still difficult to get players, who were, of course, looking for the best deal.

Generally, the Cork guys would stay, but the guys from outside, if they could go back up to Dublin and earn two or three hundred quid more, it was a no-brainer.

We had the appeal of Champions League and European football and challenging at the top, playing in front of 5,000 in the Cross every second week.

It was huge exposure for a player. If he was good enough, everyone would know him and it would be a great place to play, he'd be a big fish in a small bowl. As I've said, we did well with that pitch to players.

But those two weeks after the season finished were a nightmare, even after we won the double.

STEPHEN DOOLEY'S CONTRACT was up, and he was free to leave.

I wanted him to stay.

I was very close to him and he was a brilliant footballer, totally underrated. I couldn't believe it when I got him. I had worked so hard to sign him because Stephen had to trust you, he was a really deep, quiet guy, but I built a strong relationship with him.

Wycombe Wanderers were interested, and Dools wanted to go over on a trial for a few weeks, which he could do because his contract had expired with us.

Meanwhile, Coleraine were going for the league title against Linfield in the Irish league. Stephen's from Portstewart, outside of Coleraine, and a few of his buddies were playing for Coleraine. They were only a few months into the season, and he had the chance to join them. He was under enormous pressure to join Coleraine.

I knew it was going to be very difficult to keep him at Cork City and so it proved. Stephen signed for Coleraine, before joining Rochdale in League Two the following May. It was tough to lose him.

ALL OF A sudden, we had lost two-thirds of the forward line that won us the double – Seáni Maguire, who was now an Ireland international, and Stephen Dooley.

If Stephen Kenny hadn't said what he said in the press conference the week of the cup final, we would probably have lost Karl Sheppard too.

I went looking for a new centre-forward, someone who could get us 20 goals a season. If we got one who could do that, Cork City would be close to winning the league in 2018. I spent quite a bit of time in the UK that winter scouting players, but we couldn't really get the right fit.

Graham Cummins was the one guy who did stand out.

He was from Cork and we felt he might fit the profile of what we were looking for. Graham was playing for St Johnstone in Scotland.

Eventually, we agreed with St Johnstone to sign him on a free transfer.

Graham changed our game because his strengths were in the air – he was good in the air, so we needed to get crosses in. He wasn't going to run in behind like Seáni, that wasn't his game. We were going to have to be more direct. Cork City were going to be a different side than when we had Maguire, Dooley and Sheppard all playing together. They could interlink, play one-twos and run in behind defences.

We were phenomenal with the three of them, our intensity and our passing and the goals we scored the previous two years were electric. Graham simply had different strengths.

I brought Josh O'Hanlon in too. I thought that maybe there might be a bit of the Seáni in there, as he had been in England, it didn't work out for him and he came home. He was talented – a strong, mobile striker. But it didn't go to plan.

I wasn't expecting to find another Seáni Maguire, even if some people were saying, 'Oh, you never really replaced Maguire!'

It wasn't possible to replace him, no one could.

Ryan Delaney and Greg Bolger also left us. Ryan's loan deal was up, and he returned to England. Greg joined Shamrock Rovers as he had lost his place to Conor McCormack. We did our best to freshen up the squad again for 2018, but we weren't as strong as we had been going into the previous season.

I had to make the most of what we had.

JUST BEFORE THE 2018 season began, we got terrible news. Liam Miller had passed away after being diagnosed with pancreatic cancer.

He was just 36, and died a few days before his 37th birthday.

We had known for months that Liam was very sick, but it didn't lessen the shock. He and his family had moved home from the United States after his diagnosis and treatment. Liam's passing was incredibly sad for everyone in the club, especially Mark McNulty, who was very close to him.

Liam was very polite and nice, he had a lovely manner about him, and he was always very thoughtful in a quiet way. He had played for two of the biggest clubs in the world – Celtic and Manchester United – and had a season with us back home in Cork.

His passing shocked everyone in Cork.

Two days after Liam passed away, we played Dundalk at Oriel Park in the President's Cup. The game itself would typically be a big occasion – the meeting of the league champions and the FAI Cup winners, or, in this case, the double-winners and the league runner's up – but it was inevitably subdued.

We still wanted to go out and give a performance for Liam.

Yet, at half-time, we were two down.

The game was played in awful conditions – snow, sleet, rain and wind, the elements threw everything at us. We rallied after half-time. Karl Sheppard, Barry McNamee, Kieran Sadlier and Graham Cummins all scored, and we won 4-2. We were now seven games unbeaten against Dundalk and found a way to win without Seáni Maguire, Stephen Dooley and the guys who left.

People have said to me in the years since, 'Oh, 2018, that wasn't a great season for you!' The narrative has been that Cork City had a bad year.

But during the first half of the year, we were brilliant. We won six matches on the bounce going to into the final game before the summer break, at home to Bohemians. It looked like we weren't going to score, until the last minute, when Gearóid Morrisey smashed home a winner. Turner's Cross was still rocking.

We stayed at the top of the table with 53 points from 22 games, a point ahead of Dundalk. In seven days though, it all changed.

OUR FIRST MATCH after the break was away to Dundalk. The game was live on RTÉ on a scorching hot night and there wasn't a lot between the two teams.

Dundalk scored at the start of the second-half. I brought Josh O'Hanlon on as a substitute and he managed to get us an equaliser.

It was 1-1 going into stoppage time.

A draw would have kept us top of the table, with one more game to play against Dundalk at the Cross later in the season. Both teams were so far ahead of the rest at that point, that the result of this game was going to have a massive say in who won the league.

In the first minute of added time, one of the Dundalk players broke free out wide and crossed into our penalty area.

Pat Hoban went to attack the ball but couldn't reach it. The ball missed him, hit off Sean McLoughlin, our defender, and went in.

That was it. 2-1 to Dundalk.

Rather than us being top of the table by a point, we were now two points behind Dundalk after losing to a stoppage time own goal, one of the most unfortunate goals you're ever likely to see.

We were desperately unlucky.

A week later, we played Shamrock Rovers at Turner's Cross. Until that point, we had a one hundred percent record at home. And we looked on course to keep that going when Karl Sheppard won us a penalty. Kieran Sadlier was our penalty taker. Sads had incredible technique, both right and left foot; he had a great strike of the ball and he was unbelievable at taking penalties and free-kicks. He had scored all five of his previous penalties, including the kick that won us the double.

Sads struck his penalty to the bottom left corner, but Gavin Bazunu, Shamrock Rovers' 16 years old goalkeeper, saved it.

The match ended 0-0. You couldn't write it.

All of sudden, in a week, we took one point from six and lost ground on Dundalk. We lost it from then. Our form was okay for the rest of the season, but we never got to the levels we had in the first half of the year. Also, we lost Mark McNulty and Gearóid Morrissey to injury.

A few days after the Rovers game, we played our first Champions League match in 12 years.

We were drawn against Polish champions Legia Warsaw, who had knocked Dundalk out of the competition the previous year and reached the group stages. Legia were a serious team, but in the first 20 minutes we missed a sitter when Barry McNamee was through on goal, but he scuffed his strike.

Graham Cummins came off the bench in the second-half and went through one-on-one with the goalkeeper, who saved his shot.

Our game-plan was working, we were frustrating Legia but just couldn't take our chances. And then, 12 minutes from the end of the match, they scored a wondergoal, a strike from 25 yards out.

Turner's Cross was packed for the game, and we could feel the air suck from the crowd. The whole team, the supporters, everyone was stunned.

But that's just how it is in Europe.

For Irish teams, goals are very hard to get because we're playing opposition that are better than us. To get a result, we have to be at our absolute best and just hope our keeper plays well and the opposition have an off night.

Over the last few years, the coverage of the League of Ireland has reached its highest level. Yet, the product, the level of the teams, is more or less the same as it has been over the last 30 or 40 years.

In other European countries, football is also fully professional, it's an actual industry. Whereas, in our league, clubs are lucky to survive year-to-year and most don't pay players out of season. Inevitably, other leagues and teams are stronger and we're going to be underdogs going into most European matches. I'm not sure people factor this in when judging Irish teams.

After the game, the Legia players were looking to swap shirts with the City players. We couldn't let them… we needed the jerseys for the return leg.

That's the level Irish clubs are at.

After giving them a good game and coming close to getting something from the game in the first leg, Legia beat us comfortably in the return leg, 3-0.

CORK CITY WERE still in Europe after losing to Legia. We were drawn against Rosenborg in the Europa League. Ahead of the game, there was some false expectation from some people, thinking Rosenborg weren't that good, and we were going to beat them.

And there was a bit of talk going around, I'm not sure where it began, maybe on social media, saying… 'Sure, Rosenborg aren't that great, they're only a Norwegian team!'

It was so far off the mark. Rosenborg were an excellent team.

The first leg was at Turner's Cross and we started very well. For the first 20 minutes, we absolutely tore into them and made it difficult. But, as I learned from every European game that I was involved in with Cork City – from Bayern Munich to Galatasaray to Slavia Prague as a player… Larnaca to BK Häcken to

Genk as a manager – you must score when you get your chance and hope that the opposition have an off night.

It didn't happen that night.

Rosenborg had top players, internationals such as Mike Jensen, Jonathan Levi and Nicklas Bendtner.

You didn't have to be a genius to sit back and watch and go... *These guys are a level above Cork.*

The way they passed the ball, and the movement was top class. Rosenborg scored twice in the first-half, Levi getting both.

When the first goal went in, the crowd at the Cross went completely flat. When the second goal went in, the City players went completely flat.

We lost 2-0 and the defeat knocked us back.

We were deflated.

So much so, in hindsight, I think it would have been better if we had no European games left after the Legia defeat.

We would have got back on track and had a chance of catching Dundalk in the league. Instead, the Rosenborg game killed us. In the second leg, they hammered us 3-0. The players' confidence was knocked, they were just gutted.

Rosenborg were Norwegian champions. They had never lost in Europe against an Irish team – and knocked both Dundalk and Sligo Rovers out over the previous few years. They were a seasoned European team, with international players.

Yet, the talk ahead of the first leg in Cork was that they weren't all that good, and we should get something from the game. There were a few airheads on one of the soccer programmes saying... 'Ah, you know, Cork should get through that tie'.

They didn't have a clue.

As a result, I think that the City players thought that the gap between Cork and Rosenborg was a lot closer than it actually was.

We had always held our own in Europe. But this was the first time we had been well beaten over two legs. The players were demoralised, and they didn't get back on track for a while.

I tried to rally the troops, to get them going again, because we still had a chance to catch Dundalk.

If we won our next game, at home to St Pat's, we'd go top of the table.

Pat's scored after half-time on a blisteringly hot day in August – the match was on a Sunday afternoon – and we got a late equaliser.

We pushed and pushed for a second goal, but we were leggy after the Rosenborg game, and we had a few injuries, and our strength in depth wasn't what it had been. At full-time, it was like a balloon had been burst.

We played Sligo Rovers next at Turner's Cross. Dundalk had lost to Shamrock Rovers earlier in the week. If we won, we would have been three points behind them.

There was another big crowd at the Cross that night and we got off to a perfect start. Sheppard scored after about 10 minutes with a header.

I'm thinking to myself... *This is great, we're back in it... There's a real opportunity here!*

We battered them but couldn't get a second goal.

The Cork supporters started to get edgy and Sligo scored a soft goal. The crowd then became aggressive, you could feel the tension and the frustration.

We kept going for a second goal but were caught in the last minute. Raf Cretaro went through and scored with five minutes to go, another soft goal from our perspective.

They beat us 2-1.

I was on the sideline thinking... *Can we just rewind it back to two weeks ago?*

You can't though.

It was gone.

The players knew it. The supporters knew it.

I knew it.

But if anyone else was in any doubt about us retaining the league title, our next game against Bohemians confirmed it beyond any question.

The first-half was the worst 45 minutes I oversaw in my time as Cork City manager.

I ALWAYS KEPT in touch with footballers from Cork who were playing in the UK, because a lot of them were keen to come back to Cork later in their careers, such as Alan Bennett and Liam Miller.

Damien Delaney was one Cork guy I had stayed in touch with. Damien played left-back for Cork when he was a young lad. At the time, I was coming towards the end of my playing career.

He had a very good career in England. Damien played over 100 times in the Premier League for Crystal Palace and was with Leicester City, Hull City and Ipswich Town. He had indicated to me that he would love to come back to play for Cork City and I always said to him, 'Don't leave it too late!'

In January 2018, he told me that he would come home and join us during the summer break after his contract with Palace expired. I thought that would be perfect because it was just before our European games.

In truth though, I expected him to join a team in the Championship.

Yet, we met up when he was home at Easter and said he was definitely joining us.

He was adamant.

I was delighted.

Damien was 36, but he was fresh because he hadn't played many games for Palace that season and was still very fit. He had also played at a very high level and would be a good presence in the dressing-room.

It then came time to discuss money, and he asked how much we could offer him. 'I can't offer you anything, Damien!' I said, laughing.

I didn't have big money to give him. I certainly didn't have anything close to Premier League wages.

As every player who signed for Cork City knew, every penny was hard to get, and I ran the club like it was me parting with my own money.

Damien was a very intelligent guy and he had done well from the game. He had a house in Cork, and we agreed a reasonable wage for us – which was a couple of hundred a week.

There was later talk that Cork City were paying Damien five grand a week. Which was utter nonsense, a completely made-up figure, a lie.

Damien was a brilliant guy, great in training and a model professional, which is why it's desperately unfortunate that his time with Cork City will be remembered by some for that game against Bohemians, a result that effectively brought an end to our time as league champions. Damien came into the team when the season started to turn against us. He was there for our European games and did okay.

I shouldn't have started him against Bohemians though.

Damien's wife had their first child the week of the game and I asked him was he okay to play. Like any player, of course he said yes. But I should have pulled him from the game, I should have taken the decision myself.

Damien scored an horrendous own goal after about 10 minutes of the match. He passed the ball back to Peter Cherrie, who was in goal for us as Nults was injured – he passed from the corner of the penalty area and the pass was overhit and went into the net.

Peter was probably as responsible for that goal as Damien, but it was easier for some to slag the guy who had been playing in the Premier League a few months beforehand. It didn't get much better for Damien or City after that.

Just before half-time, after we got one back, Bohs scored again and we were 4-1 down. It was awful, the worst we ever played in my time as manager.

There was no question that I had to take Damien off. I felt desperately sorry for him, because he had such a brilliant career.

The match finished 4-2 and we lost the chance to close the gap on Dundalk to three points, ahead of our match against them the following week.

That was it for us, our title challenge was over and there was no way back.

Dundalk beat us 1-0 at Turner's Cross and went nine points clear.

AFTER BEING TOP at the summer break, the season slipped away from us and it was small margins that cost us – last minute own goals, brilliant goalkeeper performances, wondergoals. Cork City weren't as good as we had been in the double year when we won 20 out of our first 21 games, a record for the league.

It's hard to imagine any team being that good.

But small things started to go against us and then bad results affect confidence. The Rosenberg game, as I've said, killed us, knocked the players back and led to more poor results. It all seemed to flip so quickly, which is how it goes in football sometimes.

It was something similar with Damien.

He found the step back difficult. I think he thought, being a Premier League player, that it was going to be easier than it turned out to be. But the intensity is very high in the League of Ireland.

It's not about the money for players, because some only make a living from the game here. But they fight for absolutely everything and games are often decided by fine margins. It's a tight league, where momentum can change quickly and go against you.

After a couple of bad results in Europe and the league, we couldn't recover. I think maybe Damien needed a full pre-season training with us, rather than coming in mid-season, to do well.

That was the story of our season though… ifs, maybes and buts.

A bounce of the ball can change results which affects everything and how you're perceived. Overall, our team wasn't as good as in 2016/17.

By half-time in the Bohemians game at Dalymount Park, the City players' confidence was on the floor. Damien was singled out for criticism on social media. I didn't play him after that, and I think he was a disappointed with me until he left the club at the end of the season.

But I couldn't help that.

I always did what I felt was right for Cork City. I assembled the squad, coached the players, put guidelines in place and gave them all encouragement.

I was never worried about what people or the media thought.

My only responsibility was to Cork City.

BUT THE CRITICISM was soon all aimed my way.

Damien may have had a bad game, but I was the manager who signed him, so questions were being asked.

The lies circulating about the money we were supposedly paying him didn't help. After the 2018 season ended, I was at a Cork City supporters' Question and Answer evening and was asked by a fan about Damien.

'He didn't play well, what happened?'

I gave an example of a young fella, 19 or 20, going out to meet a girl on a date, and on both sides there might be the best of intentions, to do things right – they both dolled themselves up! But, for whatever reason, it didn't happen, it didn't work out. *It happens.*

That's how it was with Cork City and Damien.

We both had the best of intentions, but it didn't work out.

Considering how good Cork City had been on the pitch and with our signings over the years, and how brilliant a career Damien had, you would imagine both parties would have been given the benefit of the doubt.

Yet, at this point, patience and perspective were in short supply.

CHAPTER 23

A COUPLE OF days after the Bohemians defeat, Liam Miller's tribute match was staged at Páirc Uí Chaoimh in Cork. I was on the organising committee with Roy Keane and Michael O'Flynn, the property developer.

It was a bittersweet but really good day.

A team of Ireland and Celtic legends played against a team of Manchester United legends. The game was staged on a Tuesday afternoon, but it was still a sell-out, with 43,000 in attendance. It was the largest crowd ever in Cork for a soccer game.

The match raised one and a half million euro for Liam's family and charities in Cork. And there was a gala dinner that evening at Cork City Hall. The room was packed, everyone involved in the match was there, and the journalist Trevor Welch was on stage asking questions of the people involved in organising the game.

Trevor came to me and, in front of the audience, asked about Cork City's title challenge fading.

'Well, Trevor, I came out tonight to enjoy the night,' I said with a smile.

Even there, at a black-tie dinner, with some of the most famous footballers from Ireland and the UK to have ever played the game, there was no hiding place being Cork City manager.

Cork is a unique place to be a sportsperson.

I SAW THAT, coming in from the outside, and I always felt that there was an unbelievable confidence within the county when it came to sport.

It was a fantastic place to be when you were winning, everyone knew you and there was great pride in the team. But, at the same time, if you weren't doing well, Cork people would let you know. There was pressure all the time.

It had been 33 years since I moved to the county, and 32 years since I first played for Cork City, but not a lot had changed.

In Cork, you were expected to win.

And the crowd followed successful teams. We had achieved tremendous success between 2014 and '18. Yet, after a few bad results, the pressure was on.

'The one thing about sport that everyone in this room knows,' I continued, 'is that when you're down you get kicked and kicked again. And there is only one way to respond and that's to get back up and that's what we have to do.'

At that point, I was getting plenty of kicks.

I WAS BEING criticised by a section of City supporters, which is part of the job, especially when results go against you. But it was really starting to ramp up around the time of the Bohemians defeat. There was speculation about my position as Cork City manager.

After each disappointing result, it was… 'Oh, is Caulfield in trouble?'

I found this strange given the success we had and where the club had been before 2014.

Some people wanted to put me in a box.

If they spoke to Colin Healy, Alan Bennett, Stephen Dooley, Seáni Maguire or any of the players I had at Cork City, not one of the players would say that we went out to put 11 men behind the ball.

That never happened. *Never.*

We played to our strengths. When the pass was on, we played it.

Yes, we were strong defensively, but there was no shame in that.

We pressed ferociously, closed down the opposition all over the pitch and didn't give them a second on the ball. No other team in Ireland could match Cork City for intensity. When we had Seáni Maguire and Stephen Dooley up front with Karl Sheppard, the three of them were phenomenal. Opposition teams couldn't live with us.

We were electric, tore teams to shreds, and we had the best defensive record in the league. There was no talk of 'philosophies' when we won 21 out of 22 games in the 2017 season, a record.

In 2016 and '17, we played Dundalk 10 times and won seven times, only losing once.

We were an outstanding team.

Cork City lost top class players and the nature of Irish football means it's almost impossible to find another Seáni, an Ireland international and the only player in recent years to leave the League of Ireland and excel in the Championship.

Dooley wanted to come back to us in 2018 after the season in Northern Ireland ended with Coleraine. But we couldn't afford him, we didn't have the money. That was the reality of the situation and there was nothing I could do.

I put him in touch with Rochdale. Brian Barry Murphy was a coach there and we played together for Cork. Stephen joined and has been brilliant for them. He's a magical player. And players like that are almost impossible to replace.

So, when you can't replace them, you have to adapt.

In 2018, Graham Cummins was our centre-froward and he was good in the air, so we got the ball wide, and hit crosses into him. He wasn't going to run beyond a defence. I knew as soon as we signed him that we had to change our system. If we got the ball wide and got a good delivery into the box, he would score five or six out of 10 chances he got. But that brought more criticism, especially when we hit a bumpy patch. And Cummins wasn't as consistent as we'd hoped. I had to question his attitude, and many of the lads felt that he wasn't a team player. He had spoken about filling Maguire's boots, but he fell a long way short of that ambition.

It even affected the players.

Professional footballers nowadays are exposed to this talk more than I ever was as a player, and one or two of the City guys would probably have been thinking… *We're being criticised unfairly and don't deserve this.*

I used to say to them, 'It doesn't matter once you win, lads. There was no problem at the halfway point of the season, when we were top of the table'.

Professional football is a business. You have to compete, and you have to win. A manager could go into Cork and try to play beautiful football, record high possession statistics.

But if they don't win games, they won't last.

Some supporters in Ireland are brainwashed by English football though. They view the game here through the prism of how they follow the sport across the water. We are in an era where Irish football is totally dominated by English football, and we have almost become like English supporters, hysterical about everything.

It was never that way in the old days.

When I was a player, the manager almost decided when he was going to leave a team. There was no hype or hysteria. The City team I played in was given time to develop. But now, in every sport, if there's a bad run of form, straightaway the calls are to get rid of the manager.

It has almost become as important to manage your supporters. Most are level headed. But there is an element that mirror the impatient, English persuasion where even winning doesn't seem to be enough.

For the younger breed of supporter, there's no patience.

I think, ultimately, they forget that we're not paid millions to do this. There's no real football industry in Ireland, no investment in the sport.

There was only so much any manager could do and I had to be realistic and honest, even if others on the outside weren't.

I had spent over 20 years of my life involved with Cork City.

I had seen it all with the club.

And the one thing that could turn it all around, that could completely change people's perceptions and the narrative, was to win.

And we still had a chance to do that in 2018. We were still in the FAI Cup.

A few days after Liam's memorial match and dinner, we had a semi-final against Bohemians back at Dalymount.

BOHEMIANS WERE FRESH from beating us 4-2, when the first-half was the worst half of my time as Cork City manager.

Bohs were a very good team, plucky and in good form at the time.

The match was shown live on RTÉ on a Sunday afternoon. In the first-half we played well and had a couple of half-chances but didn't take them. It was a tight match, quite scrappy, which was inevitable in a semi-final.

In the second-half, the momentum shifted.

Bohemians took over and Dinny Corcoran scored with about 20 minutes to go. Dalymount erupted, the Bohs fans were making a big noise and I felt sick in the pit of my stomach.

That looked to be it for our season.

For the first time since 2015 we wouldn't reach the FAI Cup final. We kicked back into life and started to get a few chances. Sheppard had a volley that went just wide and Graham Cummins had a header saved. With two or three minutes left, Conor McCarthy was fouled in the box and we were given a penalty.

Kieran Sadlier stepped up.

Sads was a brilliant penalty taker and had scored every kick he had taken for us – expect the one that Gavin Bazunu, the 16 years-old Shamrock Rovers goalkeeper, saved earlier in the season, So, that was on my mind, of course, when he put the ball on the spot. Everything had seemed to go against us over the previous few months, so anything that might have looked to be a certainty before, I was no longer so sure about.

Sadlier held his nerve though and scored.

The game finished 1-1 and went to a replay.

When we got on the bus to go back to Cork, there was no doubt in my mind that we would win the replay.

In the first-half at Turner's Cross a week later, we were unbelievable. We were at it, we tore into Bohs from the start of the game and pinned them back in their half. The Cross was rocking, there was 4,000 at it and the rain was pouring down.

We scored twice in the first-half – Graham Cummins and Karl Sheppard got the goals.

It was Cork City at our best.

Bohs got a goal back in the second-half – Ian Morris scored from about 45 yards out with an incredible strike that hit the crossbar and went in.

We deserved to win though and saw out the game.

We were back in the FAI Cup final again for the fourth year in-a-row. And, for the fourth year in-a-row, we would play Dundalk in the final.

CORK CITY STOPPED Dundalk from winning the double in 2016 and had the chance to do so again.

We also had a chance to make our own history, the opportunity to win our third FAI Cup in-a-row, and be the first team to achieve that feat since the great Shamrock Rovers of the 80s.

I felt we had a chance of winning the final because we had a good history against Dundalk. I think they knew we had their game plan sussed over the previous 18 months and knew that they had to change in games against us.

Dundalk had improved in 2018, despite losing their two strikers at the end of '17, Ciarán Kilduff and David McMillan, who were great at running behind defences. I feel that they then mirrored us in a way by re-signing Pat Hoban to play up front. Hoban was brilliant at holding the ball up and laying it off, a very strong player. He helped Dundalk get up the pitch.

They began playing against us in the same way we used to play against them – high energy and high pressing; they let us make the first pass, then they would go and try to win the ball.

Dundalk had resources and money that we didn't, so that made it easier for them to rebuild if they lost a key player. I found out later they were also good at blocking players from leaving the club because they could pay them good money to keep them.

I could never keep anyone, not really. For a start, I couldn't afford to! But also, morally it felt wrong to keep a player when you'd no intention of using him. They also had the added appeal of being close to Dublin.

On paper, we shouldn't have been able to compete with them as we did. Yet, here we were, in the final against them again.

The previous finals between Cork City and Dundalk had all been extremely tight, something Stephen Kenny blamed on us trying to stifle games. We were trying to win and weren't going to play into his hands by being open.

IN THE 2018 final, we played very well. Sean Hoare scored a soft goal to give Dundalk the lead after about 20 minutes, a header from a corner.

But we went straight back down the pitch and Karl Sheppard won us a penalty.

Kieran Sadlier scored and we were level again. In every other final between us, there hadn't been a goal in normal time. There had now been two in two minutes.

We gave as good as we got in the game, and it looked like it would be going to extra time again.

And then, with about 15 minutes to go, we lost the ball in midfield.

Dundalk got the ball wide to Sean Gannon, who crossed into the box. Our defenders were running back towards the goal. Patrick McEleney ran into space in the box and scored with his header.

It was another gut punch for the Cork players.

We didn't feel sorry for ourselves though. We came back at Dundalk and created some chances to get the equaliser, but it wasn't to be.

Dundalk won, and won the double.

The final few months of the season had been tough for Cork City, and for me personally. But such is the way in football, if we had have won the cup final the whole perception of our year would have changed.

I think there was an element of fatigue or overfamiliarity amongst our supporters. There wasn't the same excitement for the cup final as there had been in previous years. Maybe it was because we had been in the final too often, but whatever it was, there wasn't the same buy-in.

The final had over 30,000 at the Aviva Stadium. But the crowd we took up from Cork was the lowest of all our finals. In many ways, it felt like the end of a cycle, possibly the end of an era.

I HAD ONE year left on my contract and I knew we were facing a massive rebuild. There were a few players leaving us and I knew we needed to rebuild the squad quickly enough so that Cork City could stay in the European places.

I felt it was possible.

We did it in 2015 and '16, on both occasions improving the team.

I identified around 10 players who could improve the team, seasoned guys, around 25 and 26. It was a tough challenge to overhaul the squad again, but it could be done.

There were talks with the chairman Pat Lyons and the co-chairman Pat Shine about altering the business model of Cork City being a fan-owned club and bringing in outside investment. It was required to keep the team competitive.

FORAS had saved the club, but the model had reached its limits.

Meanwhile, Stephen Kenny was being pushed for the Ireland manager's job. A few weeks after the cup final, he took over as under-21 Ireland manager with an agreement to become Ireland manager in 2020.

Stephen and I had our differences. Sometimes, it went too far, and other times it was nonsense. At that time there wasn't any great love lost between the camps.

And Kenny and I were never going to be buddies and go for a drink together. But I still backed him for the Ireland job.

In the League of Ireland, we get such a battering.

And sometimes, it was hard to argue against it.

But people involved in the game here have to stick together, to support each other.

The job is hard enough as it is.

CORK CITY WAS at an important juncture after the 2018 FAI Cup final.

Pat Shine agreed with me.

Pat was a founding member of FORAS, the group of 650 fans who ran the club. He was instrumental in saving Cork City. Pat was a very quiet and reserved guy, but highly intelligent and his word was gospel. He was like the godfather of the club. No one would go against him.

He and I recognised that Cork City couldn't progress any further working within the current model.

Understandably, from the supporters' point of view, they didn't want to take risks, especially as they saved the club from going bust in 2010. They didn't want to put the club in jeopardy, and, of course, neither did I.

I treated Cork City's money like it was my own money. Every cent the club spent was accounted for. And I knew, and the board knew, every cent that was coming in and out of the club.

But we had reached the limits of what a supporter-owned club could do.

We needed a model like Shamrock Rovers, or German clubs, where there was a mix of outside investment and supporter ownership.

PAT SHINE AND I agreed that this was the next step for Cork City. We were at a very preliminary stage, but we were talking about where we needed to get to. The supporters would still have a majority share, but there would be outside investment.

It needed to happen.

I had been involved with Cork City from 1986 and experienced the boom and bust cycle. From bust in 1989 to winning the league in '93; bust again in 1995 to winning the FAI Cup in '98.

It was the same story in my years away from the club, from winning the league in 2005 to almost becoming extinct in '10.

I always felt we had to stop this nonsense and put a secure structure in place. We wanted to take Cork City out of the quagmire and bring it to a level where we would always be in the top three or four.

We might not win trophies every year, but we'd be competitive. I was thinking to myself... *We must bring the club away from this nonsense of boom and bust, up and down.*

I had many conversations with Shine about it and we agreed that outside investment was needed for Cork City to continue competing. He knew we had to do something because it had become such a big job operating the club.

From taking over Cork City when it was on its knees in 2010, FORAS were now running a club where the turnover was over €2million a year. We had grown our money year-on-year, because we went from challengers to winning the FAI Cup and then the double. Cork City were a successful team, we were in Europe every season and had the biggest attendances in the country. This brought more money in, and we were getting stronger and stronger.

But success also makes a club fatter, expenses go up. We now had a General Manager, and sales and marketing personnel.

Success increases expectations too.

Yet, in truth, Cork City had been overachieving between 2014 and '18. We couldn't pay the same money as Dundalk, not by any means.

Even in 2017, when we won the double, we were probably the third or fourth highest payers in the league, behind Dundalk and Shamrock Rovers, and possibly Derry City and St Pat's. City also expanded, we now had six more teams than when I joined as manager and the operating costs all came out of the same football budget.

After the FAI Cup final, I knew the budget would be cut. It would create a strain, but I was prepared for it and was determined to try and rebuild the squad again.

YET, EVERYTHING CHANGED when Pat Shine passed away two weeks after the FAI Cup final.

It was very sad for his family and the club. Pat was widely respected.

He was close to Pat Lyons, the chairman, and between the three of us, we had a strong working relationship. I knew I had the full support of both.

Pat's passing rocked the club and had massive implications. It created a power vacuum and allowed people to go on solo runs.

At the time, we were trying to agree a budget for the new season. Two of the proposed budgets were rejected by the board. I told Pat Lyons that the club was playing Russian Roulette. We had so much success, people would be expecting it to continue but we weren't going to be able to compete for players.

I told Pat, 'There's a serious chance we could drop off with this budget!'

He said to me, 'This is the best budget we're going to get through, John'.

The third proposed budget was accepted, but just barely. There were three votes for it and three against it and Pat Lyons, as chairman, used his casting vote to get it approved.

The budget was down significantly from the previous season – by roughly €300,000, much more than I ever expected. I knew this would cause problems for City in 2019. We wouldn't be able to attract the same quality of player.

So, I took the decision with the management team that we'd try to rebuild the team. Of course, we couldn't publicly say that we weren't going to be able to compete for the league after four years of being in the top two. But that was the reality of it.

In Cork, the people really don't want to hear excuses. They'd tell you to just get on with it. And they're right in a way.

Yet, we had massively overachieved all along.

In the seasons before I took over as manager, Cork City finished mid-table. They weren't within an ass's roar of the title.

And then, 11 months later, we were in the last game of the season up at Oriel Park against Dundalk for the championship.

Did I expect that? Absolutely not.

I wanted to bring the passion back, to put systems in place and get the club competing again. Cork City came from nowhere and stayed at the top for five years.

Success causes problems though.

In City's history, we've only won three league titles and they've been every 12 years – 1993, 2005 and 2017. Which is strange.

Shamrock Rovers won back-to-back league titles in 2010 and '11 under

Michael O'Neill. They reached the group stages of the Europa League. Michael brought the club forward massively. But he left after they couldn't agree a contract for his third year.

What does that say about success and expectations?

Sligo Rovers won their first league title in 35 years in 2012, when Ian Baraclough was manager. Sligo won the FAI Cup in 2013.

Less than a year later, Ian was sacked.

It's incredible when you step back and look at it. Success brings more people on board, it creates problems, as I was about to find out. When I was appointed in 2014, FORAS struggled to get the board completed with seven members, but now there was huge competition at the AGM to get on to the same board… everyone wanted a slice of the action.

CHAPTER 24

THE BOARD WAS coming to the end of its term. After Pat Shine died, Pat Lyons stepped down. He had planned to stay for another year, but he was close to Shine and rang me two days before Christmas and said he was going to step away. I knew this wasn't good for me.

Lyons saw that there were going to be massive changes coming.

But at the same time, I was always practical and would deal with people as I found them.

The budget had been sanctioned. It wasn't what I'd hoped for, but I was just working away and trying to sign players.

We still had a lot of signings to make.

I was still having difficulty signing a centre-forward. I was just in my normal mode, getting ready for the new season.

At the AGM in January, six new members were voted on to the seven-person board of Cork City. The old board were guys involved in business, in their forties and fifties, and they had a lot of experience.

You can bounce ideas off people like that.

The people on the board are volunteers, they give up time to do the role. And maybe it's no different than being a manager, they go to games and, if the team isn't doing well, they will be asked questions and maybe they get fed up taking abuse.

FORAS members had their hearts in the right place, but as I was about to find out, you need to have business experience on the board.

The new board had a different profile. It was a younger board, for instance, with two 27-year-olds on it. In football terms, it was like scrapping your first-team squad and putting your under-19s into the first-team and saying... 'We'll let them develop'.

But that was how it worked with FORAS, any member could challenge and go on the board. It was a democracy, and these younger lads were voted in.

I knew every Cork City supporter who was regularly at Turner's Cross and these were all good people that had been voted onto the board.

They were all supporters, and they had the best of intentions.

Only time would tell if they were out of their depth.

I was there to help them.

The only one who remained from the previous board was Declan Carey, who had joined the previous year. Carey was voted in as chairman at the AGM in January. You would imagine that a newly appointed chairman should meet with the manager as soon as possible. Pat Lyons and I met every second week.

But Carey and I didn't have our first meeting until a few weeks later.

I felt that, from the moment the new board was formed, that not everybody wanted me as manager. There was little doubt in my mind about that.

So, between the FAI Cup final in November and the middle of January, my two biggest allies at the club were gone, our ideas to advance the club wouldn't be fulfilled, my budget was slashed, a new and inexperienced board was voted in – and I had a strong feeling that I wasn't part of their plans.

I had one year left on my contract and while I had aimed to rebuild the squad and drive the club forward again, it now became more about just seeing out the season.

This type of thinking was totally against the plans we had for the club about taking Cork City to the next level.

IN PREVIOUS YEARS, I would meet with the board on average once a month.

At the meetings, there would be questions and answers about the first-team and the football operations at the club.

My first meeting with the new board wasn't until April 23 – three months after they were elected.

It may seem strange, but I genuinely don't believe that the new board understood that they had to meet regularly with the manager. I'm not sure that they were given the correct information.

The meeting came a day after we drew 0-0 with Sligo Rovers at Turner's Cross on Easter Monday. After 12 games into the season, we had 12 points and were mid-table. We were having trouble with injuries and scoring goals. There were tight games that went against us, such as the opening match of the season away to St Pat's, where they got a penalty after three minutes, scored and beat us 1-0.

The players' confidence drops after results like that and it becomes tougher to pick them up for the next match.

It's a vicious circle.

I got a call to say the board meeting was going to be that evening. I had no relationship with them, so I wasn't sure what to expect.

Results hadn't been as good as they had been in previous years, and I was in the final year of my deal. I went into the meeting thinking that maybe the board would ask me to step down.

WHEN I WALKED into the room, there were eight people on the other side of the table, including Declan Carey and the board members, and the General Manager Paul Wycherley.

The meeting started with a bit of a bang.

Carey was very direct from the beginning.

He told me results weren't good enough, that the fans weren't happy. The crowds were down, he continued.

I wondered if they all wanted me to storm out of the meeting? And if it was 10 years ago, when I had more of a temper, I would have met the questioning in the meeting head-on, no problem.

But I kept my cool.

I was fearful of nothing. I had nothing to hide.

I gave up a very well-paid job in Diageo to do the job, and there was no doubt in anyone's mind that Cork City was my passion.

If they wanted to ask me questions, I'd answer them.

I sat and listened, waiting for my chance to have my say.

Carey had been on the board the year before, when none of the other members were, and he'd never been all that vocal. He barely said a word, that I could remember.

Now though, he was saying plenty.

I was told that they were having problems with cashflow and the club was in debt to the tune of approximately €130,000.

My view was that I was there to help them.

I knew it was difficult for the board. They were already being criticised by supporters and I could sense they felt that pressure.

To me, however, it didn't seem like they knew what they were doing.

I had experience, they didn't, but they almost treated me like… *Oh, he's just a football manager.*

YET, THE WHOLE football finance came from my pot. Everything, from travelling expenses to coaching wages, to running the underage teams and first-team, it all came from the one football fund. This fund also had to cover the wages of the non-football staff.

I had been managing Cork City since 2014. I had bought and sold players, rebuilt squads and overseen the growth of the club. I was there to help.

On the commercial side of the club, there were four people who had been hired since we won the double in 2017. They were paid some of the highest wages in the club, at a time when Cork City was struggling to bring in money.

People in the club had to justify themselves, of course, but it felt like it was just me on trial.

I was writing, taking notes of what they said, and after a few minutes, when there was a bit of calmness, I asked how much of the debt was due immediately?

I was told: 'The 130 grand isn't all due now!' Only €80,000 was due.

So, I drew a line through 130 on my page… and wrote 80.

They then said the crowds were down at Turner's Cross.

I had all the budgets for the gates.

'At the moment, we are down about 22 grand for the season on crowds,' I informed them. 'We're down 2,200 for the first six matches based on yesterday's game. This is a projected figure, and this is where we are.'

The chairman came in and said, 'Yes, but going forward we are going to be way down!'

I said, 'Lads… this is my first meeting with you all… and thank you for meeting me, but this club was in a much worse condition during the first couple of years I was here as manager.

'And we had plans to work around it.'

One of the members asked, 'Do you think we can turn it around?'

'Absolutely!' I told him.

I also told them all that this was the first time Cork City were going to be seeded in the European draw, which was huge. It gave us an advantage and a great chance to progress. Advancing to the next round of the Europa League was worth a quarter of a million euro. If we won the first round, there'd be no money problem.

'There is no guarantee we will win, of course, but our biggest game of the season is in two months' time in Europe.'

I was trying to get them to see the bigger picture. I said, if they wanted, we could sell some players. I had one or two players lined up to sell, including Seán McLoughlin. Seán was a local lad, a defender, who came into the team in 2018. I could have sold him to Doncaster Rovers in January 2019 for €80,000, but I refused because it was an insulting bid. I knew we could get more for him.

I told the board that at the meeting. I then said that there were players we could move on. There were a couple of the English lads brought in, for instance. We signed James Tilley from Brighton on loan and he had done okay, but I could let him go. There was also Dan Smith, who we signed on loan from Portsmouth, that we were going to let go anyway. 'There are a couple of key players that other clubs will want,' I said. 'If the situation was that bad, we could sell players. I can understand that your heads are down. You can't see any light at the end of the tunnel.

'But in football, this is the way it is.

'In football, there will be times like this when we're down.'

I felt that their heads were in the sand a little and they didn't really know how things worked in football.

Which wasn't a surprise, as it was their first board meeting with the manager.

AFTER THE MEETING, I felt that most of the board members realised I could help and most came across really well, very genuine.

I had told them we could turn the situation around.

Our upcoming European match was the key game, it could make or break our season. I told them we could still make the top four and qualify for Europe.

There were also the cups and we needed to do a bit of readjusting to the squad.

And worst case scenario, we can then clear out some players in the summer. We had that plan for the last four or five years, but we never had to use it, thankfully. It wasn't an irreparable situation.

For the previous five seasons, we were in the top two. Less than 18 months before this meeting, we won the double.

The situation could be turned around, no doubt.

The meeting lasted 45 minutes. After the confrontational start, it ended with five of the seven board members interacting and being cooperative.

It was very positive.

They thanked me and I told them I would help in any way I could. I think they appreciated what I was saying because, in my opinion, they didn't understand what was required. They didn't have the experience or knowledge.

Some of the board may not have changed their minds about me, but I stated my case and offered constructive ideas to help get the club out of a tight spot.

The board was made up of good people, they were all supporters and I was sure that they knew it was best for the club to work with me for the remainder of the season.

Seven days later, I was gone.

CORK CITY'S NEXT match was away to Derry City at the Brandywell.

We lost 2-0, another tough result.

We had a load of injuries and it was clear the team was in transition, but we just couldn't get a result.

We played Finn Harps a few days later at Turner's Cross. There were only 1,600 at the game. It was tough to see, especially considering how big our crowds had been. As I knew though from the time I came down to Cork in 1985, however, the Cork fans follow success and we were in a sticky patch.

Kevin O'Connor, who had rejoined us on loan from Preston North End, scored with a free-kick in the second-half. We had some chances to score a second but missed them. Finn Harps equalised with about 15 minutes to go.

We couldn't get a second goal and it ended as a draw.

It wasn't a good result for Cork City.

I wasn't worried for my job after the game though because it had been such a productive meeting with the board the week before.

The following morning, a Tuesday, I had everyone in at Bishopstown for a recovery session.

We were playing Bohemians on Friday and they were in very good form. As we were going out to training, I got a text from one of the security guards. He was working the night before.

He heard that the board had made the decision to sack me.

I felt a mix of everything – anger, sadness, disappointment. I was sick in the pit of my stomach, but also numb. I didn't say a word to the management or players though.

I then got an email around 10am saying that they wanted to meet me at six o'clock. I knew that was it then.

I gathered my thoughts and went out to training.

I was always very bubbly around the club. I always had this idea that you don't bring your problems to work.

I had brilliant staff and brilliant people around me at Cork City, and the motto was always… 'If you've a problem, don't bring it into work'… especially if you're part of the management team. You lead from the top and your personality dictates how the day will go.

As a manager, you're there to be bright and positive.

You have to create the atmosphere so when the players come in, there's no moaning.

Even if you're about to be sacked, or you know this is your last training session with a club to which you have given over 20 years of your life.

WE TRAINED AND there wasn't a word about my meeting that night.

When the players left, I called the coaching staff in.

I said, 'Look, I'm not one hundred percent sure but they called a meeting for six. I think I'm going to be gone this evening!'

They were all really shocked.

I had great staff… loyal, brilliant people.

I said, 'Don't say anything to anyone for now, and I'll let you know as soon as I leave the meeting. I'm hearing on the grapevine that they're going to sack me later'.

Cork City, being a supporters' owned club, meant it was almost impossible to keep a secret. The coaching staff all left.

I was alone.

There were so many things running through my head.

It was difficult to even know where to start.

I had been with Cork City from 1986.

I was there for the first few years when we were terrible, getting hammered up and down the country.

I was there when we won our first trophy.

I was there when we played our first European game, when we got battered 5-0 in Moscow.

I was there when we drew with Bayern Munich at Musgrave Park.

I was there when we won our first league title at the RDS in 1993 in the play-off.

I was there when the team almost beat Galatasaray, when we were brilliant under Damien Richardson and played tremendous football.

I scored Cork City's first goal in the Champions League. I was there when Rico walked away, when the club almost went to the wall and were in the depths in the mid-90s.

I was there when the team came back and won the FAI Cup.

I played more games for Cork City than any other player. Pat Morley and I still hold the record for most league goals for the club.

I watched on during the 2000s when Cork City won the league in 2005, and watched in horror as the club almost went to the wall.

I took over as manager in 2014 with a very simple aim – to bring the passion back, to bring the fans back and make Cork City competitive.

We did that.

We took off and went toe-to-toe with Dundalk.

We built a team, stripped it down and rebuilt it again.

I drove the length of the country countless times to scout and sign players. I took a chance on Seáni Maguire and watched him develop into the best player in the country, an Ireland international.

I watched us win 21 out of 22 games – blow teams away. No one could live with Cork City when we were at our best.

We won the double for the first time in the club's history.

I was there!

I RANG HOME and told Gráinne that they had called a meeting for that evening.

She asked me what I thought would happen?

'Yeah, I'm gone… I think!' I told her.

I went to my office and just started packing up my stuff.

I had loads of coaching books and manuals, lots of little mementos. I packed it all up into my car and drove off.

That evening, there were only three at the meeting – Declan Carey, Conor Hallahan, who was the club treasurer, and Colm McAuliffe.

Carey spoke first and said, 'We had a meeting last night, we were going to write to you, but we felt we should tell you in person'.

I said, 'Well Declan, I'm delighted you had the decency to at least tell me in person, because it would have been an insult to send that!'

Colm and Conor both thanked me, and said it was a difficult decision.

I said, 'Lads, I disagree with your decision. I think it's wrong. I think you have made a bad move. But you have the power and it's your choice.

'There is no doubt I could turn this around. We only had a meeting a week ago where I gave loads of solutions.

'But it's done now.'

I didn't want the meeting to go on, and neither did they, they seemed extremely nervous.

'I want no messing!' I told them.

'I want everything sorted with my contract!'

They said, 'Absolutely, of course.'

I asked how they were proposing to handle my exit. They said they would announce it the next day.

'Okay, fair enough,' I continued.

'What I'm going to do lads is… I'm going to come in here tomorrow morning at eight o'clock and I'm going to have everything typed up. I want you to have everything typed up and we all sign this off.'

They said they would pay me monthly for the remainder of my contract, rather than up front. We agreed to meet the following morning to sign off on my exit.

Almost six years as manager of Cork City ended in around seven or eight minutes.

I WALKED OUT and felt a sense of relief.

The sadness of leaving Cork City hadn't kicked in.

It had been a difficult season. I felt isolated.

From the new board's first day, I felt that they were not behind me. It wasn't that we were not getting on. There was no communication.

No relationship.

The team wasn't as good as it had been. I was under pressure and I felt it because I didn't have the support of the board.

I felt I was very much on my own, even though I had brilliant and loyal staff.

It was like I had been on a drug for five years. It's only when you look back, you think... *Never get yourself in that situation again.*

But because Cork City was my passion, I couldn't help it.

The club solicitor rang me, Seán Ó Conaill. He was disappointed to see me go, but he said he would draw up the terms for my dismissal. I didn't want any hassle by bringing in an outside solicitor.

I drove home and told my family the news.

The relief was huge.

Gráinne was happy it was over, which may seem strange, because she knew how much the job meant to me.

But at the same time, I think she was just on edge for five or six months because the team hadn't been doing as well as it once had.

She knew I wasn't happy, and that the pressure on me was enormous.

I was in a bubble.

Now, it had been burst.

I was relieved for my family, relieved that I wouldn't have to keep putting them through it anymore.

I SPENT MOST of the night going back and forth on emails with Seán Ó Conaill. By around eleven o'clock, we he had drawn up the agreement.

The following morning, I got into my car and left the house to drive to

Bishopstown. I turned on the radio and on the 7am news bulletin, there it was, news of me leaving Cork City.

I went into the boardroom at 8am.

We signed what we had to sign and that was it.

Jesus, it's all back to square one now.

It hurt me to think it, but my feeling at that moment was that Cork City was only going to go one way.

We… They won't be able to compete for a number of years.

The club had dropped off, and once you drop down a level, you lose the quality to attract players and it becomes a vicious circle. Also, the board was inexperienced, and didn't seem to realise that they needed to bring in money too.

I later met a buddy of mine for lunch, who I worked with for years, and he offered me a job! I said I was going away for a while and we'd see, but I hadn't even given thought to anything like that yet.

I wasn't even sure what I was going to do that weekend.

I didn't have to think about training the next day or any of those immediate thoughts that would have run through my head on a constant basis over the last six years.

WHEN I SAT down and gathered my thoughts later that day, I was still very raw about what had happened, but also very disappointed at the way the club was going.

Cork City was founded in 1984. I moved to Cork in 1985. I joined Cork City in 1986 and played for the club across three decades.

I had been there the whole way through. I saw first-hand the good times and bad times. There were now people running the club who probably had only started following it since 2005, when Cork won the league.

Or maybe they started supporting around 2003, when Pat Dolan took over as manager.

I don't think they would have been able to understand what Cork City had been through, the problems that we had to overcome to keep the club going.

I saw nothing but trouble in the months ahead for the club.

But also, I had to factor in that maybe these people didn't view it like I did, like Pat Lyons and Pat Shine did.

There was probably an element of supporters going… 'Well, we don't want the budget to go higher. We don't want outside investment. We had a few good years, some big days out. We'll be down for a few years, but we'll be grand again eventually.'

Cork City is a professional entity, though. It's a *business*.

Even when Pat Shine was talking about our plans, his concern would be how to sell it to FORAS, because there would be people going, 'It's our club, never mind everyone else!' Whereas, I had witnessed the good and the bad times at the club, the ups and the downs, the boom and bust cycle.

I desperately wanted to ensure we left that behind.

But, ultimately, it didn't happen.

WITHIN A FEW weeks of leaving, my head was clearer, and I realised… *Jesus Christ, I was under an incredible amount of pressure.*

From the day I walked into the job in November 2013 to the day I left in May 2019, I was under immense stress.

I was just flat out. But I have no regrets and would do it all again.

Cork City was my passion.

My relationship with Cork City and time with the club was absolutely phenomenal.

Nothing could taint it.

It was a privilege to play for the club, a privilege to manage the club and a privilege to win trophies for the club.

That's what I remember when I think of my time managing Cork City. How we came from absolute nowhere to challenging for the league title. That night in Oriel. How we picked ourselves up time and time again after coming close.

Going up against Dundalk, proving people wrong… the Cross packed with the biggest football crowd in Ireland every week.

I think of the memories we made, winning the FAI Cup with the last kick of the game. Seáni, Dools and Shep tearing teams apart… winning 21 games won out of 22.

Winning the double.

I think of the bond with the players and the craic we used to have.

I remember when I signed Greg Bolger from St Pat's, he told me that he had been advised, 'Why on earth would you want to go down there? Sure, all they do is run up hills! It's like the army down there!'

There was a perception that we used to spend our time in training just running up and down hills!

I never once did that in my time as a manager.

I didn't even know where the hills were, where we supposedly did this all of this running!

We just had great craic with it.

'All right lads, if you don't win tomorrow,' I'd warn them, '… we'll be running up THOSE HILLS!'

Over five and a half years, we went on a journey that no one could have predicted. I'll always cherish the memories.

As I said when I took over as manager, I wanted to bring the crowds back, to bring the passion back and make Cork City competitive again.

I feel we achieved that.

EPILOGUE

IN THE MONTHS after I left Cork City, I stayed involved in football and sport where I could.

I did some punditry work on the League of Ireland with eir Sport, and some underage coaching with the local soccer team where I live in West Cork. I was involved with St Mary's, my local GAA club, whom I joined over 35 years ago.

It was a difficult year with the Covid-19 restrictions, as it was for everyone.

I was keeping an eye on the League of Ireland and what was happening, waiting for a chance to get back into management.

I was part of a few potential takeover scenarios with one or two clubs, but nothing concrete came from them. There were other offers, but nothing that was one hundred percent right for me. And then, in August 2020, I got a phone call on a Wednesday afternoon from Galway United asking would I be interested in speaking to the board about becoming the club's new manager.

Galway United were struggling in the First Division.

But I saw great potential in the club. Galway is the third biggest city in Ireland, with a very strong soccer passion. In my playing days, they were always a strong team. Galway won the FAI Cup in 1991 and the League Cup in '97. Yet, for whatever reason, they haven't had a sustained period in the Premier Division over the last 10 or 15 years.

I wouldn't say Galway United were 'sleeping giants', because they had no history of winning league titles, but I felt the club and the area had enormous potential.

I DROVE UP to Galway that night and had a very good chat with the board members for a couple of hours.

We spoke about the club and where it could go.

It was mid-season, the team was struggling and second from bottom in the table. No players could be signed because the transfer window was closed.

It was an incredibly uncertain time. The league had only resumed a few weeks earlier after the Covid-19 lockdown and no fans were allowed at matches.

But I was interested.

We spoke again on Thursday at lunchtime and we had another long discussion. After coming to an agreement, they rang me that night and offered me the manager's job.

I accepted it.

I knew a lot of people saw me as a Cork City person, because I played for the club 650 times and managed the club for almost six years.

And I was a City supporter, of course.

At the end of the day, however, I'm a football lover.

I'm a football manager and a qualified Pro Licence coach.

I have a passion for the League of Ireland. And I wanted to manage again.

I was very excited about the opportunity with Galway United.

GALWAY IS ALSO a lot closer to Roscommon, and the home where I was raised. Once the country began to get to grips with Covid-19, I was in a position to see more of my parents.

The two people who made me the man I am.

My father was always a quiet man.

A quiet country man, in many ways, and I can never remember him raising his voice to me. Even when I had my few rebellious years as a young man, my father allowed me to carve out my own path in life. Though he was always there to advise me.

He was the man who first brought me to matches, and then during my playing days and my managing days, he has been there 'with me' still – he really liked watching Cork City play, and when City were playing in Galway or Sligo or 'up the country' he would be there for me in the ground.

He is a proud man too, and I know he has been proud of what I achieved in the game. Though at cup finals or league deciders, he would always make sure to stay in the background.

He is a quiet, always supportive, unassuming man. He was never on the pitch after any of our matches. He was never going to be seen in a photo giving me a congratulatory hug.

After some of our bigger games, I would not get to see him at all. When a manager has all his after-match duties attended to, there are fewer people left in the ground anyway. My father, for sure, would not be hanging around.

He'd be thinking of getting into the car and getting home, having a cup of tea. I'd phone him later on, of course. And find out what he thought!

My mother would be there too, at our games over the years, for the cup finals, and one or two of the more important games. At the Aviva Stadium she'd be found in one of the warm corporate boxes, chatting away to Gráinne, and my girls, and chatting to anyone who was close at hand.

Winning and losing was always less important to her than it was for my father. She'd hope I'd win but, as she always said to me... 'Once you are all safe, everything is okay!'

And she is right in that slice of wisdom.

Even though it has been difficult for me, on the sideline, to always grasp that truth.

FAMILY COME FIRST.

Again, as a football manager, this is something you have to continually remind yourself. We all get so consumed by the 'family' of players we work with, and the results the team is delivering week after week – our own family too often can come second.

Gráinne, and our girls, however, understand the pressures that come with the jobs I've had all these years.

Aideen is 25. Sinéad is 23, and both of them were living at home during the pandemic. Sinéad is working in Dublin. She studied business in UCC and graduated in 2019, and began working with Accenture.

Aideen went to Mary Immaculate in Limerick, to study primary teaching. She graduated three years ago.

Both girls are sporty by nature. Gráinne is a swimming coach, and not surprisingly both Aideen and Sinéad are both qualified beach lifeguards.

Swimming was their first love, though Sinéad was also a good runner when she was younger and was good enough to compete at the Community Games finals in Mosney. They take their love of swimming solely from their mother, not me, as I don't swim at all.

Gráinne has her own swim coaching business, and coaches swimmers in both the pool and the open water around West Cork. She has run a few marathons over the years, including Dublin, London and New York, and more recently has got into Ironman triathlon racing.

Getting the chance to support Gráinne in her sporting endeavours has always filled me with immense pride. I was with her when she ran the Dublin marathon, and New York, but because of my own working schedule I wasn't able to be in London when she ran there. I wasn't there when she competed in Ironman Sweden, but I was with her in Barcelona.

Football has seen to it that I have been a 'hit and miss' supporter of her sporting goals, but I am incredibly proud of what she has achieved.

I WALKED INTO Galway United in 2020 and found the club very low in confidence.

It was my job to lift that.

I had to put structures in place, while also working within the club's parameters.

I came in with a fresh pair of eyes, and no agenda, and the response from the players was brilliant. I also realised, immediately, how much I had missed being away from football.

But it was going to be a huge ask to get into the play-offs. There were 10 games to play and we needed to win eight or nine matches to finish in fifth place and reach those play-offs.

So, the aim was to put things in place in order to challenge for promotion the following season. I was thinking of maybe experimenting with players in the club, looking at them and giving them a chance for next season.

I was looking at the bigger picture.

And then we started winning games.

Galway United went on an incredible run.

After five wins in-a-row, I was thinking to myself... *Jesus, we might have a chance here.* We made the play-offs, but did not win promotion.

But I saw enough to know that a winning team in Galway will get the support of sports fans in the city. Galway city is less 'GAA territory' than the rest of the county, which has football dominating in the north and hurling in the south.

The city itself has more people who are interested in all sports.

But GAA does not hold the entire county in its grip.

I APPRECIATE THAT too, because I know and understand GAA. It has always been part of who I am throughout my sporting life.

Soccer became my first love, but gaelic football has always been part of my life.

I have always played the game in Cork, since first moving down from the midlands. I never stopped playing gaelic.

I transferred from St Dominic's in Roscommon to St Mary's in Enniskeane as soon I moved to West Cork, and the game has always helped me to keep in shape throughout the year. It's junior football, but junior football in Cork is a serious business – it's unbelievably tough and competitive, and the standard of the game is very high. Clubs are bursting themselves to graduate to intermediate and senior levels.

The soccer season and the GAA season dove-tailed nicely for me, when soccer was a winter season and GAA was mainly on the go in the summer months.

I was finished playing soccer, however, by the time St Mary's finally got to a county junior final. I was 40 years old, but still lining out for the parish. It was a thrill to finally win it, but it was a shame we never got to a final when I was in my prime. I would have loved that, though I was able to reach higher levels by lining out with our divisional team Carbery and that was always a great experience.

As was 1990, when I was chosen for the Cork junior team. I was a corner-forward. We won the All-Ireland title that year, beating Meath in the final in Portlaoise, and then we played Warwickshire in the 'Away' final back home in Páirc Uí Chaoimh.

There was nothing going to stop me playing both games, or even flirting with some hurling for a few summers too.

I've been a member of St Mary's all my adult life, and I've showed up on the sideline at times too, helping out, as nearly everyone in a GAA club does from time to time. It's part of your life when you live in West Cork.

And it's not something I'd ever have wanted to miss out on.

AS GALWAY MANAGER, I am splitting my time between my family home in West Cork at the weekend and Galway during the week.

In 2020, Covid-19's hold on the country meant some things were a struggle, as they were for almost everyone in 2020. Galway got to the play-off final against Longford Town in 2020, and they beat us 2-1.

It was massively disappointing. But, it was a fantastic 12 weeks from when I took over, a real rollercoaster ride, and very enjoyable. For me, it was great to be back in the game. I had missed it terribly. And I was massively looking forward to my first full season with the club in 2021. I got to work preparing for the 2021 season immediately after we lost to Longford, and that meant, unfortunately, cutting players from the squad.

We had to let fifty percent of our squad go straight away and most of the experienced lads. A lot of the older players were working full-time and incapable of fitting into our plans for full-time training for the following season, including training in the mornings. Most of those older lads were all well established in their jobs so financially it was a non-runner. In the First Division, it's impossible to even consider giving up a good job for full-time football.

I knew we needed to bring younger blood into the team. I kept about 12 of the younger lads that we had and went looking for players who could fit into what we were looking for.

It was full-time training and low wages – a lot of our players are students on amateur contracts – and we needed them to buy into what was happening.

I looked forward to the 2021 season as much as I had looked forward to any season in my whole career and, just like when I formally began my time as Cork City manager in 2014, I sought to bring passion to the game in Galway and I sought to bring the supporters back in serious numbers.

Passion and support are the two most important building blocks for every successful team.

A MEMOIR • EPILOGUE

I'M A DREAMER.

I suppose I always have been. And I dream of the League of Ireland becoming everything it deserves to be, with more money coming into the game, and with the attention of the whole country doubled and trebled – with people seeing how good the game in Ireland is, and how much better it can be with the right support and backing.

We got a glimpse of that when Dundalk recently continued to do the game here proud and qualified for the group stages of the Europa League, and got to play the likes of Arsenal and Molde and Rapid Wien.

Dundalk lost all six games, scoring eight times and conceding 19 goals. They were competitive, and watching them meeting Arsenal in the Emirates Stadium was a proud evening for everyone who loves the League of Ireland.

They did not let us down. Every man stepped up to the plate. And, as a dreamer, I was left feeling at the end of it all how amazing it would be if more Irish clubs got to walk onto that magnificent stage.

How much good it would do our game if we saw our best teams competing against the biggest and most glamorous teams in the world. Every single game against a team like Arsenal would raise the profile of our own game here at home. It would nourish our game here. Those games would tell people that there is very little wrong with our game, and that more and more people should come out and support the game here!

Yes, I'm a dreamer.

I dream of a League of Ireland with more people watching.

A league with a higher profile. And a league which also fits itself into the dreams of young lads all over the country.

I HAVE BEEN a Cork City fan all my adult life.

Despite how my time as manager ended, I never wished to seem them meet hard times again, and I always hoped that they would avoid relegation in 2020.

They didn't, and hard times has been the recurring story of football in Cork. I was honoured to be Cork City manager, and to have served the club for so long.

It saddened me to see what happened, as much as it delighted me to see Dundalk run out at the Emirates Stadium and welcome Arsenal to the Aviva Stadium.

What happened to Cork City in 2020 shows what can happen when the eye is taken off the ball. Once the club made sweeping changes to the board and missed out on European football, there were always going to be difficult times around the corner. It has been a sharp and horrific fall for a club that won the double a few years earlier.

Because I love Cork City and always will, no matter who I manage, it pains me to see where the club now finds itself.

FOOTBALL MANAGEMENT IS, ultimately, a results game.

It's one of the few jobs where you know you've a certain shelf life, and one that could be quite short if you start losing games.

It's a high pressure job.

We're in it because we love it and we're mad, that's just the way it is.

Everyone in every job is under pressure at the moment.

But football is one of those jobs where you can't be in it for too long, because it doesn't allow you to be in it for long.

But it's something I love.

When I went back into it, for my first game with Galway United, I was building myself up all day. I was thinking... *Jesus, am I really back to this again?*

I suppose I could have stayed away from football, gone back to my old job for a few years and had an easier life.

But I'd be dead without football.

I live for the buzz, to see if I can improve a player or make a team better, to try and achieve something. For good or bad, that's what I enjoy doing.

I love managing and trying to build something.

Sometimes in a match, when a decision goes against you, or you have a bad night, you're questioning why you're doing it.

There are easier professions. But that's just the way it is.

I wouldn't want it any other way.

It's my passion. My life.

It's who I am.

MY WIFE GRÁINNE (inset above), and our daughters Aideen and Sinéad, were unstinting in their support of my desire to make Cork City the best team in the land, and nobody deserved to share the glory with the team more than my family. When my time at Cork City ended suddenly and unexpectedly, I wanted to stay in the game and the offer to take over at Galway United in 2020 was one I was delighted to accept.